Queer Voices in Hip Hop

TRACKING POP

SERIES EDITORS: JOCELYN NEAL, JOHN COVACH,
ROBERT FINK, AND LOREN KAJIKAWA

RECENT TITLES IN THE SERIES:

Queer Voices in Hip Hop: Cultures, Communities,
and Contemporary Performance
by Lauron J. Kehrer

Critical Excess: *Watch the Throne* and the New Gilded Age
by J. Griffith Rollefson

Soda Goes Pop: Pepsi-Cola Advertising and Popular Music
by Joanna K. Love

The Beatles through a Glass Onion: Reconsidering the White Album
edited by Mark Osteen

The Pop Palimpsest: Intertextuality in Recorded Popular Music
edited by Lori Burns and Serge Lacasse

Uncharted: Creativity and the Expert Drummer
by Bill Bruford

I Hear a Symphony: Motown and Crossover R&B
by Andrew Flory

Hearing Harmony: Toward a Tonal Theory for the Rock Era
by Christopher Doll

Good Vibrations: Brian Wilson and the Beach Boys in
Critical Perspective
edited by Philip Lambert

Krautrock: German Music in the Seventies
by Ulrich Adelt

Sounds of the Underground: A Cultural, Political and Aesthetic
Mapping of Underground and Fringe Music
by Stephen Graham

Rhymin' and Stealin': Musical Borrowing in Hip-Hop
by Justin A. Williams

Queer Voices in Hip Hop

Cultures, Communities, and
Contemporary Performance

Lauron J. Kehrer

University of Michigan Press • Ann Arbor

For questions or permissions, please contact um.press.perms@umich.edu

Published in the United States of America by the
University of Michigan Press
Manufactured in the United States of America
Printed on acid-free paper
First published November 2022

A CIP catalog record for this book is available from the British Library.

Library of Congress Control Number: 2022942046

ISBN 978-0-472-07568-3 (hardcover : alk. paper)
ISBN 978-0-472-05568-5 (paper : alk. paper)
ISBN 978-0-472-90301-6 (open access ebook)

DOI: https://doi.org/10.3998/mpub.11306619

Open Access publication of this book is supported by the H. Earle Johnson Book Publication Subvention from the Society for American Music and the AMS 75 PAYS Endowment of the American Musicological Society, supported in part by the National Endowment for the Humanities and the Andrew W. Mellon Foundation.

The University of Michigan Press's open access publishing program is made possible thanks to additional funding from the University of Michigan Office of the Provost and the generous support of contributing libraries.

For all the queer and trans musicians who made it possible for me to be me.

Contents

Acknowledgments   ix

Introduction. "I Don't Have Any Secrets I Need Kept Anymore":
    Out in Hip Hop   1

1 • Hip Hop's Queer Roots:
    Disco, House, and Early Hip Hop   18

2 • Queer Articulations in Ballroom Rap   42

3 • "The Bro Code":
    Black Queer Women and Female Masculinity in Rap   67

4 • "Nice For What":
    New Orleans Bounce and Disembodied Queer Voices
    in the Mainstream   94

Outro. "Call Me By Your Name":
    Demarginalizing Queer Hip Hop   124

Bibliography   131

Index   143

Digital materials related to this title can be found on the Fulcrum platform via the following citable URL: https://doi.org/10.3998/mpub.11306619

Acknowledgments

I am grateful to the many, many people in my personal and professional lives who helped to model potential paths for me to complete this project and who supported and guided me as I sought out my own course. While this feels like a partial list, what follows is an attempt to acknowledge those who in some way helped me to write this book and to whom I am grateful.

First and foremost, I am grateful to the folks at University of Michigan Press who saw the potential in this project and nurtured it forward. Mary C. Francis was the acquiring editor who brought me and my project on board and helped me with many conceptual considerations at the beginning of writing this book. Even after she moved on to become the director of a different press, Mary continued to encourage me. Sara Jo Cohen took over after that departure, but the care and encouragement with which she handled this project me made it feel as if I had been working with her from the beginning. Many thanks also to Anna Pohlod for helping with the nuts and bolts of getting this project over the finish line. Loren Kajikawa, Tracking Pop series co-editor, mentor, and friend, deserves all of my gratitude. He read every draft of every chapter, sent me sources and ideas whenever he came across something relevant, and has been nothing but supportive. This project truly is indebted to his attention and passion for hip hop scholarship.

The genesis of this book was my dissertation, which I defended in spring of 2017. My dissertation committee, Lisa Jakelski, Honey Meconi, and Elliott H. Powell pushed me to develop my ideas on intersections of race, gender, and sexuality while simultaneously being the most supportive committee a student could ever hope to have. Since then, Elliott has become a good friend and mentor who continues to share his intellectual generosity with me. He is one of the folks who has most deeply influenced my thinking about hip hop, race, and queer identity, which I believe is reflected throughout this book.

I've been fortunate to have various kinds of institutional support for this project. Fieldwork that I conducted in New Orleans in 2016 was supported by an Adrienne Fried Block Fellowship from the Society for American Music and a Glenn Watkins Traveling Fellowship from the Eastman School of Music. Funding from a Faculty Summer Research Grant from the College of William and Mary supported writing during the summer of 2018. The Society for American Music and the American Musicological Society supported Open Access publication of this book in the form of the H. Earle Johnson Publication Subvention and an AMS 75 PAYS subvention grant, respectively. I presented several iterations of this research at conferences of the American Musicological Society, the Society for American Music, the Society for Ethnomusicology, and the International Association for the Study of Popular Music, with funding support from the Eastman School of Music, the Susan B. Anthony Institute at the University of Rochester, the College of William and Mary, and Western Michigan University. I appreciate the feedback from attendees, session chairs, and fellow panelists that these occasions afforded. I also had the opportunity to present parts of this research for the music departments at the University of North Carolina at Chapel Hill, University of Nevada, Reno, and the University of Iowa and would like to thank the faculty and students at both institutions for their engagement with my work.

While conducting my fieldwork in New Orleans that informed what would become chapter 4, I was able to interview a few people directly involved in the bounce scene. I am grateful to Jay Pennington, aka Rusty Lazer, who sat with me and then connected me to other artists. Rappers Ha Sizzle and Keno both took the time to share their insights with me, as did others whom I was not able to formerly interview. I am thankful that they met with a then-graduate student to talk about their music so candidly, and I deeply admire their passion for New Orleans and its well-established and more recently emerging traditions. Thanks also to CJ Johnson, my friend since college, for their on-the-ground perspectives and support.

This book is indebted to the community of scholars, writers, mentors, and friends who in turn encouraged and challenged me to do my very best work. One such group was the 2020 cohort of the AMS Popular Music Study Group Junior Faculty Symposium. I'm grateful to all the mentors and attendees who offered feedback on my work, but especially my mentors Sherrie Tucker and Tammy L. Kernodle. Other music scholars in my intellectual community who, whether they know it or not, have in some way shaped this project, include Kevin Bartig, Amy Coddington, Lisa Cooper Vest, Sarah Fuchs, Kaleb Goldschmitt, Carol Hess, Mark Katz, Matthew D.

Morrison, Amanda Sewell, Tes Slominski, Kira Thurman, and Brian Wright. Gayle Murchison has been a wonderful friend and mentor and helped me come up with the title for this book. I'm thankful to everyone I've named here and those whose names I have inadvertently left out.

I am also grateful to be part of an amazing community of musicians at Western Michigan University, and I deeply appreciate my colleagues' support and friendship. My students, especially those who took my Hip Hop Music and Culture seminar in my first semester at WMU in the fall of 2019, also contributed to this book. I am thankful every day that I get to work with such a great group.

My family has always supported my endeavors, even when there was no blueprint or clear roadmap. My parents, Laurie Jockwig-Kehrer and Ronald Kehrer, made sure I received an excellent music education, both formal and informal. My sister, Kaitlin Kehrer-Scharphorn, along with Joe and Oliver always keep me grounded. My aunt Julie Finney has also been a great support. *Grazie anche alla mia famiglia italiana per l'amore e i sorrisi.*

No one, and I mean no one, has been a stronger support or influence in my life than my wife, Maria Cristina Fava. She has been my colleague, my editor, my harshest critic, my most ardent advocate, and my best friend since 2009. I could not have finished this book without her. *Grazie mille tesoro per tutto—ti amo.*

Introduction

"I Don't Have Any Secrets
I Need Kept Anymore"

Out in Hip Hop

On July 4, 2012, prior to the release of his debut studio album, *Channel Orange*, R&B singer and songwriter Frank Ocean posted an open letter on his tumblr blog that was originally intended to be part of the thank-you's in the album's liner notes.[1] In the letter, Ocean writes about unrequited love that he had for another young man, whom he calls his "first love":

> 4 summers ago, I met somebody. I was 19 years old. He was too. We spent that summer, and the summer after, together. Everyday almost. And on the days we were together, time would glide. Most of the day I'd see him, and his smile. I'd hear his conversation and his silence . . . Until it was time to sleep. Sleep I would often share with him. By the time I realized I was in love, it was malignant. It was hopeless. There was no escaping, no negotiating with the feeling. No choice. It was my first love, it changed my life.[2]

While Ocean never openly identified himself as gay or bisexual, the message was clear that he did not identify as straight. Furthermore, the fact that this coming-out story was framed as part of the acknowledgments section of the liner notes to his forthcoming album suggests that Ocean's music was in some ways influenced by his personal relationship with another man.

At the end of the letter, Ocean remarks, "I feel like a free man. If I listen closely . . . I can hear the sky falling too."[3] While Ocean's trepidation was

---

1. Frank Ocean, "thank yous," tumblr, July 4, 2012, http://frankocean.tumblr.com/post/26473798723.
2. Ocean, "thank yous."
3. Ocean, "thank yous."

certainly understandable, his open letter was met with a generally positive response by fans, critics, and other members of the hip hop community. Jay Z, for example, posted an essay by filmmaker and writer dream hampton titled "Thank You, Frank Ocean" on his curated news website, *Life+Times*, thereby endorsing Ocean.[4] Russell Simmons also demonstrated his support, stating in response to the open letter, "Today is a big day for hip-hop. It is a day that will define who we really are. How compassionate will we be? How loving can we be? How inclusive are we?"[5] Even Ocean's fellow Odd Future member, Tyler, The Creator, who, before coming out as queer himself, was criticized for his excessive use of the term "faggot" in his music, supported his colleague in a tweet: "My Big Brother Finally Fucking Did That. Proud Of That Nigga Cause I Know That Shit Is Difficult Or Whatever."[6] The outpouring of support for Ocean from some of the most important figures in hip hop is remarkable and certainly would have been unimaginable just a decade before. It also begs the question, Would some of these figures have offered the same kind of open support had Ocean not already established his professional career and public profile? Or was his coming out and the subsequent approval made possible only by the level of celebrity he had already achieved?

Taken at face value, the positive reception of Ocean (who won two Grammys in 2013) would seem to suggest that hip hop is ready for openly queer artists to represent the genre in the mainstream. The catch, however, is that Ocean is not really a rapper in the traditional sense of the word; his delivery style is primarily singing, not rapping. Moreover, his music, while undeniably falling within the malleable boundaries of hip hop culture, is more accurately characterized as R&B or pop, not rap per se. Thus, Ocean can exist as queer within hip hop without challenging the normative rapper figure; rap remains strictly in the realm of the heterosexual male. While the outpouring of support of Ocean in the wake of his coming out demonstrates hip hop's openness to queer identities, mainstream rap in particular has been slow to broaden its borders. As Snoop Dogg stated in response to Ocean's revelation

4. dream hampton, "Thank You, Frank Ocean," *Life + Times*, July 4, 2012, http://lifeand-times.com/thank-you-frank-ocean.

5. Russell Simmons, "The Courage of Frank Ocean Just Changed the Game!" *Globalgrind*, July 2012, http://globalgrind.com/1857832/russell-simmons-letter-to-frank-ocean-gay-bi-sexual-comes-out-photos/.

6. Tyler, The Creator, "My Big Brother . . ." Twitter, July 4, 2012, https://twitter.com/tylerthecreator/status/220409501487079424, accessed September 30, 2016. As a white scholar, I do not use any iteration of the n-word unless it is a direct quote or song lyric, in which case I retain the original use and spelling to preserve the words of quoted artists.

and its aftermath, "Frank Ocean ain't no rapper. He's a singer. It's acceptable in the singing world, but in the rap world I don't know if it will ever be acceptable because rap is so masculine."[7]

Perhaps unbeknownst to Snoop Dogg, queer rappers of all types already exist. And yet, as Snoop's response demonstrates, there is still resistance to rappers whose identities fall outside of the normative rapper identity matrix. In her essay to Ocean, hampton writes:

> You fulfill hip-hop's early promise to not give a fuck about what others think of you. The 200 times Tyler says "faggot" and the wonderful way he held you up and down on Twitter today, Syd the Kid's sexy stud profile and her confusing, misogynistic videos speak to the many contradictions and posturing your generation inherited from the hip-hop generation before you. I'm sure you know a rumor about Big Daddy Kane having AIDS and with it, the suggestion that he was bisexual, effectively ended his career. You must have seen the pictures of pioneer Afrika "Baby Bam" from the Jungle Brothers in drag and read the blogs ridiculing him, despite the fact that he's been leading a civilian life for nearly two decades. I know as a singer you love Rahsaan Patterson and bemoan the fact that homophobia prevented him from being the huge star his talent deserves. Only last month Queen Latifah unnecessarily released a statement denying that her performing at a Gay Pride event meant she was finally affirming her identity for thousands of Black girls. Imagine if Luther [Vandross] had been able to write, as you closed your letter, "I don't have any secrets I need kept anymore.... I feel like a free man."[8]

hampton demonstrates that while Ocean's coming out was a major event in hip hop, it falls within a preexisting discourse on homosexuality in hip hop and related Black music genres. She marks this event as an important milestone in hip hop history while also acknowledging that Ocean is not the first, nor the last, gay artist in the genre. Ocean's coming out furthered the conversation in the mainstream during a period when the legal and social landscape for LGBTQ people was rapidly evolving.

Less than a decade later, the conversation surrounding Ocean's coming

---

7. Snoop Dogg, quoted in Adam Bychawski, "Snoop Lion Says He Doesn't Know Whether Homosexuality Will Ever Be Seen As 'Acceptable' in Rap Music," Nme.com, April 6, 2013, http://www.nme.com/news/snoop-dogg/69594, accessed September 30, 2016.

8. hampton, "Thank You, Frank Ocean."

out has made space for one of rap's most visibly queer mainstream artists yet: Lil Nas X. As his songs top hip hop and pop charts, Lil Nas X has brought a queer sensibility and visibility to rap that is in many ways unprecedented but also closely connected to social and legal recognition that LGBTQ people have gained in the United States since Ocean's disclosure. It is tempting to position Lil Nas X's as an unexpected success story, but reflecting on Frank Ocean's coming out, as well as the longer history of queer involvement in hip hop, we can see instead that the stage had in many ways already been set for the rapper's stardom.[9]

In the larger discourses about popular music and culture, it is okay to be queer in hip hop, but it is nearly impossible to be an openly queer rapper, and even more so to be a queer rapper who exhibits anything other than a hyper-masculine gender presentation. As C. Riley Snorton reminds us, "The frequency with which news outlets report on the question of who is out in hip hop is indicative of a symptomatic amnesia in hip hop reporting, which seems to forget, if not actively repress, its pasts."[10] When a rapper does come out as queer, the media tends to treat them as the first and therefore an anomaly. Gender expression is still problematically tied to sexual orientation; queer men such as Ocean are presumed to be effeminate and unable to convincingly perform rap's masculinity. Women in hip hop, on the other hand, are expected to be traditionally feminine in appearance but emulate the masculine language and stances of the men in their profession. If they fail to maintain that precarious balance, they could be labeled pop stars instead of rappers, pushed outside the boundaries of hip hop or, at the very least, to its fringes. Many distance themselves from any suggestion that they are queer, thus reinforcing the notion that there are no gay rappers and that to be queer in a hip hop context should be a source of shame. If they were to openly embrace their queer identities, however, they would run the risk of losing fans and the support of an industry that is both hostile to women and invested in presenting only a heteromasculine ideal of rap or a hyperfeminine approach that does not overtly undermine that ideal. Furthermore, there is no mention of transgender, gender nonconforming, or nonbinary identities in this rap discourse. Openly queer and trans rappers may exist, but they are frequently relegated to the hip hop underground, limited to a particular local scene or circuit of LGBTQ-focused venues and events.

There are many ways to be a rapper, and that includes a plethora of sexu-

---

9. I discuss Lil Nas X at length in the "Outro" chapter of this book.

10. C. Riley Snorton, "On the Question of 'Who's Out in Hip Hop,'" *Souls: A Critical Journal of Black Politics, Culture, and Society* 16, no. 3–4 (2014): 287.

alities and gender identities and expressions. In the mainstream, however, few artists have managed to become commercially successful while also negotiating their non-normative identities. Black queer artists are diverse, with some drawing on the lineages of their cities, especially New York City and New Orleans, to create a local sound that can translate to a national stage. What they all have in common, however, is that they must negotiate the expectations of the genre, which positions rappers as primarily hetero-sexual, hypermasculine, cisgender Black men. The strategies that Black queer artists use to navigate these expectations necessarily depend on the particu-larities of their own intersectional identities, and their reception must be understood through a similarly intersectional lens.

Queer Voices in Hip Hop: Cultures, Communities, and Contemporary Per-formance positions openly queer and trans rappers not as anomalies or newly emerging phenomena but as musicians within a long-standing Black queer musical lineage. I reclaim queer involvement in hip hop by repositioning the genre's beginnings within Black and Latinx queer music-making practices and spaces. I then examine contemporary performance and politics, demon-strating that openly queer and trans rappers draw on Ballroom and other cultural expressions particular to queer and trans communities of color in their work in order to articulate their subject positions. Taking an intersec-tional approach, I explore ways that gender, race, and sexuality are co-constructed and performed in these artists' work. By centering the perfor-mances of openly queer and trans artists of color and exploring both the historical and contemporary queer expressions found within hip hop, *Queer Voices in Hip Hop* positions contemporary artists within a lineage of Black queer music making and thus situates them within a long history of queer and trans communities of color.

Coming Out to Queer Hip Hop

Growing up, I was discouraged from listening to hip hop. As a child of the 1980s and 1990s, just around the height of the Parents Music Resource Center campaign to label explicit music and the discourses about gangsta rap (which also became the style that captured a lot of white America's attention), I was fed the typical lines about rap being violent and misogy-nistic. As a white girl child especially, I picked up on the message that I was to be protected from this sort of music, which could be damaging to me. This is not to say that I did not encounter the genre. By the time I was in elementary school, hip hop was everywhere. MC Hammer and Vanilla Ice had had top hits, and school curricula had started to incorporate rapping as a (some say misguided) way to reach students (I recall in particular an elementary school assembly on school bus safety that deployed a rapping school bus robot). In this way rap was always part of my sonic environment but one of which I was taught to be particularly suspicious.

It wasn't until I was in college, doing fieldwork at the now-defunct Michigan Womyn's Music Festival (MWMF) that I encountered queer rap—or, rather, queer rap artists. By the time I began attending in 2008, there was an established dedicated hip hop day stage at the festival. I saw performers such as God-des and She (who around this time also appeared on the Showtime lesbian television drama, *The L Word*), Medusa, JenRo, Skim, and others—queer women, rapping about loving or having sexual relationships with other women. I saw a part of myself in these performances—a cross-racial identification to be sure, but they were expressing my queer desires. I realized I had internalized the discourses about hip hop's supposedly inherent misogyny and homophobia. But how could that be the case when these women were rapping here at a predominantly lesbian festival?

I was also acutely aware of the racial discourses around the genre. While the performers I saw were racially diverse, I also realized that many of the other white women attendees did not know how to place the Black butch women on stage. They enjoyed the high-energy performances but felt that some of the acts expressed misogyny in their lyrics. The policing of Black expressions and bodies in a space where gender boundaries were so highly regulated illustrated to me how race, sexuality, gender, and gender expression are co-constructed. How one understood hip hop's musical and gender expressions in this and any other space has to do with one's own positionality and points of reference.

I am a queer, gender nonconforming person, and, as such, I recognize many queer cultural practices manifested in hip hop that have often been overlooked or downplayed by scholars. I am invested in furthering queer representation in hip hop studies as well as popular music studies more generally. I am also white, which means that I may miss some codes that are specific to these communities, and I am not drawing the same lived experience as the artists about whom I write. For that reason, throughout this book, I privilege frameworks theorized by Black scholars especially and queer and trans people of color where possible. Any misreading or misinterpretations here, however, are my own. While this book addresses the ways gender, sexuality, and race intersect in hip hop and argues for a centering of queer and trans artists of color in hip hop studies, I do not claim that it does the work of decolonizing queer studies. I believe that is an admirable pursuit and one that I hope future scholars will take up, but as a white settler scholar, that is outside of my purview, and I do not wish to deploy the work of the artists I discuss here in such a way. I do, however, hope that scholars will take up this idea in the future, perhaps building on the work that I offer in this book.

Studies of Black women's experiences of and relationships to hip hop demonstrate the potential of an intersectional analysis to illuminate how issues of race and gender work in tandem. Yet the literature that elucidates the connections between these identities typically emphasizes the importance and nuances of (implicitly) heterosexual female sexuality, disregarding non-heterosexual queer identities that are a crucial part of the matrix of identity politics. With few exceptions, including the work of Shanté Paradigm Smalls, Elliott H. Powell, and a special edition of the journal *Palimpsest: A Journal on Women, Gender, and the Black International*, existing scholarship offers queer readings of mainstream heterosexual artists rather than focusing on issues of queer identity in hip hop or the music of queer artists.[11] In her essay in the special issue of *Palimpsest*, Imani Perry highlights important reasons for "queering" our understanding of mainstream hip hop, writing, "Intellectual projects framed as pursuing inclusion often simply reinscribe the center. And so, I'm not interested in just 'adding' queer subjects to hip hop. I'm interest[ed] in understanding that Black working class and poor

---

11. See, for example, Shanté Paradigm Smalls, "'The Rain Comes Down': Jean Grae and Hip Hop Heteronormativity," *American Behavioral Scientist* 55, no. 1 (2011): 86–95; Shanté Paradigm Smalls, "Queer Hip Hop: A Brief Historiography," in *The Oxford Handbook of Music and Queerness*, ed. Fred Everett Maus and Sheila Whiteley, published online September 2018, https://doi.org/10.1093/oxfordhb/9780199793525.013.103; Elliott H. Powell, "Unmastered: The Queer Black Aesthetics of Unfinished Recordings," *Black Scholar* 49, no. 1 (2019): 28–39; and Elliott H. Powell, "The Ghosts Got You: Exploring the Queer (After) Lives of Sample-Based Hip-Hop," in *The Oxford Handbook of Hip Hop Music*, ed. Justin D. Burton and Jason Lee Oakes (Oxford University Press, published online August 2018); and the special edition of *Palimpsest: A Journal on Women, Gender, and the Black International* 2, no. 2 (2013), ed. T. Denean Sharpley-Whiting and Tiffany Ruby Patterson-Myers. Other important exceptions include Andreana Clay's "Like an Old Soul Record': Black Feminism, Queer Sexuality, and the Hip-Hop Generation," *Meridians* 8, no. 1 (2008): 53–73; and Mark D. Wilson's "Post-Pomo Hip-Hop Homos: Hip-Hop Art, Gay Rappers, and Social Change," *Social Justice* 34, no. 1 (107) (2007): 117–40. In the *Palimpsest* special issue titled "The Queerness of Hip Hop/The Hip Hop of Queerness," only the contributions by Moya Bailey ("Homolatent Masculinity & Hip Hop Culture"), Tavia Nyong'o ("Queer Hip Hop and Its Dark Precursors"), Richard T. Rodríguez ("Hip Hop Spice Boyz"), Mecca Jamilah Sullivan ("Fat Mutha: Hip Hop's Queer Corpulent Poetics"), and Rinaldo Walcott ("Boyfriends with Clits and Girlfriends with Dicks: Hip Hop's Queer Future") offer any mention of queer artists, and they do so only in passing.

landscapes are as much queer as they are straight, both theoretically and literally."[12] Perry argues that focusing on queer subjects separates queer identities from others, such as Black and poor, which problematically gives the impression that artists and listeners are either/or—that is, either Black *or* queer rather than Black *and* queer. Furthermore, she suggests Black and poor *are* queer, in that they are all illegible within the hegemonic white culture that values heteronormativity. While there is a strong case for queering mainstream hip hop, I argue that focusing on heterosexual artists perpetuates the marginal status of artists outside the commercial or cultural mainstream, especially those who are queer-identified.[13]

In this project I focus on the work of Black rappers who openly identify themselves as queer, trans, or otherwise within the loose category of LGBTQ identities. Shanté Paradigm Smalls helpfully delineates three methods of "marking about queer(ed) Black bodies": bodies that are perceived as queer; bodies that nominate themselves as queer; and bodies that queer or disrupt their own images.[14] Smalls adds that these options are not exhaustive, but they are useful for thinking through the relationships between Black bodies and authentic heteronormativity. In this book I am primarily concerned with the second category. While I refrain from using the framework of "Black bodies" and instead use language that centers Black people, I am focused on those who, in Smalls's parlance, nominate themselves as queer or trans. I seek to center the musical and performative expressions of openly queer and trans artists who have been under-discussed in studies of hip hop and popular music, not artists who have been perceived to be LGBTQ or closeted in some sense. While I do not mean to be exclusive in this focus, I wish to avoid ascribing identity labels onto individuals without their input and try, where possible, to use the language that artists use for themselves. I do hope, however, that this discussion of how non-heteronormative genders and sexualities might manifest in hip hop is useful for understanding a myriad of other artists as well as the ways in which hip hop and hip hop artists can be queer.

Queer Voices in Hip Hop is indebted to Smalls and other scholars of color who have demonstrated the overwhelming whiteness of queer studies and advanced an intersectional approach.[15] For example, José Esteban Muñoz's

---

12. Imani Perry, "Untitled," *Palimpsest* 2, no. 2 (2013): 166–67.

13. Mark Anthony Neal, "Trafficking in Monikers: Jay-Z's 'Queer' Flow," *Palimpsest* 2, no. 2 (2013): 156–61; and Sullivan, "Fat Mutha."

14. Smalls, "'Rain Comes Down,'" 89.

15. This book is also indebted to recent work by scholars on queerness and Black music traditions, such as Alisha Lola Jones, *Flaming?: The Peculiar Theopolitics of Fire and Desire in Black Male Gospel Performance* (New York: Oxford University Press, 2020).

framework of "disidentification" is useful for thinking through how the artists in this book situate themselves both in and against hip hop's mainstream discourses.[16] Disidentifying is a way of creating a "minoritarian" identity in relationship to cultural texts or discourses of the mainstream. Many of the queer and trans artists in this book disidentify not with hip hop per se but with the heteronormalizing aspects of mainstream hip hop. Disidentification is about working against but from within; queer artists working in hip hop push against the expectations of heteronormative gender and sexualities of the genre. They *are* hip hop, but they also open up additional possibilities for hip hop expressions. They push against boundaries imposed by some artists and listeners who have tried to shape hip hop to fit only certain heteromasculinist discourses. Throughout this study, I want to avoid reinscribing the message that hip hop is always homophobic; at the same time, I want to acknowledge that some hip hop is at times homophobic, but that fact doesn't preclude or even prevent queer artists from participating in or challenging those discourses through the medium itself.

This book is not meant to be a comprehensive study of all LGBTQ hip hop artists. Instead, its goals are to situate queer hip hop artists within a Black queer musical lineage, reposition hip hop as already queer from its beginnings by reclaiming queer involvement in hip hop history, and offer analyses that can be applied to other artists beyond those that I discuss here. In *Queer Voices in Hip Hop*, I seek to offer a way of discussing queer and trans hip hop artists that does not presume that they are new or coming from outside of hip hop itself or that hip hop is always already inherently homophobic.

"If I Were Gay, I Would Think Hip Hop Hates Me": Confronting the Myth of Black Homophobia

The idea that hip hop is inherently homophobic has been echoed by hip hop artists themselves and is often deployed in a way that positions hip hop and the Black communities that create it as oppositional if not antagonistic to queerness. Often presented under the guise of pro-LGBTQ activism, this argument ignores the historical and contemporary overlap between hip hop, queer identity, and Black experiences in the United States. One of the clearest examples of this is manifested in white, cisgen-

---

16. José Esteban Muñoz, *Disidentifications: Queers of Color and the Performance of Politics* (Minneapolis: University of Minnesota Press, 1999), 31.

der, heterosexual rapper Macklemore's assertion in his and Ryan Lewis's pro–marriage equality anthem, "Same Love," that "If I were gay, I would think hip hop hates me."

The fourth single from the duo's album *The Heist*, "Same Love," was recorded as part of the Music for Marriage Equality Project that worked to approve Washington State's Referendum 74, which legalized same-sex marriage in that state.[17] Following that successful campaign, "Same Love" rose up the charts in 2013 as the US Supreme Court prepared to rule on challenges to the federal Defense of Marriage Act, and quickly became a nationally recognized anthem for marriage equality and LGBTQ rights.[18] American rock critic Robert Christgau wrote that the track was "the best gay marriage song to date in any genre and as corny as it damn well oughta be," implying that it was sentimental in a way that might move listeners.[19] Writing for the pop culture website *A.V. Club*, Chris Mincher described the song as a "refreshing" reminder that "hip-hop can be an effective tool in advocating social transformation," problematically suggesting that other contemporary hip hop singles were apolitical.[20] The *New York Times* noted that "Same Love" was "the first song to explicitly embrace and promote gay marriage that has made it into the Top 40," indicating that unlike so-called gay anthems such as Lady Gaga's 2011 hit single, "Born This Way," Macklemore and Lewis's track actually named marriage equality and LGBTQ rights as its focal point.[21]

The track's breakthrough on the *Billboard* Top 40 charts followed the success of the duo's "Thrift Shop" and "Can't Hold Us," both of which fit comfortably in the sonic realm of pop as well as hip hop and R&B genres, even if they were not marketed as such by promoters.[22] Macklemore and

17. Leanne Naramore, "Hip-Hop's Macklemore x Ryan Lewis Release Beautiful Video for 'Same Love,'" *HRC.org*, October 3, 2012, http://www.hrc.org/blog/entry/hip-hops-macklemore-x-ryan-lewis-release-beautiful-video-for-same-love, accessed April 2, 2015. The duo donated much of the proceeds from the song to the advocacy group Washington United for Marriage. See James C. McKinley Jr., "Stars Align for a Gay Marriage Anthem," *New York Times*, June 30, 2013, http://www.nytimes.com/2013/07/01/arts/music/stars-align-for-a-gay-marriage-anthem.html?_r=0.

18. McKinley, "Stars Align."

19. Robert Christgau, "Customer Guide Review: Macklemore & Ryan Lewis," *robertchristgau.com*, http://www.robertchristgau.com/get_artist.php?name=macklemore.

20. Chris Mincher, "Macklemore & Lewis' 'Same Love' is more than a pro–gay marriage anthem," *AV Club*, January 24, 2014, http://www.avclub.com/article/macklemore-amp-lewis-same-love-is-more-than-a-pro--200929.

21. McKinley, "Stars Align."

22. Eric Weisbard notes that the promoters of "Thrift Shop" "first targeted alternative

Lewis's crossover appeal can be at least partly attributed to their music's sonic characteristics, which share a pop aesthetic with other chart-topping hip hop and R&B tracks of that summer.[23] "Same Love" opens with a held chord, reminiscent of the opening of a church hymn. A hesitant-sounding piano introduction enters over this chord, closely followed by delicate string tremolos. These sounds then drop out to make space for the opening piano melody, based on the beginning of the 1965 single "People Get Ready," a gospel-tinged R&B track written by Curtis Mayfield and initially performed by the Impressions. It is not until about halfway through Macklemore's first verse that the beat, which consists of soft drum set sonorities, is added, and it remains tertiary to the song's melodic and lyrical content. Indeed, the instruments used, especially the sustained organ chord and melodic piano, suggest churches and suburban spaces rather than the landscapes often invoked in commercial rap, such as the hip hop club or city streets. The inclusion of the melody from "People Get Ready," a song that is very much rooted in African American freedom song traditions and that features Underground Railroad imagery, invokes comparisons between the mid-century civil rights movement for racial equality and the contemporary mainstream LGBTQ rights movement.[24]

---

rock, then rhythmic Top 40, and then mainstream Top 40," and that the song "in no way sought to belong to R&B as a format—and by extension to the R&B format's privileging of black listeners." Eric Weisbard, *Top 40 Democracy: The Rival Mainstreams of American Music* (Chicago: University of Chicago Press, 2014), 262. This may or may not have been Macklemore and Lewis's decision, but it does speak to the way their sonic approach combined with their racial identities to allow them to pursue radio formats beyond those focused on Black music genres and Black listeners.

23. For example, the only other hip hop songs on the Top 40 during the week of June 29, 2013, when "Same Love" reached the number 33 position, were Macklemore and Lewis's own "Can't Hold Us" and "Thrift Shop" (numbers 3 and 19, respectively), "Power Trip" by J. Cole (featuring Miguel) at number 21, Wale's "Bad" (featuring Tiara Thomas or Rihanna) at 23, Drake's "Started From the Bottom" at 35, "U.O.E.N.O." by Rocko (featuring Future and Rick Ross) at 36, and Lil Wayne (featuring 2 Chainz), "Rich as F**k" at 38. Most of these songs were similarly pop crossovers. At the top of the hip hop and R&B singles for that same week was the pop chart topper "Blurred Lines" by white singer Robin Thicke featuring T.I. and Pharrell. Rap songs that did not share pop elements were relegated to much lower positions on the *Billboard* charts.

24. As Joseph G. Schloss argues, samples in hip hop are not necessarily used to make particular intertextual references; more often, producers or DJs use samples that are obscure and thus more difficult for the average listener to identify. *Making Beats: The Art of Sample-Based Hip-Hop* (Middletown, CT: Wesleyan University Press, 2004). In "Same Love," however, the borrowed melody, or quotation, is not an electronic sample but rather is performed on an acoustic instrument and is easily recognizable, thereby invoking a historical reference to music of the civil rights era.

Macklemore begins his first verse with a personal story about growing up with stereotypical ideas about what it means to be gay, revealing that while he himself is straight, he has a gay uncle. He finishes the verse with a critique of religious and political conservatives for their anti-gay positions:

America the brave still fears what we don't know
And "God loves all his children" is somehow forgotten
But we paraphrase a book written thirty-five hundred years ago

Additional references to anti-gay sentiment in churches recur throughout the track. In the second verse, for example, he raps, "It's the same hate that's caused wars from religion," and "When I was at church they taught me something else / If you preach hate at the service those words aren't anointed / That holy water that you soak in has been poisoned." The critique of religion—or, more accurately, the homophobic use of religion and religious rhetoric—is particularly apt here, as the campaign against Referendum 74 was heavily championed by religious organizations such as the state's three Catholic dioceses.[25]

Although Macklemore's "Same Love" does not at first blush appear to engage in racial politics, the circumstances surrounding the song's success, particularly when considering Macklemore's own position as a white, straight, cisgender male working within the genre of hip hop, point to the racial politics of the mainstream American LGBTQ rights movement. Macklemore's critiques of hip hop, that if he were gay he would think hip hop hates him, erase the Black music genre's history of grassroots activism and draw on rhetoric often used by proponents for marriage equality that creates a false dichotomy between Black communities and LGBTQ individuals. This false dichotomy, which demonizes "Black homophobia" as a particularly large hurdle for (white) LGBTQ Americans on the road to legalized same-sex marriage, was perhaps most evident in the backlash against Black voters following the passing of California's Proposition 8 (hereafter Prop 8), an amendment to the state constitution that banned same-sex marriage in that state.

Early exit polls, later proven inaccurate, estimated that 70 percent of Black voters, most of who voted for President Barack Obama, also voted in favor of Prop 8, and several of the biggest media outlets in turn cited this

25. Joel Connelly, "Same-Sex Marriage Leads in Washington, Passes in Maryland, Maine," *Seattle PI*, November 6, 2012, http://blog.seattlepi.com/seattlepolitics/2012/11/06/same-sex-marriage-leads-in-washington-maryland-and-maine/.

statistic as fact.[26] This prompted many white marriage-equality supporters, such as gay writers Dan Savage and Andrew Sullivan, to decry "Black homophobia" as the root cause of the setback to marriage equality.[27] As *Slate* contributor Jamelle Bouie points out, this scapegoating of Black voters, like Macklemore's scapegoating of hip hop, is part of a larger phenomenon of "invented black pathology," in which "behaviors present among other groups of Americans become pathologies when they're exhibited by blacks."[28] Citing the report released by the National Gay and Lesbian Task Force in January 2009 that found that only 58 percent of African American voters supported Prop 8, Bouie noted, "Prop 8 didn't win because of blacks or Latinos, it won because millions of Californians—white as much as black or brown—opposed same-sex marriage."[29] By painting homophobia as a uniquely Black problem, rather than an American problem that cuts across all ethnic and racial communities, white LGBTQ leaders position themselves as wiser, more progressive, and thus better situated as leaders of a mainstream movement that can "fix" the problems within communities of color. It also further marginalizes queer people of color who are left primarily outside of this discussion unless they are invoked as infantile subjects in need of saving from their own communities.

Macklemore's assertion in "Same Love" that "If I were gay I would think hip hop hates me" functions in much the same way as the backlash against Black voters following the passing of Prop 8 in that it also relies on the exaggerated concept of Black homophobia as a threat to LGBTQ people. Rather

---

26. In a study released by the National Gay and Lesbian Task Force Policy Institute, Patrick J. Egan and Kenneth Sherrill found that only 58 percent of Black voters voted "yes" on Prop 8. *California's Proposition 8: What Happened, and What Does the Future Hold?* (San Francisco: National Gay and Lesbian Task Force, 2009), http://www.thetaskforce.org/static_html/downloads/issues/egan_sherrill_prop8_1_6_09.pdf, accessed September 15, 2017. Articles that cited this statistic include Karl Vick and Ashley Surdin, "Most of California's Black Voters Backed Gay Marriage Ban," *Washington Post*, November 7, 2008, http://www.washingtonpost.com/wp-dyn/content/article/2008/11/06/AR2008110603880.html; and Farhad Manjoo, "Props to Obama: Did He Help Push California's Gay-Marriage Ban over the Top?" *Slate*, November 5, 2008, http://www.slate.com/articles/news_and_politics/politics/2008/11/props_to_obama.html.

27. Dan Savage, "Black Homophobia," *The Stranger*, November 5, 2008, http://slog.thestranger.com/2008/11/black_homophobia, accessed April 22, 2015; Andrew Sullivan, "The Grim Truth," *The Atlantic*, November 5, 2008, http://andrewsullivan.theatlantic.com/the_daily_dish/2008/11/the-grim-truth.html.

28. Jamelle Bouie, "Blacks Don't Have a Corporal Punishment Problem," *Slate*, September 19, 2014, http://www.slate.com/articles/news_and_politics/politics/2014/09/blacks_and_corporal_punishment_why_we_invent_black_pathologies.single.html.

29. Bouie, "Blacks Don't Have a Corporal Punishment Problem."

than emphasize the role that churches played as a source of communities' bigotry, he targets the cultural institution of hip hop, but the accusation still relies on an invented Black pathology that locates homophobia in hip hop but not in other, predominantly white genres. While it is true that some mainstream hip hop features anti-gay slurs and attitudes, Macklemore's position as a white rapper and the lack of any openly queer Black performers on his track complicates his criticism of the genre. Rather than combating homophobia in hip hop, his claims bolster his own strategic performance as a self-conscious, socially aware white rapper while engaging in rhetoric that perpetuates a false dichotomy of Black versus gay.

The idea that hip hop is especially homophobic renders queer and trans hip hop practitioners, many of whom are Black, invisible. Yet, queerness and hip hop are and always have been interrelated. Macklemore's lyrics are the result of decades of some heterosexual hip hop practitioners' distancing from Black queer expressions, not a reflection of some innate characteristic found in the genre. The remainder of this book is focused on hearing those very voices that "Same Love" erases. I ask us to listen for and to the Black queer resonances in hip hop that have often been ignored.[30]

Situating Queer Voices in Hip Hop

This book begins by locating the queer foundations of hip hop. In the first chapter, I argue that hip hop evolved from music genres that began in queer spaces, especially disco, and as such has probably always had queer practitioners and most certainly has queer roots. As Alice Echols notes, the earliest rap performances used disco records, as is evident in the first rap record, the Sugarhill Gang's "Rapper's Delight" (1979), which was built on the bass line and other elements of Chic's 1979 single, "Good Times."[31] As rap evolved, however, many of its practitioners distanced themselves from the dance genres that were perceived as inherently gay or too white, engaging in homophobic, revisionist narratives that attempted to separate hip hop from other dance genres that have queer or feminine associations. Here, I reposition hip hop in a specifically Black queer musical and cultural lineage that begins with disco in the 1970s (or even earlier, if we consider its rela-

---

30. For more on Macklemore, see Lauron Kehrer, "A Love Song for All of Us?: Macklemore's 'Same Love' and the Myth of Black Homophobia," *Journal of the Society for American Music* 12, no. 4 (2018): 425–48.

31. Alice Echols, *Hot Stuff: Disco and the Remaking of American Culture* (New York: W. W. Norton, 2010), 217.

tion to Black queer Harlem of the 1920s and 1930s) and house music of the 1980s. House and hip hop developed along separate paths, but both continued to have queer participants, even if those participants remained much more visible in the former than in the latter. This chapter demonstrates that without Black queer music making, there would be no hip hop.

In chapter 2, I argue that a group of openly queer and trans rappers based in New York City, including Leıf, Azealia Banks, Cakes da Killa, and Zebra Katz, use cultural signifiers of Ballroom culture to express a particularly Black and/or Latinx LGBTQ identity, blending aspects of Ballroom culture with those found in hip hop in order to render those identities legible in a genre that I call "Ballroom rap." Critics and journalists tend to discuss these artists together as evidence of a rise in the number of popular queer hip hop artists, and several of them, specifically Azealia Banks and Leıf, have been on the brink of real commercial success but have not yet reached the large national audiences that, for example, Macklemore has. The chapter problematizes the grouping of these artists together as simply "gay rappers" but suggests that they do share some stylistic characteristics in that each of them draws on aspects of Ballroom culture. I illustrate three main ways in which rappers reference Ballroom in their music: lyrically, visually, and musically. Applying the genre label "Ballroom rap" to the work of these specific openly queer or trans Black artists based in New York City positions their musical texts in relationship with each other in such a way that their multifaceted identities and musical styles are no longer collapsed into the contested category of "gay rap." Instead, this genre accounts for the shared cultural reference point that has led music journalists and listeners to already profile these artists in relation to each other while also making visible the often unnoticed heritage of Black queer culture in the city over the past century and acknowledging that this culture is not monolithic and is constantly in flux.

One group that has been largely erased from hip hop discourses is openly queer Black women, especially those with more masculine gender presentations. In recent years, artists such as Young M.A and Syd have spoken openly about their experiences being queer rappers while simultaneously achieving commercial success, a rare feat in the genre. And yet, theorizations of queer hip hop artists have largely focused on men. In chapter 3, I explore the strategies that Young M.A and Syd engage in order to navigate expectations of mainstream rappers as queer Black women who are androgynous or masculine-of-center. I argue that these artists face a double bind in which they are both hypervisible and invisible. Both successful in the commercial mainstream, Young M.A and Syd have very different musical styles, but they are both Black, queer, non-femme women rappers who must navigate the hypervisibility/invisibility paradox. Their musical expressions and the ways they have defined themselves in public, especially in response to homophobic comments made against them or in their professional circles, are both clear assertions of queer identity and resistance to being pigeonholed by non-queer listeners as essentially queer rappers. As butch women artists, Young M.A and Syd do not fit into the previously established categories for women rappers, but they also do not assert their own category. This approach helps them navigate the hypervisible/invisible paradox to which, as queer women of color, they are particularly susceptible.

In chapter 4, I consider the influences of queer and trans bounce artists in the mainstream. For the past decade, queer and trans rappers have been the dominant force in New Orleans bounce, a dance-centric hip hop genre specific to that city. Recently, artists such as Beyoncé and Drake have sampled some of these artists in their own hit songs, such as the former's "Formation" (which samples Big Freedia and the late Messy Mya) and, more recently, Drake's "Nice For What" (which also samples Big Freedia). However, the queer artists sampled in these and other examples, including the openly queer and gender nonconforming Big Freedia, are rarely given much *visibility* as collaborators; they seldom appear in music videos, for example, and instead become purely audible samples in which their queer identities are erased. This chapter, which draws on fieldwork I conducted in New Orleans in 2016 and is informed by relationships I've maintained since then, rounds out the book and brings together these tensions between mainstream/lesser-known, queer/non-queer, exploitation/representation that are embedded throughout the previous chapters and reframes questions about sampling and ethics through a queer lens.

I close the book with an "outro" in which I consider hip hop's most visible openly queer artist in the mainstream to date: Lil Nas X. Tracing queer expressions from his first breakthrough hit, "Old Town Road," through his first full-length album, *MONTERO*, and his cover of Dolly Parton's "Jolene," I listen not only for the queer resonances that place him in the Black queer musical lineage that I outline in the previous chapters but also for the ways Lil Nas X blurs genre boundaries. I argue that while Lil Nas X's visibility and mainstream success as an openly queer rapper is in many ways unprecedented, we should not view his as a stand-alone success story. His emergence is better described as a recent development within the decades-long history of queer involvement in hip hop, albeit one that challenges contemporary mainstream notions of hip hop authenticity and masculinity.

Notions of hip hop authenticity, as expressed both within hip hop communities and in the larger American culture, rely on the construction of the rapper as a Black, masculine, heterosexual, cisgender man who enacts a narrative of struggle and success. While there is considerable racial, gender, and sexual diversity among hip hop practitioners, including rappers, those who fall outside of this matrix of normative hip hop identities are always in conversation with rap's specific notion of Black masculinity. These artists, especially queer and trans artists, employ performance strategies that engage with and challenge this construction in order to render themselves legible (and audible) to hip hop audiences. *Queer Voices in Hip Hop* examines some of these strategies through a combination of musical, textual, and visual analysis and reception history. I hope that this book helps us reconsider what hip hop studies, and indeed popular music studies more generally, might look and sound like if Black queer and trans identities were no longer at the margins of scholarship but were instead centered within it.

1 • Hip Hop's Queer Roots

Disco, House, and Early Hip Hop

While Macklemore's "Same Love" and the discourses around hip hop and LGBTQ rights in predominantly white communities have constructed a dichotomy of Black or gay that often precludes Black *and* gay, there is another false dichotomy that began to take root decades earlier as hip hop artists attempted to define their nascent genre: rap or disco and, later, rap or house. Rap was and continues to be positioned at odds with these dance music styles that are largely associated with Black and Latinx LGBTQ social spaces. A musical history shows that these genres grew out of similar approaches to technology, especially manipulation of prerecorded sound and playback equipment, including turntables and tape decks. Yet the messaging over the last few decades suggests that they developed largely independently from each other both musically and in terms of the spaces where they were heard and the identities of those involved. Aside from some discussion of the role of disco records and sometimes disco clubs in early hip hop, narratives about the development of the genre rarely acknowledge their shared social histories. Indeed, some of these narratives actively assert the development of hip hop as *distinct* from disco, albeit retroactively. For example, as Loren Kajikawa notes, Def Jam cofounder Rick Rubin situated the sound of rap artists on his label in the mid-1980s with rock rather than disco, stating, "Rap records are really black rock and roll records, the antithesis of disco."[1] While Kajikawa illustrates the ways this fashioning of rap worked to "elevate rap's standing by appealing to the same anti-disco sentiments that had pigeonholed black musicians in rap's first years as a commercial genre," we might also think of this rhetoric as part of the beginning of commercial hip hop's distancing from anything considered queer.[2]

---

1. Rick Rubin, quoted in Loren Kajikawa, *Sounding Race in Rap Songs* (Oakland: University of California Press, 2015), 69.

2. Kajikawa, *Sounding Race in Rap Songs*, 69–70.

But what happens if we marginalize homophobia in hip hop the way we have historically marginalized queerness in the genre? If we reconsider the genre's development and put it more closely in conversation with those music traditions associated with Black and Latinx queer club cultures, we thus reposition hip hop in a Black queer musical and social lineage. In this chapter, I push back against the assumption that hip hop is inherently homophobic by looking at its roots and overlapping histories with disco and house, two genres closely associated with Black and Latinx LGBTQ subcultures. I examine the rise and fall of disco and its significance in queer spaces and then discuss the emergence of house music following the homophobic and racist backlash against disco. These developments are significant to early hip hop, both musically and socially. In addition to shared musical styles and techniques, early hip hop overlapped in spaces with disco especially, putting Black queer subcultures in proximity with the earliest hip hop performances. As early hip hop participants began to distance themselves from disco, a homophobic tendency to separate that new genre from musical styles and spaces associated with LGBTQ people developed. Rather than positioning hip hop as always already homophobic, however, I consider how that homophobia was constructed over the ensuing decades and was not inherent in the genre.

The proliferation of online and print articles in the mid-2010s profiling openly queer and trans rappers such as Big Freedia, Leif, Mykki Blanco, Zebra Katz, and others, as well as more recent writing on Lil Nas X, suggests that the success of these artists is newsworthy because they are anomalies.[3] Hip hop, however, evolved from music genres that began in queer spaces, especially disco, and as such has probably always had queer practitioners and most certainly queer roots. As Alice Echols notes, the earliest rap performances used disco records.[4] Furthermore, there was demonstrable overlap in spaces and social practices in which disco and early rap were performed and consumed. As Nadine Hubbs notes, "The most consequential and neglected

3. See, for example, Clare Considine, "Zebra Katz, Mykki Blanco, and the Rise of Queer Rap," *The Guardian*, June 8, 2012, http://www.theguardian.com/music/2012/jun/09/zebra-katz-rise-of-gay-rappers; Carrie Battan, "We Invented Swag: NYC's Queer Rap," *Pitchfork*, March 21, 2012, http://pitchfork.com/features/articles/8793-we-invented-swag/; Billy Nilles, "Why Lil Nas X's Last Year Is Such a Big Deal," *Eonline*, January 25, 2020, https://www.eonline.com/news/1060868/why-lil-nas-x-breaking-billboard-records-is-such-a-big-deal.

4. Alice Echols, *Hot Stuff: Disco and the Remaking of American Culture* (New York: W. W. Norton, 2010), 217.

aspect of queer identity . . . [is] more social than sexual."[5] Musical practices associated with queer socialities and queer spaces connect early hip hop to queer cultures of the 1970s and 1980s.

As rap evolved, however, some of its heterosexual creators intentionally distanced themselves from the dance genres that were perceived as inherently gay or too white. Rapper Chuck D of Public Enemy, for instance, articulated such a stance on house music:

> My thing is I don't like house music. I first heard it as a DJ, when I was doing radio shows, and I said then that I thought the beats lacked soul. . . . And I dislike the scene that's based around house—it's sophisticated, anti-black, anti-culture, anti-feel, the most ARTIFICIAL shit I ever heard. It represents the gay scene, it's separating blacks from their past and their culture, it's upwardly mobile.[6]

Chuck D's resistance to house, while seemingly based on musical preferences, is rooted in homophobia. It is an example of revisionist narratives that attempt to separate hip hop from other dance genres that have queer or feminine associations. To counter this problematic narrative, which erases the contributions of Black queer artists, we can instead place hip hop, especially its contemporary queer expressions, within a Black queer musical lineage. Rather than focus on openly queer individuals, in this chapter I examine the musical and social overlap between early hip hop and the Black dance genres of disco and house, which were both intricately tied to Black queer spaces. As this context demonstrates, it was that lineage that produced rap's predecessors: without Black queer music making, there would be no hip hop.

Disco as Black Queer Lineage

Scholars have widely acknowledged that the birth of disco can be traced largely to the Black and gay clubs in New York City at the end of the 1960s and beginning of the 1970s.[7] However, in their efforts to emphasize the

---

5. Nadine Hubbs, *The Queer Composition of America's Sound: Gay Modernists, American Music, and National Identity* (Berkeley: University of California Press, 2004), 5.

6. Chuck D, quoted in Brian Currid, "'We Are Family': House Music and Queer Performativity," in *Cruising the Performative: Interventions into the Representation of Ethnicity, Nationality, and Sexuality*, ed. Sue-Ellen Case, Philip Brett, and Susan Leigh Foster (Bloomington: Indiana University Press, 1995), 167.

7. Walter Hughes, "In the Empire of the Beat: Discipline and Disco," in *Microphone*

multiculturalism of disco's origins, as well as the homophobia that fueled the backlash that resulted in its decline in the mainstream, many scholars have failed to acknowledge the specifically Black queer influences on the genre. I do not intend to essentialize disco by declaring it solely a Black gay genre; rather, here I pull together existing scholarly threads to highlight how Black gay communities and individuals were a major yet often under-emphasized force behind the genre and its successors.

Disco is a constellation of spaces, sounds, and performances centered on communal dance experiences. As a musical movement of the 1970s, it often played an important role in the social lives of individuals from various marginalized communities who were engaged in challenging their position in society. Walter Hughes describes disco as "not only a genre of music and a kind of dancing, but the venue in which both are deployed," especially for gay men.[8] He continues:

> It is, as its name suggests, site-specific music, the music of the discotheque. The name also defines it as music that is technologically reproduced, "on disk," not performed. . . . For urban gay men, "disco" is where you dance and what you dance to, regardless of the technicalities of musical innovation and evolution.[9]

Nadine Hubbs similarly regards disco as "a musical, social, and cultural space with critical African-American, Latino/a, and variously *queer* involvements."[10] Echols notes that disco developed in relation to social movements and helped to broaden "the contours of blackness, femininity, and male homosexuality."[11] Disco, as both music and space, reflected newfound freedoms brought about by activist movements that began in the preceding decade and was the soundtrack for several marginalized communities finding their groove.

David Mancuso's dance parties, which he organized in his private space known as the Loft, were among the earliest and most influential and became

---

Fiends: Youth Music & Youth Culture, ed. Andrew Ross and Tricia Rose (New York: Routledge, 1994), 147–57; Anthony Thomas, "The House the Kids Built: The Gay Black Imprint on American Dance Music," reprinted in *Out in Culture: Gay, Lesbian, and Queer Essays on Popular Culture*, ed. C. K. Creekmur and A. Doty (Durham, NC: Duke University Press, 1995), 437–46.

8. Hughes, "In the Empire of the Beat," 148.

9. Hughes, "In the Empire of the Beat," 148.

10. Nadine Hubbs, "'I Will Survive': Musical Mappings of Queer Social Space in a Disco Anthem," *Popular Music* 26, no. 2 (2007): 232. Emphasis in the original.

11. Echols, *Hot Stuff*, xxv.

the model not only for gay discos but also for many of the clubs that proliferated in the 1970s. Mancuso drew inspiration for these early gatherings from the tradition of rent parties, a mainstay of Black communities in Harlem especially during the early twentieth century.[12] Eric Garber has chronicled Black queer life in Harlem during the years of the Harlem Renaissance (approximately 1920–1935), noting that during the Great Migration that brought an influx of African Americans from the South to northern industrial cities such as Chicago, Detroit, and New York, Black lesbians and gay men formed social networks and institutions, some of which are still in place today.[13] While rent parties were an important focal point of Black life, Garber writes that they were especially important for Black queer individuals in that they provided the relative safety of privacy.[14] In addition to the practical benefits of raising funds, rent parties also provided a private space where Black (and sometimes white) lesbians and gay men could gather together and hear blues musicians perform songs that reflected their own queer experiences, dance in same-gender couples, and participate in a particularly Black queer culture.

Mancuso's Loft parties were inspired by these rent parties and were known for attracting a very diverse crowd, much more so than the clubs that existed in New York City during this time. Disco historian Tim Lawrence writes that the crowd included many Black and Latinx gay men but that "it was also very mixed . . . cutting across the boundaries of class, color, sex, and sexuality."[15] Although Mancuso's parties were not specifically Black or gay, many Black gay participants found a home at the Loft, including Larry Levan and Frankie Knuckles, who would later become influential disco and house DJs themselves.

Spaces serve as important factors in the evolution of disco, as they were influenced by and reflective of the social and political climate of the time. Before the Stonewall riots of 1969 sparked a new wave of pro-LGBTQ activism in the United States, there were few options for LGBTQ people to socialize together in groups. House parties, which were held in private homes, offered discretion but required invitations and a network of connected individuals. Public spaces were limited to gay bars that were fre-

12. Tim Lawrence, *Love Saves the Day: A History of American Dance Music* (Durham, NC: Duke University Press, 2003), 22.

13. Eric Garber, "A Spectacle of Color: The Lesbian and Gay Subculture of Jazz Age Harlem," in *Hidden from History: Reclaiming the Gay and Lesbian Past*, ed. Martin Duberman, Martha Vicinus, and George Chauncey Jr. (New York: Meridian, 1990), 318–31.

14. Garber, "Spectacle of Color," 321.

15. Lawrence, *Love Saves the Day*, 22.

quently mafia-owned and were subject to constant police raids, which often resulted in patrons' arrests and their names being published in local newspapers. This act of public outing and shaming had dire consequences for some, including losing their jobs and experiencing increased stigma from society as well as families. In the years following the Stonewall riots, public spaces for members of gay communities, especially white gay men, evolved drastically. Not only did laws change (slowly but surely, thanks in part to new resistance to those laws), but an ethos of pride also began to develop among members of the LGBTQ community. This included a desire to celebrate gay identity in public ways; dancing was one of the expressions of that celebration. As Gillian Frank has noted, disco emerged as the "music of liberation for gay white men" because it "coincided with—and provided a focal point for—the process of becoming politically visible and winning civil rights within American culture."[16] Discos played an important role in the development of a politically active and increasingly visible population because they provided spaces where LGBTQ people could "imagine a sexual community and coordinate their gay identity."[17]

While gay-owned discos that featured a largely gay clientele blossomed during the early 1970s in New York City especially, they were not always the multiethnic and multiracial utopias that many would like to remember. The LGBTQ community was not immune from the rampant racism of mainstream American culture, and this racism played out in the policing of some disco spaces. For example, the Flamingo, a predominantly gay club that opened in Manhattan (the center of gay nightlife in New York City) in December 1974, was overwhelmingly white, thanks in part to an expensive membership system.[18] As Lawrence notes, club owners claim to have not consciously turned away numbers of Black patrons but that doing so helped foster a friendly relationship with the club's neighbors and attracted an upscale crowd.[19]

Despite disco's queer roots, enthusiastic gay audiences, and popularity in gay clubs, very few artists who performed in the genre (aside from DJs and producers) were openly gay-identified. The gender-bending singer Sylvester, whose singles "You Make Me Feel (Mighty Real)" and "Dance (Disco Heat)" were club hits in both the United States and Europe, is a notable exception. Early in his career Sylvester performed with a nontraditional theatrical drag

16. Gillian Frank, "Discophobia: Antigay Prejudice and the 1979 Backlash against Disco," *Journal of the History of Sexuality* 16, no. 2 (2007): 284.

17. Frank, "Discophobia," 285.

18. Lawrence, *Love Saves the Day*, 139.

19. Lawrence, *Love Saves the Day*, 139.

troupe, the Cockettes, who were not interested in passing as women and instead performed in women's clothes and wigs but with their beards intact.[20] Unlike other members of the troupe, who viewed themselves as transcending all social categories, Sylvester was largely invested in performing his Black identity.[21] He was deeply inspired by Black blues women, such as those who were mainstays of the aforementioned Harlem rent parties, and drew on their legacy in his own performances. As a disco artist, his vocal style featured a sustained falsetto, and his appearance, while androgynous, leaned toward the feminine. Walter Hughes suggests that "You Make Me Feel (Mighty Real)," with its gospel-inflected vocalizations of desire and repetitiveness, "performs the representative hypostatization of [Sylvester's] gay identity":

> His impassioned repetition becomes as orgasmic as Donna Summer's in "I Feel Love," insisting that, for the gay black man, the realization of the self can have the ecstatic force of a revelation. . . . This is a "gay" realness that flickers into being with a "touch" and a "kiss"—at the moment of homosexual physical contact.[22]

Rather than mapping their same-sex desire onto the performances of Black women divas, gay men, particularly *Black* gay men, were able to hear it reflected in Sylvester's voice and the words he sang.

And yet, as Hughes also points out, even though Sylvester's identity as a Black gay man should make sense in a genre that originated as one that was primarily vocalized by Black (usually straight) women and enjoyed by gay (usually white) men, "he is nevertheless rendered invisible if not impossible by the dominant culture's potent alliance of homophobia and racism."[23] In other words, Sylvester's open performances of his own Black gay identity were not only a rarity in disco in particular and popular music more generally, but his career often goes unmentioned in histories of the genre, not because it lacked impact but because the particular intersections of Blackness and queerness are so often subsumed under either race or sexuality—that is, Black *or* gay, not Black *and* gay.

The erasure of Black queer identities in narratives of disco is also a result of some scholars' focus on multiculturalism, on the idea that disco was enjoyed across social boundaries. This emphasis on a multicultural commu-

---

20. Echols, *Hot Stuff*, 141–42.
21. Echols, *Hot Stuff*, 141.
22. Hughes, "In the Empire of the Beat," 154.
23. Hughes, "In the Empire of the Beat," 153–54.

nity of listeners and dancers, however, decentralizes the influence that Black individuals, especially Black queer individuals, have had in disco's development. Echols and others note that disco was played in gay clubs long before reaching a larger audience, but gay listeners in scholarly accounts are nearly always assumed to be white.[24] When scholars discuss gay people of color at all, they do so primarily in the context of the multiracial gay club, where their experiences are subsumed under a universalized white gay male narrative. For example, Gillian Frank highlights some of the ways in which early disco especially resonated with multiple marginalized groups at various points of intersection:

> From its origins, disco music was associated with cultural difference. At the beginning of the 1970s many disco artists were Latinos or African Americans, and many were African American women. The audiences for the first wave of disco were predominantly urban straight and gay African Americans, straight and gay Latinos, and white gay men dancing in African American and gay night clubs in major urban centers like New York and Chicago.[25]

Frank positions early white gay audiences within African American *and* gay nightclubs, but this construction makes it unclear whether these clubs catered to an African American gay clientele or to those who were either African American *or* gay. Furthermore, he explains that white gay men reinterpreted disco music, especially those tracks that featured Black artists, as expressive of their own experiences of marginalization and coming together as a community. This explanation is offered without regard to how that community often reinscribed racial hierarchies in white gay spaces, as noted above.[26]

I push back against the idea of a utopic, multiracial gay disco dance floor, however, not to essentialize all disco experiences as simultaneously Black and gay but to draw attention to how multicultural discourses erase the contributions of Black queer communities. In relocating disco's origins at the intersection between Blackness and queerness, I wish to situate successive Black queer cultural productions in similar Black queer spaces. The public backlash that eventually pushed disco and dance music back underground at the end

---

24. For example, Echols writes, "By the time Vince Aletti wrote about what he called 'party music' and 'discotheque rock' in a fall 1973 issue of *Rolling Stone*, gay men had been dancing in discos for three years" (*Hot Stuff*, 2).

25. Frank, "Discophobia," 284.

26. Frank, "Discophobia," 284.

of the 1970s provides a useful illustration of the ways homophobia and racism intersected in this genre and in the music's reception.

Like most popular music styles of the United States, disco is rooted in Black popular music traditions and technological changes. During the Stonewall era, recorded music was the main form of entertainment at both private parties and in gay bars, and it was the record that became the site of the musical and technological innovations that fueled the emergent genre.[27] Drawing on the sound associated with Detroit's Motown label, the house band of producers Kenneth Gamble and Leon Huff's Philadelphia International Records label, MFSB (Mother Father Sister Brother), transformed the beat and tempo and produced the "Philly sound" that became the foundation for the new recorded dance music. Drummer Earl Young describes how he created the disco beat:

> I thought the Detroit sound was unique. Motown used four-four on the snare—khh, khh, khh, khh—and the heartbeat on the bass—dmm-dmm, dmm-dmm, dmm-dmm, dmm-dmm—and they also used four-four on the tambourines. . . . I would use cymbals more than the average drummer, and I realized that if I played the four-four on the bass I could work different patterns on the cymbals.[28]

The new beat, with its four-on-the-floor emphasis in the bass, provided a framework that allowed DJs to transition more easily between records and keep dancers on the dance floor for longer stretches. Later, this somewhat standardized beat would facilitate new approaches by prominent DJs who, paralleling similar contemporaneous developments in hip hop, would loop, lengthen, and remix their own versions of dance singles.

Disco was not limited by these rhythmic characteristics, and DJs, the real stars of the scene, played music according to their own tastes. In tandem with disco's emergence as a mainstream phenomenon, an increasing number of white performers, including rockers such as Rod Stewart and the Rolling Stones, began to record their own disco singles. Michael Fresco, the owner of the Flamingo, suggests that it was the distinction between DJs' musical choices (i.e., the ability to select musical styles closely associated with predominantly white or predominantly Black artists) that primarily influenced the racial makeup in his club.[29] In fact, a combination of factors, including musical selec-

27. Frank, "Discophobia," 284.

28. Earl Young, quoted in Lawrence, *Love Saves the Day*, 120.

29. Michael Fresco, quoted in Lawrence, *Love Saves the Day*, 139.

tion, door policies, and general feel of a particular club, had an impact on a club's racial demographics. As noted above, some clubs catered to primarily white audiences, including gay clubs, which left Black gay participants to create their own spaces as well as their own social and professional networks. Rather than assert that there are particular musical styles and sounds that divide audiences among racial lines, I contend that it was involvement and socialization in these networks that might have led to a shared musical taste and style that contributed to the racial division found in many disco spaces.

This intersection of racism and homophobia led to the establishment of what Lawrence calls the Black gay network within the scene, and it was in this informal social and professional network that participants, including DJs, interacted and shared musical ideas. In her study of gay American modernist composers in the mid-twentieth century, Nadine Hubbs argues that through their shared marginalized identities as homosexuals, gay composers, including Aaron Copland and Virgil Thomson, formed professional and social circles in which they influenced one another's compositional techniques and approaches.[30] This does not suggest that there is an inherently queer form of composition; rather, their queerness influenced gay composers' personal and professional lives in such a way that it had an impact on their musical output. Similarly, I do not wish to suggest that there were specific records or artists that provided the soundtrack for Black queer spaces exclusively. Instead, it was the formation of spaces that acknowledged and welcomed Black queer participants and the networks that emerged out of necessity that might have led to a perceived or actual distinction between the musical styles that were preferred by different racialized groups.

By the late 1970s there was a large and vocal movement proclaiming that "Disco Sucks!" This anti-disco sentiment coalesced in the now-infamous "Disco Demolition Night" that took place on July 12, 1979, at Chicago's Cominsky Park during a baseball game between the Chicago White Sox and the Detroit Tigers. Steve Dahl, a radio DJ for Chicago's WLUP-FM 98, inspired tens of thousands of his listeners to bring disco records to be destroyed during the intermission, and the result was a riot in which attendees stormed the field, rushed the gates, and wreaked havoc on the stadium.[31] As Hubbs, Frank, and others have argued, at the root of this demonstration and its participants' rallying cry of "Disco Sucks!" was a desire to reclaim white masculinity's dominance in mainstream music by privileging album-oriented rock (AOR) over dance music. Frank writes:

---

30. Hubbs, *Queer Composition of America's Sound.*
31. Frank. "Discophobia."

The sexual and gender politics of the antidisco backlash marked a moment in which a primarily white male and middle-class audience sought to assert their masculinity within heterosocial spaces. Put differently, the backlash against disco saw heterosexual men attack disco music because they believed that disco culture limited their ability to interact with women, excluding them from heterosocial spaces, imperiled their heterosexuality, and privileged an inauthentic form of masculinity.[32]

Although the relationship between homophobia and discophobia has therefore been clearly outlined, Frank de-emphasizes the ways in which the "authentic" form of masculinity that anti-disco protesters championed was also racialized. He acknowledges that the participants in the anti-disco movement were primarily white men but fails to stress how masculinity and whiteness are co-constructed and performed and that the backlash against disco was fueled not by homophobia alone but by the intersection of homophobia and racism. As Hubbs argues, participants in the Cominsky field demonstration were "defending not just themselves but society from the encroachment of the racial other, of 'foreign' values, and of 'disco fags.'"[33] She suggests that the backlash against disco demonstrated participants' recognition that disco "constituted a coalition around shared experiences of difference," not of sexuality, gender, or race alone but across these differences.[34]

House Music and Black Queer World-Making

The homophobic and racist (as well as sexist and classist) backlash against disco did not kill the genre, but it did succeed in pushing disco back underground to the Black and gay (and Black gay) clubs from which it had emerged. The music industry distanced itself from the controversy by relabeling disco as "dance music," and the scene moved back into underground clubs and away from mainstream attention.[35] In the crucible of predominantly Black queer spaces, several regional offspring genres emerged, including what came to be known as "house," so named for the Chicago club from which it emerged, the Warehouse. As a direct descen-

32. Frank, "Discophobia," 280.

33. Hubbs, "'I Will Survive,'" 231.

34. Hubbs, "'I Will Survive,'" 241.

35. Kai Fikentscher, *"You Better Work!": Underground Dance Music in New York City* (Hanover, CT: Wesleyan University Press, 2000), 29.

dent from disco and attributed primarily to the innovations of former Loft attendee and DJ Frankie Knuckles, house music is the sound that accompanied Black gay dancers in the Warehouse and other Chicago spaces. It found its way across the Black gay urban American landscape, eventually returning to New York City partly through the work of another former Loft devotee, DJ Larry Levan.

Scholars have undoubtedly located house's musical beginnings in Chicago, but it is worth noting that the so-called godfather of house, Warehouse DJ Frankie Knuckles, was a former Loft devotee who cut his teeth DJing in New York City discos. At the Warehouse, which opened in 1977, he found that the local Black gay patrons, or "kids," wanted high-energy music to fuel their dancing from very late Saturday nights through Sunday afternoons. Knuckles and other local DJs began pushing the tempos to 120 beats per minute (bpm) or faster in order to satisfy these dancers. Like disco, therefore, house developed as a series of DJ-promoted technological innovations designed to enhance the dancing experience. In addition to increasing the tempo to create a high-energy sound, Knuckles and other Chicago DJs began to make their own mixes of disco and other records (including soul, Philly, and R&B) by looping, remixing, and adding electronic rhythm tracks. The new style maintained disco's four-on-the-floor bass drum rhythm but introduced electronically programmed drumbeats and more complex cross-rhythms. In house, everything and everyone became subservient to the rhythm; vocal and instrumental sounds were reduced and reintroduced as rhythmic flourishes and repeated motives, not as focal points.

There is no question that house music originated in a particular Black queer location. Like disco, house is both a sound or musical style and a scene, and, as such, it cannot be divorced from the Black gay clubs in which it developed. As Anthony Thomas points out, not all of those involved in the house music scene were gay, and not everyone who was gay was involved in the scene, but there is an important connection between the groups and the musical developments.[36] He writes, "The sound, the beat, and the rhythm [of house] *have* risen up from the dancing sensibilities of urban gay Afro-Americans."[37] The Black queer origins of house, like many contributions of queer and trans people of color to the struggle for LGBTQ rights and visibility, have been subject to revisionist whitewashing. Writing in 1995, Thomas noted that house had begun to radiate out to white gay communities as well and expressed concern that listeners would cease to remember house's roots

---

36. Thomas, "House the Kids Built."
37. Thomas, "House the Kids Built," 438.

in African and African American musical traditions.[38] Brian Currid confirms the existence of a universalist narrative that places Black queer cultural production under the umbrella of an un-raced (i.e., white) gay tradition, arguing that while "house serves as a site where queers create historical narratives of continuity across time and space," it also "powerfully accesses the primary contradictions of 'we are family,' as it is used simultaneously to mobilize a notion of community which performs the ontological stability of the 'we' across time and space, and to defer that very stability, critically problematizing who and what this 'we' is."[39] Currid not only places house in a queer lineage with disco but also emphasizes the Black queer lineage, pointing to clubs as spaces where Black queers could avoid the homophobia of predominantly straight Black clubs and the racism of predominantly white gay clubs, and challenge the existing narratives of queer history that marginalize, rather than center, the roles of Black queers in the construction of gay identity and community.[40]

Despite Currid's and Thomas's warnings against downplaying its Black queer origins, much house music scholarship has indeed largely erased this history.[41] An illustrative example is a 2001 article by Stephen Amico, who discusses house music and its relationship to queer dancing without even mentioning race, despite the important ways in which race and sexuality are co-constructed, including in queer spaces.[42] Amico examines how "various symbols of stereotypical masculinity operate to inform the musical discourse" at a specific New York City club.[43] Despite his focus on the relationship between physical appearance and musical discourse, and the problematic use of terms such as "African war dance" and "tribe," which one of his informants used to describe communal experiences in a queer dance space, and which pass unremarked upon, the only time Amico mentions race is to note the prevalence of Black women singers in house music. Not only is this study disconnected from the particular Black queer history of house, but it also erases Black queer and trans participants from any contemporary dance music scene and participates in the problematic universalization of gay culture, which Currid urges us to resist.

---

38. Thomas, "House the Kids Built."

39. Currid, "'We Are Family,'" 173.

40. Currid, "'We Are Family,'" 173.

41. An excellent exception is Micah E. Salkind's recent book, *Do You Remember House?: Chicago's Queer of Color Undergrounds* (New York: Oxford University Press, 2019).

42. Stephen Amico, "'I Want Muscles': House Music, Homosexuality, and Masculine Signification," *Popular Music* 20, no. 3 (2001): 359–78.

43. Amico, "'I Want Muscles,'" 359.

In addition to the importance of Black queer artists to the development of the aforementioned musical genres, I hope to have also illustrated the significance of Black queer spaces where this music has been created, performed, and enjoyed. These spaces are important sites of queer world-making—specifically, Black queer world-making. In her ethnographic study of New York City's queer club cultures, Fiona Buckland, drawing on the work of Lauren Berlant and Michael Warner, discusses the significance of the club as such a space, noting that such "third spaces of recreation" are important for self-fashioning as well as communal fashioning.[44] She uses the term "world-making" to refer to "a production in the moment of a space of creative, expressive, and transformative possibilities, which remained fluid and moving by means of the dancing body, as it improvised from moment to moment."[45] The sounds of disco and house contributed to fashioning of such world-making sites by providing a reason for the space as well as sonic signifiers of a shared community. However, as Buckland notes, the borders of such sites are malleable and in these cases overlapped with sites of early hip hop development, as I will discuss below.

(Un)Queering Hip Hop

Rap and disco, and later house music, are more closely connected than they may often appear. As I mentioned at the beginning of this chapter, the earliest rap was closely related to disco, in terms of both the actual records the early hip hop DJs were spinning and the places where they were spun. For example, in a November 2020 Facebook post, Rocky Bucano, the executive director and CEO of the Universal Hip Hop Museum relates a story about getting records for his first professional gig at the Stardust Ballroom from David Mancuso at the Loft, adding that the two became "dear friends" after that meeting in 1975.[46] In his substantive study of the history of hip hop business, Dan Charnas demonstrates the role of disco DJs such as DJ Hollywood in the development of rap music.[47] He notes, for example, how DJ Hollywood embraced turntable techniques and setups similar to those of

---

44. Fiona Buckland, *Impossible Dance: Club Culture and Queer World-Making* (Middletown, CT: Wesleyan University Press, 2002), 6.

45. Buckland, *Impossible Dance*, 4.

46. Rocky Bucano, "True story . . . ," Facebook, November 15, 2020, https://www.facebook.com/1304512998/posts/10219362243949207/?d=n, accessed May 29, 2021.

47. Dan Charnas, *The Big Payback: The History of the Business of Hip-Hop* (New York: New American Library, 2010).

the earliest hip hop DJs and began rapping rhymes over those beats like the earliest MCs. The social spaces and musical developments of the two genres had a significant amount of overlap in the 1970s.

Indeed, Charnas, Kajikawa, Lawrence, and others have situated both musical and cultural overlap between the genres that initially were marked more by social scenes than any distinct musical characteristics. Both genres highlighted the role of the DJ, who took an active role in manipulating pre-recorded music and developing techniques on turntable equipment to engage dancers. The actual records used by both disco and hip hop DJs were very similar at first, and, as noted above, DJs often even frequented the same record shops. As Kajikawa writes:

> Given these multiple points of overlap, it would be a mistake to assume that rap and disco were immediately understood as distinct and opposed genres. . . . In fact, printed materials and recorded evidence of hip hop music in the years leading up to "Rapper's Delight" give no indication that "disco versus hip hop" was a meaningful topos. There are numerous examples of hip hop DJs, MCs, and promoters embracing the term "disco" to describe their events and performance practices.[48]

Hip hop's early history, then, is much more connected to disco than later narratives would seem to suggest.

Yet, as Charnas notes, the emerging hip hop culture also sought to set itself apart from disco, which by the end of the decade had become a target for animosity. Charnas's discussion of this distancing is worth quoting here at length:

> The first rap records were released into an environment that was arguably the most hostile to Black music in American history. Whipped into a fury by the "death to disco" movement, many Americans—mostly young, White males who became alienated from Black music when their favorite rock stations stopped playing Black artists in the mid-1970s—declared "rap" to be disco's insipid offspring in need of ridicule and, if possible, a lynching. Disco's White opponents took great advantage of the fact that rap rhymed with "crap."
> Of course, many of the founders of the b-boy movement rejected disco, too, and with it the upscale, older rapping disco DJs like Hol-

---

48. Kajikawa, *Sounding Race in Rap Songs*, 42–43.

lywood. The enmity toward the glitzy disco scene was the reason why they had become b-boys and b-girls in the first place. To people like Fred Brathwaite and Afrika Bambaataa their culture was more than "rap," as rapping had been a part of Black culture since the first slaves arrived in America, and went all the way back to Africa. *What we're doing in the streets of New York*, they claimed, *is something new.* Soon, figures like Bambaataa and Brathwaite began using the term "hip-hop" to distinguish themselves from disco and to name an entire street culture that had, until then, been nameless.[49]

As Charnas points out, this distancing was twofold. First, there was distancing from the genre that invoked the racism and homophobia of so many white, mostly male listeners. But there was also a distancing from the perceived ills of disco—the "glitz," which has connotations of both class and gender, that, as Charnas notes, was seen as being at odds with the nascent street culture. There was also, on another level, the desire for the emerging hip hop culture to stake its claim as a new, unique practice, unassociated and unindebted to its disco predecessors.

Disco historians have also noted both the overlap and distancing between the two genres in the 1970s and their underlying gender and class politics. For example, in his history of 1970s disco, Tim Lawrence identifies Grandmaster Flash as one of the first to articulate a distinction between rap and disco just as disco was on the decline:

Flash's version has subsequently been transformed into the official history of rap versus disco. "It was [DJ Kool] Herc who saw possibilities of mixing his own formulas through remixing prerecorded sound," writes Houston A. Baker Jr. "His enemy was a dully constructed, other-side-of-town discomania that made South and West Bronx hip hoppers ill. Disco was not *dope* in the eyes, ears, and agile bodies of black Bronx teenagers . . . and Queens and Brooklyn felt the same." Baker goes on to form an unspoken alliance with Dahl's homophobic army when he notes that the "club DJs were often gay, and the culture of Eurodisco was populously gay" before concluding, "Hey, some resentment of disco culture and a reassertion of black manhood rights (rites)—no matter who populated discotheques—was a natural thing."[50]

---

49. Charnas, *Big Payback*, 59.
50. Lawrence, *Love Saves the Day*, 383.

Here the relationship between anti-disco sentiment and homophobia (and femmephobia) is more clearly articulated and further illustrates how this distancing began quite early on in hip hop's history and was motivated by intersecting gender and class politics.

Hip hop's distancing from disco, then, also marked a distancing from queerness. In the podcast series *Trapped in a Culture*, hip hop radio personality Troi "STAR" Torain notes that the period in which Afrika Bambaataa and the Zulu Nation were recording some of their most influential records was also a period of early hip hop when there continued to be much overlap with queer subcultures:[51]

> [It] definitely was a time that a closeted homosexual would not want to come out in hip hop. Right? But it also was a time that that same person, through hip hop, could've been exposed to homosexual subculture. And what I mean by that is like, hip hop was a subculture and so was, you know, the homosexual community at that time. So we actually used to share a lot of the same clubs. Ok? On Thursday it might be gay night and on Friday it's hip hop night. There were even clubs that had different rooms with different music. One might be some disco and the gay people in there, but then upstairs they got hip hop, one thing's they got, you know, reggae: everybody's co-existing. And it wasn't the way they tried to make you feel, that hip hop was always so homophobic and all of that, even though I don't buy that term, but I say all this to say that, no we weren't. No, we weren't. We allowed that to co-exist with us.[52]

The framing of this statement simultaneously resists narratives about hip hop's inherent homophobia and upholds those narratives. Torain clarifies how space, particularly sonic space, is used to delineate subcultures while also asserting that the boundaries between these subcultures—physical, sonic, and cultural—were malleable. He also asserts himself, as he self-identifies with hip hop, as a gatekeeper who allowed for this overlap. This framing strips queer practitioners of early hip hop of their agency to assert themselves and suggests some discomfort at their presence.

Further context for this interview helps to clarify Torain's position.

---

51. Troi "STAR" Torain, in Leila Wills, "2 Can Y'all Get Funky," January 2020, in *Trapped in a Culture*, podcast, streaming audio, 15:07, https://trappedinaculture.com/podcast. This podcast series examines the allegations of child sexual abuse and statutory rape by several men, including Afrika Bambaataa.

52. Torain, quoted in Wills, *Trapped in a Culture*.

Trapped in a Culture is a documentary film project and podcast series created by Chicago-based journalist Leila Wills that investigates the allegations of child sexual abuse made against hip hop pioneer Afrika Bambaataa. Torain's interview positions a period of hip hop when Bambaataa and his Zulu Nation were growing their influence in close proximity to queer subcultures. This positioning also problematically associates homosexuality with pedophilia and abuse. I want to be clear—the allegations of sexual abuse leveled at Bambaataa should be taken seriously but should not be used to suggest that early queer practitioners in hip hop were predators or pedophiles. We must be careful not to replicate arguments long used against LGBTQ rights that conflate the two. I present this evidence here not to divorce it from the real issues of abuse but, by emphasizing the role of space, to show just how closely related early hip hop and LGBTQ communities could be.

Torain's wording also indicates the bifurcation of queerness and hip hop that I examined in the introduction to this book. He positions LGBTQ people near hip hop but still outside of it. His wording—"we allowed that to co-exist with us"—does not suggest an easy integration, and it upholds a power imbalance in which heterosexuals assert control over who can or cannot be associated with a subculture. Disco is associated with gay subcultures, while hip hop is in physical (and sometimes musical) proximity to but remains outside of those social spaces. This framing speaks to the distancing of the emerging genre from disco and queerness even as it attempts to account for hip hop's relationship to them.

A similar distancing persisted as disco was pushed back underground and transformed into new dance genres such as house. House music DJs like Frankie Knuckles were innovating with music and technology, in many ways drawing on the same tools and techniques as hip hop DJs. House music culture scholar Micah E. Salkind identifies an enforced dichotomy of house and hip hop, predicated on house music's queerness and perceived femininity:[53]

> It is critical to hear and feel house music in a post-1970s American cultural context where visual, sonic, and kinesthetic hip hop signifiers were, and are, often assumed to authenticate Blackness in ways that cover over the heterogeneity of Black American, let alone Afro-Diasporic, cultures. Although house was hardly a fixed corporate genre during the early 1980s, it was already being positioned by industry gatekeepers as a cultural antithesis of hip hop. Remember[ing] the ways that house and hip hop became competing subcultural affilia-

---

53. Salkind, *Do You Remember House?*, 70–71.

tions in Chicago youth cultures, performer Felicia Holman recalls the social pressure she felt to choose between the two camps: "Even despite the fact that you had . . . these mergers and blends of parallels of hip hop and house, for the most part, among the populace, you had to choose. Are you house, or are you hip hop."[54]

The distancing from disco on the intersecting bases of class, gender, and sexuality carried over to disco's successor.

House and hip hop were sometimes positioned as being on parallel, not overlapping, paths. Some DJs and later producers in hip hop have acknowledged the importance of innovations happening in house music and the overlap in their repertoire but have largely been careful to navigate the discourse around these connections in a way that keeps them safely distanced from house's queer connotations. For example, in an interview with Troy L. Smith, New York–based DJ Quick discusses a record that both he and Larry Levan played:

TROY: Give me a classic break that you would use in a battle against say a legendary crew!

QUICK: If I were going to battle the L Brothers back in the day, this next record would have stunned them to the point that they might not have been able to recover so easily; especially when the underdog comes back at you hard. Tribe: "Ethnic Stew" was a bad record and it cost $20 at Downstairs' on 34th street never to be seen again in any of their stores. Furthermore it was back in the fall of '76 and the cut was "Think People," I do believe Troy. So on a scale of 1 to 10, in terms of how difficult it was to find. I would have given it a 1, except back in '83 when I was playing garage music it turned out that Larry Levan from the Paradise Garage was playing "Smoke" which was a cut from that album. So it was at Vinyl mania for $20.

So I have to say that the album was a 3; even though I was out the game and had no idea what was happening uptown. Smoke was a great tune and Larry was one of the all-time greatest legends. *Great club, but I did not care for the atmosphere and only attended the place twice.*[55]

---

54. Salkind, *Do You Remember House?*, 70.

55. Troy L. Smith, "From the D.J. Quick of Queens, New York Series: Part 1," Facebook, July 10, 2015, https://www.facebook.com/troylsmith21/posts/10206308633131191, accessed May 29, 2021. Emphasis mine. Downstairs Records was an important record store for both disco and early hip hop DJs (see Charnas, *Big Payback*; and Lawrence, *Love Saves the Day*).

This excerpt again demonstrates the musical overlap between hip hop and house in the early 1980s, but it also subtly illustrates the way that heterosexual hip hop artists might distance themselves from the queer spaces and cultures associated with house music. DJ Quick acknowledges Levan's contributions and, indeed, the similarities in their tastes but expresses discomfort at the atmosphere of the Paradise Garage, which, as noted above, was a predominantly queer space. Even as some hip hop artists can acknowledge the musical relationship between the genres, the social significance of those spaces was difficult for some to reconcile.

As a result of this distancing, the sonic markers of underground dance music and hip hop came to signify queerness and a certain masculinized heterosexuality, respectively, in different social spaces. One of these spaces was the Ballroom scene, which I discuss in chapter 2. In these spaces, house music is used to underscore queer or feminine gender categories while hip hop signifies hardened masculinity or even straight-passing performances. In his ethnographic study of Black men and the "down low," Jeffrey Q. McCune provides a thick description of the ways house and hip hop sonically delineate space on Black queer dance night in a club called the Gate.[56] He first describes entering a "house room," a space where house music was played that was "charged with homoerotic energy and rhythmic impulses."[57] He then describes a "hip-hop room," noting that there was "something rough and rugged about the way people moved in this space."[58] Reflecting on how the two spaces "occupy two distinct modes of expression," McCune writes:

> While the house room and music were "fabulous," it was clear that the hip-hop room and music were deemed "cool." If one simply observed the house room, where one witnesses voguers in high fashion from DKNY to Prada, dancers wearing traditional Kenneth Cole, and the classic tight shirt/tight jeans models, he or she would recognize it as a place where "I'm fabulous and I don't care what you think" is the general sentiment. Whereas the predominant look in the hip-hop room was more uniform—demonstrating people's desire or consciousness of specific fashion trends traditionally associated with hip-hop music and its consumers. This is not to suggest that fabulousness and coolness are determined by fashion. However, clothes are one way that

---

56. Jeffrey Q. McCune, Jr., *Sexual Discretion: Black Masculinity and the Politics of Passing* (Chicago: University of Chicago Press, 2014).

57. McCune, *Sexual Discretion*, 77.

58. McCune, *Sexual Discretion*, 77.

individuals in space can display both their individuality and conformity. Although this binary description may imply otherwise, it is
important to note that I am not claiming that hip-hoppers and house-
heads, as they are often called, don't share space or blur the lines. Yet,
. . . the distinctions between the two spaces are important as they
reflect a larger dominant shift/divide in the black gay cultural experience at this historical moment.[59]

McCune connects the role of music as it delineates queer spaces. This dichotomy, underscored by the fashion choices and sexual behavior of participants
in each space, is predicated on the same distancing that early hip hop artists
enacted away from disco and house in the 1970s and 1980s, respectively.
Writing in the 2000s, McCune illustrates that this dichotomy in some ways
remains intact, but hip hop is still present in queer spaces and is a part of
Black queer world-making.

The uneasy relationship between house, whose sounds in some ways
reached the mainstream in some iterations in the late 1980s and early 1990s,
and hip hop continued into the end of the twentieth century. We hear house
influence in Queen Latifah's "Come into My House" from *All Hail the
Queen* (1989). Like a Ballroom commenter, she repeats on the track, "Give
me body," and she regularly plays on the possible double (or even triple)
meaning of the term "house"—the music, a house party, the houses of Ballroom culture are all possible references over a house-inspired beat. While
Queen Latifah long resisted responding to rumors that she is queer, she has
more recently performed in LGBTQ contexts and acknowledged her long-
term partner, Eboni Nichols, during an acceptance speech for a BET Lifetime Achievement Award in June 2021, which makes this track retroactively
even more open to queer readings.

Some hip hop artists, perhaps eager to position hip hop as a more "seri-
ous" (and heterosexual) genre as it was gaining commercial momentum in
the early 1990s, made fun of house through their own music. De La Soul's
"Kicked Out the House" (1991) is an example. The song opens with the dis-
claimer "In no way are we trying to disrespect any sort of house or club music
but we're just so glad that we're not doing it" over a house beat. The repetitive
hook goes "Kicked out the house, you got / Kicked out the house, hip house
/ Kicked out the house for good." The tongue-in-cheek song clocks in at just
under two minutes long and seems to poke fun at fellow Native Tongues acts
such as the Jungle Brothers, whose "I'll House You" (1988) is often cited as

---

59. McCune, *Sexual Discretion*, 78.

one of the first hip-house tracks released outside of Chicago, and even Queen Latifah, whose aforementioned "Come into My House" has even more overtly queer resonances. As the 1990s went on, the delineation between house and rap became even more sonically and culturally apparent.

As I have traced here, hip hop is often placed as antithetical to Black dance music associated with queer subcultures. Early hip hop DJs sought to distance themselves from disco in the 1970s, and throughout the 1980s and 1990s hip hop artists similarly made clear a distinction between their work and house music cultures, even when there was some sonic overlap. There were several motivations for this distancing, including a need for the emerging genre to set itself apart from others and to stake its claim in the Black American soundscape. However, there were also more nefarious motivations, including a desire to distance hip hop from anything associated with queerness. A closer examination of the histories of disco, house, and hip hop, however, illuminates how these genres are closely related. In addition to musical relationships, there are spatial and temporal relationships as well—hip hop's development is not so easily divorced from that of Black queer dance genres and spaces. We can look at this history, though, and begin to tease out the origins of the commonly held belief that hip hop is inherently homophobic, even while we dismantle this notion.

Hip Hop's Queer Pasts, Present, and Futures

It is an undeniable yet unfortunate fact that there have always been instances of homophobia in commercial rap. The first commercial rap record, "Rapper's Delight," included the following lines in its full version:

I said, "By the way, baby, what's your name?"
[She] said, I go by the name Lois Lane
And you could be my boyfriend, you surely can
Just let me quit my boyfriend called Superman"
I said, "He's a fairy, I do suppose
Flyin' through the air in pantyhose
He may be very sexy or even cute
But he looks like a sucker in a blue and red suit"

As early men rappers established a heterosexual style of braggadocio aimed at impressing women, they sometimes resorted to this kind of homophobia to position themselves as more desirable than the men competing for female attention in their narratives. Grandmaster Flash and the Furious Five's "The Message" also contains offhanded mention of a former "fag-hag"-turned-bag-lady, placing a negative connotation on association with queers. This lyrical homophobia has continued, with persistent use of the word "faggot" by artists such as Eminem and more subtle digs at real or perceived queerness, such as Nicki Minaj's lines about Young Thug wearing dresses in "Barbie Dreams," even as she later raps about "Young M.A, Lady Luck, get the strap for this pussy." Anti-queer lyrics persist, even as some artists have begun calling for more sensitivity and an end to homophobia in rap.

Yet, as Shanté Paradigm Smalls notes, there has also always been queer involvement in hip hop.[60] In their brief historiography, Smalls traces this queer involvement from the first recording by an openly queer hip hop group, Age of Consent, in 1981 to the beginning of the twenty-first century as a watershed moment for queer hip hop. They write, "Queer hip hoppers can note that they have been in the rap game since 1981, some 30-plus years, at this point."[61] Smalls notes the alignment of queer hip hop history with the history of recorded rap but also points to the "sonic future of queer hip hop and queer artists making hip hop music."[62]

Throughout this chapter I hope to have expanded our view of queer involvement in hip hop beyond a few notable artists to the very root of the music culture itself. Hip hop's earliest expressions reflect an entanglement with Black and Latinx queer cultures, which some artists later tried to undo. By repositioning hip hop historically within a lineage of Black queer music practices we can understand queer hip hop history not just as an example of standout artists or moments of increased visibility; rather we can position queerness at the heart of the genre. While there has been and continues to be evidence of homophobia especially in hip hop's most commercial iterations, this repositioning reminds us that hip hop is not *inherently* homophobic. What we can understand as hip-hop's homophobia is rooted in some practitioners' desire to distance themselves from hip hop's queer roots and its queer siblings in other Black dance music styles.

We can also understand the homophobic strand of hip hop as being a by-product of what Joseph C. Ewoodzie Jr. calls the masculinization of hip hop.[63] He describes the ways in which hip hop became a masculinized space

60. Shanté Paradigm Smalls, "Queer Hip Hop: A Brief Historiography," in *The Oxford Handbook of Music and Queerness*, ed. Fred Everett Maus and Sheila Whiteley (published online September 2018), https://doi.org/10.1093/oxfordhb/9780199793525.013.103

61. Smalls, "Queer Hip Hop," 11.

62. Smalls, "Queer Hip Hop," 19.

63. Joseph C. Ewoodzie Jr., *Break Beats in the Bronx: Rediscovering Hip-Hop's Early Years*

that made it difficult for women to engage as performers but that also "forced non-heterosexual participants to hide their sexuality, so we don't know much about the sexual diversity of participants during the early years of hip-hop—histories of hip-hop have often presumed most participants to be heterosexual."[64] In connecting the paucity of women performers with male heterosexual artists' performances of masculinity, Ewoodzie articulates the intersections of gender and sexuality that often go unmarked in histories of early hip hop. He also draws attention to the lack of archival evidence for queer involvement in the earliest years of the genre and the assumptions that historians often draw as a result. If we instead presume that hip hop has always had queer involvement, even before the earliest queer recordings, we can begin to rectify queer absence in these histories.

The narratives that insist that hip hop and queerness are incompatible have largely been created by heterosexual artists who have a stake in divorcing rap from its queer roots. But by reclaiming this queer past, one that considers broader social and musical spaces rather than unique individuals, we can reposition LGBTQ musicians and audiences within a Black queer musical lineage. This lineage is important because it challenges the idea that each new wave of openly queer artists is a brand-new phenomenon. Of course, recent legal and cultural battles have made it easier for queer and trans artists to be out about their identities, and, as we will see, some have managed to obtain a degree of mainstream success. To fully understand this shift, we need to reconsider our narratives of hip hop history. Thinking about rap's queer past helps make space not only for its queer futures but also for a reconsideration of its queer present.

(Chapel Hill: University of North Carolina Press, 2017).

64. Ewoodzie, *Break Beats in the Bronx*, 142.

2 • Queer Articulations in Ballroom Rap

On March 13, 2014, the New York City–based producer-turned-rapper Leif appeared as a musical guest on the *Late Show with David Letterman*, where, dressed in a blue skort (combination shorts and skirt) and white calf-high sneakers, he performed his 2012 single "Wut." With lines such as "I'm getting light in my loafers" and "I'm the kind of john closet dudes wanna go steady on," his performance left little doubt regarding his queer sexuality. For years, critics writing for publications such as the *Guardian* and *Pitchfork* had been predicting the rise of "queer rap." Leif's appearance marked the first time an openly gay rapper performed on a major network's late-night show and seemed to suggest that "queer rap" was indeed finally having its mainstream moment.[1]

In the 2010s, Leif was frequently cited as part of a larger trend of emerging queer hip hop artists, especially in and around New York City, such as Zebra Katz, Cakes da Killa, Mykki Blanco, Azealia Banks, and others.[2] In *Pitchfork*, for instance, Carrie Battan wrote, "If there's ever been a time for an artist to rip hip hop identity conventions to shreds, it's now. The genre is the furthest left-of-center it's been in a long time—or at very least, the line between mainstream stardom and underground oddballism is blurring beyond recognition."[3] Writing for the *Guardian*, Clare Considine similarly noted in 2012 that "a whole wave of fearless gay New York rappers are step-

---

1. See, for example, Clare Considine, "Zebra Katz, Mykki Blanco, and the Rise of Queer Rap," *The Guardian*, June 8, 2012, http://www.theguardian.com/music/2012/jun/09/zebra-katz-rise-of-gay-rappers; Carrie Battan, "We Invented Swag: NYC's Queer Rap," *Pitchfork*, March 21, 2012, http://pitchfork.com/features/articles/8793-we-invented-swag/; Rich Juzwiak, "Rapper Leif's *Letterman* Terrific Performance Was Also Important," *Gawker*, March 14, 2014, http://gawker.com/rapper-le1fs-letterman-terrific-performance-was-also-i-1543798565, accessed January 4, 2016.

2. Considine, "Zebra Katz, Mykki Blanco and the Rise of Queer Rap," and Battan, "We Invented Swag" are two illustrative examples.

3. Battan, "We Invented Swag."

ping out and sticking two well-manicured fingers up to the notion that there is no room for them in hip hop."[4]

Many journalists, such as the authors of these two articles, have jumped on the notion of gay rap because it is seemingly antithetical to the aesthetics and values of hip hop, at least as it has been understood in the mainstream. As I discuss elsewhere, even socially progressive rappers like Macklemore continue to suggest that hip hop and queerness mix like oil and water, creating a false dichotomy between Black and gay that erases queer and trans people of color.[5] As Bakari Kitwana argues, however, hip hop has become ubiquitous among several generations of American youth from all racial and ethnic backgrounds, and thus it should come as no surprise that the diversity of hip hop practitioners extends also to sexual orientation and gender identity.[6] Black queer rappers have perhaps always existed at the intersection of LGBTQ communities, communities of color, and hip hop culture but are just now becoming visible and audible.

While historically mainstream hip hop has been antagonistic toward queer folks, there has been a shift in recent years with major artists such as Jay Z, Kanye West, Common, and A$AP Rocky publicly voicing opinions in support of the LGBTQ community, or at the very least discouraging discrimination against them.[7] And although it may be difficult to challenge the heteronormative narrative of hip hop's origins and to seek out queer voices from among the pioneers of the genre, a changing national climate has helped to increase the visibility of contemporary queer and trans artists. Considering this public shift, journalists and music critics seem to forget that there have always been queer hip hop practitioners, including dancers, listeners, DJs, and, yes, rappers.

Despite the critical acclaim that he has received in large part for his openly queer content and performances, Le1f himself has stated that he prefers not to be known as a purveyor of gay rap. He told Natalie Hope McDonald in an interview for *Philadelphia* magazine, "I'm proud to be called a gay

---

4. Considine, "Zebra Katz, Mykki Blanco, and the Rise of Queer Rap."

5. See Kehrer, "Love Song for All of Us?"

6. Bakari Kitwana, *Why White Kids Love Hip-Hop: Wankstas, Wiggers, Wannabes, and the New Reality of Race in America* (New York: Basic Civitas, 2005).

7. Admittedly, interviews with many of these artists, especially A$AP Rocky, indicate a level of discomfort with non-heterosexuality, with most of them stating that sexuality is irrelevant to their careers or that they do not care, which is not the same as openly engaging with LGBTQ communities on an advocacy level. (For a short rundown of recent statements made by rappers, see "A History of Rappers Standing Up for Gay Rights," *Complex Magazine*, May 15, 2012, http://www.complex.com/music/2012/05/history-rappers-not-being-homophobic/).

rapper, but [my work is] not gay rap. That's not a genre."[8] Scholarship and media coverage, however, has continued to consider all queer artists together, tending to situate them as individual artists fighting to be heard within an inherently homophobic genre and thereby focusing on their shared identities rather than their music, an approach that artists such as Leif try to resist. While these comparisons do highlight the importance of the work of openly LGBTQ rappers, it also collapses a diverse group of artists into one identity-based category. The music of a rapper like JenRo, a queer woman from California's Bay Area who is influenced by the region's gangsta rap, for example, cannot necessarily be considered part of the same genre as Big Freedia, who hails from New Orleans and whose work epitomizes bounce music. "Gay rap," as Leif suggests, does not exist, because the queer identity that many rappers share is not a sufficient basis upon which to define a genre.

The New York City rappers who *Pitchfork* and other outlets have considered together, even if musically quite diverse, do share an important but often downplayed feature: a connection to the city's Ballroom scene, a vital focal point of the local Black and Latinx queer culture. Leif describes the influence of Ballroom on his music and performances:

> When I first found out about voguing as a teenager, it was an eye-opening experience because it felt like an innate way of moving. And a lot of my music is made with the intentions of movement and dance. But it's the cultural side—the experience of being *at* a ball—that's affected what I rap about. The fact that there's a scene that's existed for so long with such a rich history, and is ceremonial, is really nice.[9]

Leif acknowledges that his familiarity with Ballroom has affected his performances, and he gestures toward his own participation in its cultural lineage. He notes that this lineage has had the greatest impact on his lyrics, but it has also influenced his music, a point to which I will return. Leif explicitly connects his work with the Ballroom scene, and it is evident that drawing on the slang, gender categories, and other aspects of the culture is one strategy that Leif employs that allows him to articulate his own Black queer subject position through his music.

---

8. Natalie Hope McDonald, "America's Next Top Gay Rapper? Leif Responds to Homophobia in Hip Hop. Plus: Watch His Latest Music Video," *Philadelphia*, July 24, 2012, http://www.phillymag.com/g-philly/2012/07/24/gay-rapper/.

9. Leif, quoted in Battan, "We Invented Swag."

Hip hop genres have often been defined by a combination of geography, production techniques, musical stylistic characteristics, or thematic lyrical content. Artists such as Leif, Cakes da Killa, Zebra Katz, and Azealia Banks, in addition to sharing a geographical center, share Ballroom culture as an important cultural reference point that ties their music together into a hip hop genre we might refer to as Ballroom-influenced rap, or simply "Ballroom rap." This genre is not based on shared queer identity but rather shared references to cultural aspects of queer communities in which they participate. These references appear in their work and place them within a Black queer cultural and musical lineage that is central to LGBTQ communities of color in New York City.

In this chapter I examine how some of these openly queer rappers lyrically, musically, and visually reference the city's Ballroom scene in order to invoke a specifically Black queer musical and cultural lineage. In the previous chapter I traced the roots of this lineage in 1970s disco, as well as the emergence of house music as an underground response to the homophobic and racist backlash against disco's success. Here, I consider the role of house music in Ballroom culture and Black LGBTQ communities, paying particular attention to how participants use music in the creation and performance of the Ballroom gender system in which gender and sexuality are co-constructed. I then demonstrate how the aforementioned rappers use aspects of Ballroom culture as a means to perform a Black queer identity, and I suggest that Black queer rap that shares this cultural reference point can indeed be considered a hip hop genre.

House Music and Ballroom Culture

Even though its origins can be traced to the queer club spaces of Chicago, house music also took root in New York City, where Black queer disco began. In addition to influencing the soundscape of the city's Black queer clubs, such as the Paradise Garage, it became the soundtrack for another important queer Black and Latinx cultural institution: the Ballroom scene. Ballroom culture, or ball culture, is a largely underground community network that consists of a structure of "houses" whose members compete in balls where participants dress up and engage in highly gendered performances. Consisting primarily of Black and Latinx LGBTQ members, ball culture first emerged in the 1960s in Harlem, where Black drag queens, largely excluded from white drag balls, began to host their own events, making it a development that was contemporaneous and sometimes intersecting with the disco scene.[10] Participants formed houses, often named after fashion labels, such as House of Chanel or House of Dior, and began to host balls where participants competed against members of other houses in categories such as Best Dressed. According to DJ David DePino, in the early 1970s Paris Dupree, founder of the House of Dupree, began adding dance moves and poses given in time to the music heard outside Footsteps club:

> Paris had a *Vogue* magazine in her bag, and while she was dancing she took it out, opened it up to a page where a model was posing, and then stopped in that pose on the beat. Then she turned to the next page and stopped in the new pose, again on the beat. Another queen came up and did another pose in front of Paris, and then Paris went in front of her and did another pose. This was all shade—they were trying to make a prettier pose than each other—and it soon caught on at the balls. At first they called it posing, and then, because it started from *Vogue* magazine, they called it vogueing [*sic*].[11]

While voguing styles have changed and developed over the past several decades, as documented in Jennie Livingston's well-known Ballroom documentary, *Paris Is Burning* (1990), and, more recently, in the television series *POSE* (2018–2021), and in Marlon M. Bailey's ethnographic account of the contemporary Detroit scene, it remains perhaps Ballroom's most enduring legacy and the one most easily recognized by outsiders.[12] This recognition can be partly attributed to the popularity of Madonna's 1990 hit, "Vogue," despite the controversy over whether or not her use of the dance styles associated with Ballroom culture were appropriative.[13]

Ball houses are not simply the equivalent of teams in a competition; they

---

10. See Michael Cunningham, "The Slap of Love," *Open City Magazine*, no. 6 (1996), 175; Lawrence, *Love Saves the Day: A History of American Dance Music Culture, 1970–1979* (Durham, NC: Duke University Press, 2004), 46.

11. David DePino, as quoted in Lawrence, *Love Saves the Day*, 46–47.

12. Marlon M. Bailey, *Butch Queens Up in Pumps: Gender, Performance, and Ballroom Culture in Detroit* (Ann Arbor: University of Michigan Press, 2016).

13. For more about this controversy, see Jesse Green, "Paris Has Burned," *New York Times*, April 18, 1993, http://www.nytimes.com/1993/04/18/style/paris-has-burned.html?pagewanted=all. For more recent commentary on issues of vogue and appropriation, including contemporary resonances, see Benji Hart, "Vogue Is Not for You: Deciding Whom We Give Our Art To," *Radfag*, May 31, 2015, https://radfag.com/2015/05/31/vogue-is-not-for-you-deciding-whom-we-give-our-art-to/.

are more akin to familial units, comprised of chosen families often led by a house mother or house father. Bailey connects the kinship networks of houses to a longer history of Black LGBTQ kinship practices, noting that chosen families are formed out of necessity for LGBTQ people who may have been rejected by their families of origin:

> Through houses Ballroom members challenge conventional notions of marriage, family, and kinship by revising gender relations and redefining gendered labor within the kin unit. Primarily, the house is a social configuration, the principle through which the kin unit is organized. Yet the house can also be a space where the members congregate, and it can be a literal home for Ballroom members. . . . While, in some ways, houses reify the gender hierarchies and social arrangements that are characteristic of the biological families from which members have been excluded, these houses also take on the labor of care that the biological kin of Ballroom members often fail to perform.[14]

Chosen LGBTQ families are often necessary for LGBTQ folks, whether they have been kicked out of their homes or not, because they provide a structure in which older or more experienced members might help newer members of a community learn social norms. Houses are one manifestation of Black LGBTQ kinship networks.

Ballroom culture has its own gender system that determines in which categories of competition one will compete. Bailey identifies six gender categories, which are really categories in which sex, gender, and sexuality converge:

1. *Butch Queens Up in Drag* (gay men who perform in drag but do not take hormones and do not live as women).
2. *Femme Queens* (transgender women or MTF [male to female] at various stages of gender transition involving hormonal or surgical processes, such as breast implants).
3. *Butches* (transgender men or FTM [female to male] at various stages of gender transition involving hormonal therapy, breast wrapping or removal, and so on or masculine lesbians or females appearing as men irrespective of their sexuality).
4. *Women* (biological females who live as women and are lesbian, straight identified, or queer).

---

14. Bailey, *Butch Queens*, 80.

5. *Men/Trade* (biological males who live as men, are very masculine, and are straight identified or nongay identified).

6. *Butch Queens* (biological males who live and identify as gay or bisexual men and are or can be masculine, hypermasculine [as in thug masculinity], or very feminine).[15]

As Bailey notes, this system both relies on and challenges the more widely accepted male/female gender binary. It also provides more options for people who were assigned a male gender at birth than people who were assigned female, placing Butch Queens in a particularly privileged position.[16] Additionally, because these categories exist within the framework of a predominantly Black and Latinx subculture, they can be understood as implicitly racialized gender categories as well. Drawing on E. Patrick Johnson's concept of racial performativity, Bailey argues that Ballroom participants "take up, coconstruct, and rehearse the normative but shifting scripts of Black femininity and masculinity to have them judged by the 'experts,' as it were, in the Ballroom community."[17] The Ballroom gender system, while offering options outside a normative binary system, relies on a traditional dichotomy of masculine and feminine gender expression, as well as racialized constructions of normative gender and sexuality, that shapes the performance/competition genres and is further underscored by musical choices that accompany competitions.

House music plays an important role in the construction, performance, and maintenance of these gender categories. As a popular music idiom that developed in Black queer clubs, that association with Black queer culture translated to its use in Ballroom culture, as it did for disco in the early years of the balls.[18] Bailey observes that while the musical styles played by DJs at balls have expanded to include R&B and hip hop, house music has remained important to the scene.[19] His description of the use of music during competitions is worth quoting here at length, as it provides insight into the close relationship between Black LGBTQ history and contemporary music, dance, and gender performance:

I have participated in balls in which the DJ played R&B songs to un-

---

15. Bailey, *Butch Queens*, 36.

16. Bailey notes that in Ballroom, as in the larger Black LGBT community, men occupy a privileged position (Bailey, *Butch Queens*, 44).

17. Bailey, *Butch Queens*, 57.

18. Bailey, *Butch Queens*, 152.

19. Bailey, *Butch Queens*, 152–53.

derscore Sex Siren categories for Butch Queens, Femme Queens, or female figured participants. Because of their sensual, smooth, and sexy sound, R&B songs like "Love Hangover," recorded by Diana Ross, an iconic figure for Ballroom members, and "Nasty Girl" by Vanity 6 are frequently played. Another song that continues to maintain popularity is "Love Is the Message," by MFSB, a tune from the early Black gay club scene in Chicago. This has become the signature song for Old Way Vogue. . . .

Yet I want to highlight the beats of house music because of how important it is to New Way Vogue performance, a dance form and competitive category that best exemplifies the crucial function of the performance system and its actors and the ritualized practices that undergird this system at ball events. . . . Many of my interlocutors said that the prominence and repetition of the beat in house music guides their performance, putting them in a zone that enables them to block everything out of their minds and focus on their walk while still feeling and hearing the beat and the support from their fellow Ballroom members on the sidelines.[20]

As Bailey describes, certain styles and even particular songs are used to reinforce the style and gender expression tied to any particular competitive category, with house music serving as one of the most constant and well-recognized genres that invokes a history of Black LGBTQ life. He also acknowledges that while hip hop has gradually become more and more popular and included in Ballroom, it is often situated as dichotomous to house music, as it has been outside of the subculture, with house music representing a more feminine expression and hip hop articulating a hardened Black masculinity that serves to underscore performances in masculine categories. In their use of music genres, then, Ballroom members reinforce binary gender categories while simultaneously broadening them and challenging their normative constructions. This usage also draws out differences in the ways hip hop and house are received (i.e., as masculine or feminine genres, respectively), while also placing them together in a queer context that complicates their gendered boundaries and calls attention to their shared Black queer roots.

Like the DJs at Ballroom competitions, I position house in a specifically Black queer musical and cultural lineage that begins with disco (or even earlier if we consider its relation to Black queer Harlem of the 1920s and 1930s)

20. Bailey, *Butch Queens*, 153–54.

and put it in conversation with contemporary hip hop. House and hip hop developed along separate paths, but both continued to have queer participants, even if those participants remained much more visible in the former than in the latter. Contemporary Black queer rappers based in New York City are not, therefore, an anomaly, nor are they antithetical to hip hop's values. They are, however, among the first to be openly identified as queer and to receive much mainstream visibility. In this chapter I build on the foundation laid in chapter 1 to demonstrate how New York City's Black queer heritage contextualizes these rappers' Black queer subjectivities and the ways they perform race, gender, and sexuality through hip hop.

Ballroom Rap

Many openly queer Black rappers based in or around New York City reference aspects of Ballroom culture in their work in order to articulate their Black queer identities and position themselves in conversation with Black queer cultural practices that are largely native to New York City. Black gay male rappers specifically, including Leif, Cakes da Killa, and Zebra Katz, negotiate the assumed masculine stance of most male rappers through references to Ballroom and other aspects of Black queer life to signify that their hardness comes not from heteronormative masculinity but from their experiences of queer community and survival within a homophobic world. Like the Ballroom gender system itself, these and other rappers use Ballroom language to open additional possibilities for being within the realm of hip hop.

I place these New York City–based Black and openly queer artists within the emergent and shifting genre of Ballroom rap. As noted above, many of these artists resist the idea that their work constitutes a genre of queer or gay rap, especially given their musical diversity and sometimes divergent subject matter. However, they all invoke a shared cultural reference point in order to articulate a Black queer identity, and in that way their work situates them not only within a lineage of Black queer cultural and musical production within that city and other northern American cities but also in conversation with each other. As part of a shared musical genre, each of these artists reflects some of the norms of American hip hop, including a shared vocal rap delivery and bragging lyrics, but they also incorporate elements of New York City's distinctly Black queer musical and cultural lineage that is manifested in the Ballroom scene.

As members of a shared genre, Ballroom rap artists negotiate the pervasive heteronormativity of mainstream rap with more or less explicit references to Black queer culture. Considering these artists as part of a genre grouping allows us to analyze the similarities that place them in conversation with one another, which journalists have already observed by lumping them together in trend pieces. These articles create a framework from which listeners understand New York City's Black queer rappers, but they also highlight ways in which this framework already existed. Eric Drott argues that genres can be understood not just as groupings of music that share structural or even stylistic similarities but also as unstable and nonexclusive categories that are constantly being created and reconstructed.[21] He notes that situating genre as relational "sheds light on the conflicts of interpretation to which music can give rise—conflicts that take place not just between separate persons and groups but within the individual subject, as different musical competences and different sites of aesthetic investment intersect, interact, and interfere with one another."[22] In the genre I have outlined here, musical competences include not just knowledge of hip hop but also knowledge of Ballroom culture and other aspects of Black queer life. Additionally, these artists demonstrate how these two cultures (hip hop and Ballroom) can relate to each other. Through their negotiations of these seemingly divergent but related cultures, they enact a new genre that is not based on Black queer identity alone but on the cultural expressions developed within Black queer communities in both historical and contemporary contexts.

Ballroom rap artists use different modes to reference Ballroom culture and other aspects of a Black queer cultural and musical lineage specific to New York in order to articulate a particular Black queer identity in their performances. In her study of Five Percenter rap, Felicia M. Miyakawa identifies four ways in which Five Percenters share the teachings of or reference their faith through music: (1) lyrics; (2) flow, layering, and rupture; (3) sampling and musical borrowing; and (4) album packaging and organization.[23] Similarly, Ballroom rap artists embed their references through different means. They use lyrics that employ Ballroom slang or conjure up aspects of the Ballroom scene. Their musical approaches can be quite diverse, but some invoke the sounds of house music as a way to reinforce

---

21. Eric Drott, "The End(s) of Genre," *Journal of Music Theory* 57, no. 1 (2013): 1–45.

22. Drott, "End(s) of Genre," 4.

23. Felicia Miyakawa, *Five Percenter Rap: God Hop's Music, Message, and Black Muslim Mission* (Bloomington: Indiana University Press, 2005), 5.

their musical and cultural lineage or use vocal samples from Ballroom members in their tracks. Visual images presented through album artwork and music videos also enable rappers to access aspects of Ballroom culture, including dance, fashion, and gender presentations, that are more closely aligned with the Ballroom system than with a strict male/female binary. In the following section, I examine how Black queer rappers use lyrics, sonic characteristics, and visual images to place them in a distinctly Black queer musical and cultural lineage.

Lyrical References

Leif, the artist with perhaps the most visible profile of this cluster of queer New York City rappers (as evidenced by his performance on a major network late-night show), also has among the most explicitly sexual lyrics for a queer rapper. His songs leave little room for confusion that he is interested primarily in sex with other men. In his lyrics he also articulates his Blackness, incorporating Jamaican slang terms, such as "batty man," and other phrases that signify the experiences of growing up in multiethnic New York City neighborhoods. Most importantly, the combination of all these references, and his use of Ballroom slang and culture, articulates the overlapping communities with which he identifies.

Take, for instance, "Wut," the track that Leif performed during his appearance on the Letterman show. The performance was significant not only because Leif was the first openly queer rapper to perform on a late-night television program but also because he was explicit about that identity through his performance. Following an introductory rap that includes the first part of the chorus, the first verse of the song opens with the line "Came through in the clutch / Stomping like I'm up in Loubitons." In this first line Leif combines typical rap braggadocio (performing through adversity or difficulty) with a reference to the Ballroom scene, specifically to the gender performance category that Bailey identifies as Butch Queens Up in Pumps. Another Ballroom reference appears at the end of the second verse, when Leif asks "[I'm] Mother of the house. Care to see me in a new pose?" These references point to the importance of Ballroom in the construction and performance of his Black queer identity.

Leif draws on many different influences and interests in "Wut" and embeds them in his lyrics. The intersection of many of his identities is evident in the hook:

Wut it is? Wut is up? Wut is wut?
What it do? Wut it don't?
Wut it is? Wut is up? What is wut?
What it do? Wut it don't?
I'm getting light in my loafers
And I stay getting life 'til life's over
I'm butter like cocoa
L O L O L O L I'm loco

The line "I'm getting light in my loafers" reclaims a slang phrase that has been used at least since the 1950s to refer to homosexual men, who were also stereotypically considered effeminate. Gay men have also historically used "light in the loafers" as a euphemism to identify each other without explicitly outing someone as gay. "I stay getting life" also draws on Ballroom slang that has crossed over to straight communities and is derived from the saying that something is "giving me life," meaning it is something to be very excited about. In this context, Leif suggests that he is living his life to the fullest. "I'm butter like cocoa" is a play on several word meanings, such as being smooth like butter, specifically cocoa butter, which is both a skin care product highly associated with Black Americans and a slang term for semen coming from a Black male. Finally, in using "loco," a Spanish term for crazy, to refer to himself in combination with later lyrics such as "Rolling up a personal and chomping on a mango," references the blended influences of Black and Latinx cultures in New York City specifically. Thus, this short hook, in the context of the entire track, provides much information about Leif's identity(s), particularly his intersecting cultural and geographical reference points.

"Hey," the title track off Leif's 2014 EP, is also full of references to Ballroom and other aspects of Black queer life. Lines such as "If you feeling cunt enter circles with your bubble butt" and "I'll be serving my body telling them, 'About face'" invoke the language and rituals of competitive balls and employ them in a sexually suggestive way. Specifically, the term "cunt" is used in Ballroom circles to mean feminine and to describe certain vogue categories that emphasize femininity, such as "Vogue Femme Soft and Cunt." It can also mean fabulous or diva-like, depending on the context. Other competition categories include face and body categories, in which contestants are judged on their facial or physical appearance, respectively. Leif invokes these well-known categories but imbues them with additional meaning; rather than describing the actual walks or competitions, he uses the language of the ball to speak to members of primarily Black (and Latinx) queer communities who are familiar with that language. Similarly, the hook of the song uses Ballroom language to engage in rap braggadocio:

> I steps into the cut and all the kids say (hey)
> I get through to the showroom and the assistant say (hey)
> I grace the floor and the children say (hey)
> If you getting it how you live, let me hear you say (hey)

Terms like "the kids" and "the children" reference the kinship and hierarchical structures of Ballroom houses, where house mothers and house fathers serve as leaders who take responsibility for the performance and well-being of their "children," or other members of their house.[24] Club culture and Ballroom culture are also conflated here, where "kids" could refer to club kids or house kids, a population with a large degree of overlap. The "floor" could be either a dance floor or the floor of Ballroom competitions. "Hey," the title of the song and recurring response in the hook, evokes the familiar vocal patterns and cadences of many effeminate men's voices greeting each other. Following the hook, Leif's electronically manipulated voice sings "Now get down, g-g-get down" twice across registers, from high to low, not only offering a moment of word painting but also sonically suggesting a range of feminine to masculine gender expressions embodied in one person's voice. This range, in the context of the lyrical content, reflects the multiple gender positions of the Ballroom gender system, challenging hip hop's traditional gender binary.

Zebra Katz's best-known hit, "Ima Read" (featuring Njena Reddd Foxxx, 2012) is a perfect example of the crossover of Ballroom elements into hip hop culture. To "read" someone in Ballroom vernacular means to tell someone about themself, generally in an honest but negative way. The entire song is a read about reading someone, unfolding over a minimalist track in a nearly monotone delivery. After a repetitive introduction section, Katz raps in the first verse:

> Ima read that bitch
> Ima school that bitch
> Ima take that bitch to college
> Ima give that bitch some knowledge

And in the second verse:

---

24. For more on the kinship structure of the houses, see Bailey, *Butch Queens*.

School's in Ima read that bitch
Ima write a dissertation to excuse my shit
When I act out of line and I spit and I kick
And I rip and I dip and I yah trick
What bitch you don't like my shit?
What bitch you wanna fight me trick?
In the back of the classroom sittin' talking shit
Better shut yo ass up before I reach you real quick

If one is familiar with the culture and ritual of balls, it is easy to picture a scene unfolding that involves the dips and turns of a competitor walking, responding to the competition with witty banter and threatening to read them or more. With trophies on the line, one can picture a confrontation escalating from shit-talking to physical confrontation, but here that competitive tension meets rap braggadocio, and the tension is released lyrically.

Unlike Leif, whose lyrics are graphic and focus on sex acts between men, Katz's lyrics are less sexually explicit but rely on cultural references to code them as gay. Katz has stated:

It's a fine line that I'm playing here. I'm trying to see how cleverly I can walk a tightrope. You have [fans from] the ball culture, and then you have hip-hop heads who are gonna say this is hard because it's very minimal and to-the-point.[25]

Katz intentionally draws on aspects of Ballroom culture to reference his own Black queer identity rather than incorporating graphic sexual lyrics that leave little room for doubt. Ballroom slang in this track becomes coded lyrics that, while certainly enjoyable to the average hip hop listener, carry additional queer meanings to audiences familiar with the particular Black queer culture from which the language comes.

Like Leif, Cakes da Killa uses sexually explicit imagery to articulate an unquestionably gay identity, and he also refers to aspects of Ballroom culture in his lyrics. He is perhaps best known for his track "I Run This Club," which certainly invokes the gay club that has historically played an important role in Black queer communities (and possibly the hip hop club as well), but other tracks draw clearer connections between his work as an openly queer Black rapper and his cultural lineage that relates to the Ballroom scene: lines such as "I know niggas be gagging" and "kikiing in multi-million dollar man-

---

25. Katz as quoted in Battan, "We Invented Swag."

sions" in "Living Gud, Eating Gud" from his *Hunger Pangs* mixtape (2014); "I keep a trade in the clutch" in "Goodie Goodies" from his mixtape *The Eulogy* (2013); and "I mean it's shade on the panel / how you claiming legend when ya shit is all samples" in "Oven Ready," also from *Hunger Pangs*. The titles of tracks "It's Not Ovah" and "Get 2 Werk" (*Hunger Pangs*) also draw explicitly on Ballroom slang.

Cakes uses Ballroom vocabulary generally in service of his style of brag rap; he combines the competitive nature of balls with the long tradition of rap boasting to suggest that he is both highly desirable to other men but also street smart and capable of inflicting harm on those who would threaten or offend him. He also uses terms such as "cunt" and "pussy" in the way that they are often used in the Ballroom scene to indicate femininity, especially his own, yet he also suggests that femininity does not necessarily indicate weakness but can be a characteristic from which men such as himself can draw strength. This ideal is one that is firmly rooted in Ballroom culture, where Butch Queens occupy a privileged position in the gender system.

Musical References

In addition to lyrical references, many New York City artists make musical gestures that recall Ballroom culture and the music with which it is closely tied. These musical references add an additional layer of meaning and place them directly in a musical lineage stemming from the Black queer experiences that prompted the emergence of disco and house music. There are two main ways in which musical references appear: samples of music that recalls this lineage, especially disco or house hits, and more general use of styles that recall these genres and incorporate shared musical aspects.

One clear example of the sampling approach is found in "Soda," a track by Leif and his frequent collaborator Boody from their EP *Liquid* (2012). The track heavily samples Masters at Work's "The Ha Dance," which, as Bailey notes, is a widely used track for Ballroom walks, especially in New Way Vogue categories.[26] While the sample is at times distorted, anyone familiar with the original track, as all Ballroom participants or spectators are, would immediately recognize it and associate it with the Ballroom scene. This relationship is underscored in the music video for the track, which features dancers performing different styles, including vogue.

Cakes da Killa also uses musical samples to reference a Black queer musi-

---

26. Bailey, *Butch Queens*, 154.

cal and cultural lineage. He opens his 2013 full-length mixtape, *The Eulogy*, with a sped-up sample of Donna Summer's performance of "MacArthur Park" (1978), manipulating and slightly distorting the voice of one of the most recognizable disco divas as she sings a line that mentions cake. This sample allows him to play on his own name, Cakes da Killa, while also invoking the queer associations of disco. The aforementioned "It's Not Ovah," from *Hunger Pangs*, also features a sped-up sample, this time of First Choice's 1977 hit "Let No Man Put Asunder," which has been used in multiple house music tracks, including Frankie Knuckle's own 1983 remix.

On the *Eulogy*'s "Life Alert," rather than a musical sample Cakes includes an interlude that consists of a clip from the 1990 documentary *Paris is Burning* of a Ball participant saying, "I'm one of the top upcoming children, legendary. You have legendary children and upcoming legendary children." Not only does this recording bring Ballroom culture directly into the track to position Cakes's music within a Black queer ethos, but it also connects the unnamed participant's self-confident bragging with the long tradition of rap boasting. Cakes draws connections between two seemingly disparate cultures—hypermasculine heterosexual rap and queer Ballroom—demonstrating that they need not be incompatible.

Other artists, such as Zebra Katz, are subtler in their musical choices, avoiding samples and producing music in a style reminiscent of 1980s and 1990s house, the era that provides much of the soundtrack for balls. Katz's tracks "Tear the House Up" (2014) and "1 Bad Bitch" (2014) both sound like house tracks, from the four-on-the-floor beats with snare and hand-clap embellishments, to the minimalist, at times static synthesized bass lines with timbres reminiscent of those created using the Roland TB-303 bass line machines that were so popular in dance music during the last two decades of the twentieth century. The biggest difference between Katz's tracks and those produced by house artists is that in his work the lyrics play a more centralized role rather than serving as additional rhythmic material or momentary accents. In this way, Katz, like Cakes da Killa, combines musical elements of two styles that are already closely related but frequently understood to be at odds: the beats and synthesized sounds of house with the wordplay and sharp delivery of rap.

House music also plays an important role in the musical output of Azealia Banks, the artist from this cluster of New York City rappers who has received the most widespread attention outside of the local scene. As hip hop critics Ebro Darden and Peter Rosenberg have noted, the incorporation of house is in fact a distinctive aspect of Banks's musical style that, along with her lyrical abilities, sets her apart from her peers.[27] She is best known for her first break-through single, "212," released on the *1991* EP. At the end of the first verse of this track, Banks offers a blatant description of a queer sex act in a brief break from her threatening lyrics:

> Now she wanna lick my plum in the evenin'
> And fit that tongue, tongue d-deep in
> I guess that cunt gettin' eaten

The last line is repeated several times while the music builds until the bass drops out, a common gesture in various dance music genres but especially in house. Like Leif and Cakes da Killa, Banks is graphically explicit in this track, but there are no overt references to Ballroom culture other than in its musical style. Similarly, the tracks "Chasing Time" (*Broke with Expensive Taste*) and "That Big Big Beat" (2016) share the house music sound, from the danceable beat to the synthesizer accents. She also sings on these tracks, alternating between vocals reminiscent of the divas whose voices appear over house tracks and her tough rapper persona.

Like other Black women rappers, Banks must negotiate the racialized gender expectations placed upon her both within hip hop and in the larger culture. As James McNally argues in his study of "212," Banks rearticulates Black female identity by "confronting the listener and viewer with lyrics and images that assert her sexuality, while at the same time presenting herself as independent and empowered and avoiding the kind of objectification common in the music and videos of previous female rappers who had achieved mainstream success [such as Nicki Minaj]."[28] In support of this argument, McNally points to Banks's use of the term "cunt" in "212," noting that not only does her use of the word in this context highlight her bisexual identity, but it also presents a reframing of "cunt" in a positive light, contrary to its derogatory connotations in most other hip hop contexts. He writes:

> Banks's willingness to discuss and validate sex with another woman . . .
> distinguishes her from most mainstream female rappers and chal-
> lenges prevailing heteronormative standards in hip-hop. Taken

---

27. "Azealia Banks Goes Off on TI, Iggy + Black Music Being Smudged Out," YouTube video, 47:30, from an interview conducted by Ebro Darden, Laura Stylez, and Peter Rosenberg, posted by HOT 97, December 18, 2014, https://www.youtube.com/watch?v=uFDS-VEEl6w.

28. James McNally, "Azealia Banks's '212': Black Female Identity and the White Gaze in Contemporary Hip-Hop," *Journal of the Society for American Music* 10, no. 1 (2016): 62.

together, Banks's use of "cunt" permits her to reassert her sexuality on her own terms. To be sure, Banks's use of the term to denigrate a female rival raises potential charges of hypocrisy; despite this possibility, she has characterized the word as empowering: "To be cunty is to be feminine and to be . . . aware of yourself. Nobody's fucking with that inner strength and delicateness."[29]

McNally's assessment of Banks's rearticulation of Black female identity is correct but incomplete, as it fails to fully take into account the rapper's use of Ballroom aesthetics to rearticulate a Black *queer* female identity. As noted above, "cunt" or "cunty" has evolved in Ballroom parlance to mean exactly what Banks defines it as: feminine and strong. While butch queens or transfeminine individuals within Ballroom culture use the term most often, Banks, a cisgender woman, draws on that usage as she also negotiates racialized gender expectations. Furthermore, while McNally notes Banks's preference for house-influenced tracks, he does not acknowledge house music's relationship to Black queer communities in New York City generally and Ballroom culture specifically, a relationship that is embedded in Banks's work. The influence of Ballroom culture is also evident in some of her performance choices; for example, on June 3, 2012, she hosted a performance she called the "Mermaid Ball," a clear reference to competitive balls that featured other Ballroom-influenced artists such as House of LaDosha, a performance collective that includes the musical artists La'fem Ladosha (formerly Dosha Devastation) and Cunty Crawford and whose musical collaborations include "B/M/F" (Black Model Famous), a remix of rapper Rick Ross's "B.M.F." (Blowin' Money Fast), and "Burning Like Paris."

Banks not only rearticulates Black female identity; she also rearticulates a Black *queer* female identity, and she does so using Black queer terms. Positioning Banks within the genre of Ballroom rap and locating her within a Black queer cultural lineage specific to New York City illuminates certain stylistic and aesthetic values and cultural reference points she shares with other artists in this genre. Drott proposes that by "relating a piece of music with one set of texts and not some other, individuals (including analysts) make an implicit judgment regarding what kinds of knowledge are relevant for 'correctly' understanding the work in question."[30] Indeed, I suggest that,

---

29. McNally, "Azealia Banks's '212,'" 65. Here he cites Banks in an interview with Colleen Nika, "Q&A: Azealia Banks on Why the C-Word Is 'Feminine,'" *Rolling Stone*, September 10, 2012, https://www.rollingstone.com/culture/culture-news/qa-azealia-banks-on-why-the-c-word-is-feminine-181176/, accessed February 8, 2022.

30. Drott, "End(s) of Genre," 14.

as McNally's study demonstrates, Black queer knowledge, or at least knowledge of the particular location of Black queer identities, is necessary for if not a "correct" understanding Banks's work, at least a more complete understanding. Placing Banks's work in conversation with that of other Ballroom rap artists helps make visible the influence of Ballroom and other Black queer cultures on their work.

Visual References

Ballroom culture places a large emphasis on the visual, with most competition categories focusing on appearance above all else. Many Ballroom rap artists similarly incorporate visual aspects of queer culture into their performances, some of which reference the Ballroom scene. Haute couture fashions, voguing, and drag find their way into rappers' stage appearances and music videos. Often these images rely on the close association of fashion with ball culture. The video for Katz's "Tear the House Up" has the rapper appearing in a number of designer outfits, to the extent that an entire MTV.com article is dedicated to a look-by-look analysis of the styles (the music video is available on YouTube: https://doi.org/10.3998/mpub.11306619 .cmp.1).[31] Fashion has always been an important aspect of Ballroom; the original houses were named after designer brands, and there are specific Ballroom categories dedicated to emulating fashion shows in both walking style and appearance. Indeed, the very term "house" comes from the fashion industry, so it makes sense that artists would honor that past by engaging in visual aesthetics of the culture.

Additionally, artists often feature recognizable styles of dance and performance, especially voguing, in their music videos. As mentioned above, the video for Leif's track "Soda" features a dancer performing vogue moves, and the rapper himself engages in voguing in the video for "Koi," a track off his 2015 EP *Riot Boi*. Thanks in part to Madonna's 1990 hit "Vogue" and its accompanying music video, voguing has become perhaps the most recognizable aspect of Ballroom culture to nonparticipants. Incorporating vogue dance styles in music videos is therefore the clearest technique an artist can use to reference Ballroom culture in a way that resonates with audiences who are not Ballroom participants.

---

31. Jessie Peterson, "Zebra Katz's 'Tear the House Up' Music Video: Look by Look," MTV.com, June 3, 2014, http://www.mtv.com/news/2520801/zebra-katzs-tear-the-house-up-music-video-look-by-look/.

Drag also plays an important role in Ballroom's visual aesthetic. Not all Ballroom participants compete in drag; as Bailey notes, despite being such a highly visible aspect of the culture, drag is only one of many practices in the scene.[32] Ballroom members who compete in drag participate in categories such as realness, vogue performance, and body and face categories, all of which require the participant to "pass," or appear as cisgender women by mainstream standards.[33] Realness, according to Bailey, is a "theory of urban performance that emerges from the Ballroom community" in which race, gender, and sexual identity are co-performed.[34] He explains:

> The range of performative gender and sexual identities that are performed at the balls are framed within a discourse of blackness. Mirroring forms of Black gender and sexual performance by means of which members are largely oppressed, the Ballroom community understands that the material realities of their lives (including their safety) are largely contingent on how they are interpellated, how they are *seen* by, and within the optic lens of White supremacy on the one hand and Black heteronormativity on the other.[35]

The criteria for realness, then, for both Butch Queens and Femme Queens, is established by the Ballroom community as a strategic response to mainstream constructions of race, gender, and sexuality that both resists and reinscribes those constructions.

Within realness competitions, however, there is one category, usually performed by a Butch Queen, called Realness with a Twist in which the competitor "displays both extremes of the masculine-to-feminine spectrum in one performance."[36] The goal of this performance is to enact both "thug realness," or heightened heterosexual masculinity, and "soft and cunt" femininity successfully. Performers who compete in the Realness with a Twist category highlight how all gender expressions are performative but also reliant on normative notions of masculinity and femininity.

Mykki Blanco, the stage persona of performance artist and rapper Michael Quattlebaum Jr., embodies some aspects of the Realness with a Twist performance but also challenges both the concept of realness as a desirable category and the dichotomous construction of feminine and masculine. Blanco's per-

---

32. Bailey, *Butch Queens*, 38.
33. Bailey, *Butch Queens*, 60.
34. Bailey, *Butch Queens*, 65.
35. Bailey, *Butch Queens*, 65.
36. Bailey, *Butch Queens*, 65.

formances and music videos feature the performer in various states of drag but never a drag that would satisfy Ballroom judges' requirements for realness. He often appears with a wig, makeup, perhaps a feminine bottom, but often without a shirt, exposing his masculine tattooed chest and torso. He offers a gender performance that pushes against both the well-worn binary and the Ballroom gender systems, offering a critique of both that opens up new modes of gender, especially in hip hop.

In the music videos spanning his career so far, such as "Wavvy" (2012) and "Coke White, Starlight" (2015), for example, Blanco alternates between appearing in and out of drag, but his drag persona never completely offers an illusion of cisgender womanhood. Instead, Blanco appears in blonde, red, or brown wigs, makeup, and feminine clothing, but without a shirt (the music video for "Wavvy" is available on YouTube: https://doi.org/10.3998/mpub .11306619.cmp.2). The videos never suggest that Blanco is occupying two different subject positions or using drag to present two separate characters; instead, Blanco embodies both feminine and masculine qualities at once, sometimes highlighting one over the other but always offering them as different aspects of the same person. In "High School Never Ends" (2016), Blanco appears only in drag but again in an intentionally unconvincing manner. The video reinterprets the Romeo and Juliet tale in contemporary Germany, with Blanco playing the lover of a white German man whose violent neo-Nazi friends resist both sexual and racial difference. In flashbacks to the lovers' youth, the young Blanco is presented as a cisgender boy. While Blanco's adult character in the video could be interpreted as a trans woman, a gay man in drag, or a person with an altogether different nonconforming gender identity, viewers still understand that it is the same person. Blanco challenges the idea that gender performance needs to adhere to heteronormative binary ideas to be convincing or that gender performance needs ever be convincing at all.

Blanco's play between masculine and feminine through the medium of hip hop is especially acute in the video for "She Gutta" (2014). Opening as a parody of reality crime television shows such as *Cops*, the video follows a fictional underworld of Los Angeles gangland where queerness and stereotypical thug masculinity go hand in hand. Breaking from his typical approach, Blanco does not appear in drag, but the video does feature women who could be trans as well as muscular, tattooed Black men, including one with whom he engages in sexual acts. Stan Hawkins argues that the video for "She Gutta" does political work for LGBTQ communities:

Artists such as Blanco turn to a progressive sexual politics in the guise of transgendered representations in order to advance an awareness of the reality of violence and sexual discrimination in the US today. The video performance of "She Gutta" is a fearless attempt to forge a path for imagining civil rights and social justice in the future. At the same time, the outrageous shifting between a dark blond female and a sexually active young black gay male, wrapped up into one person, demystifies queer sexualities. Thus, Blanco insists on his/her equal right by stating explicitly in a narrative of explosive force. Authorizing this is a tactic of deferral that is, in actual fact, a disavowal of shame.[37]

Blanco's performances, in "She Gutta" and elsewhere, do push against the notion of shame and implicitly call for civil rights. However, they also draw attention to co-constructions of race, gender, and sexuality in ways that also invoke an element of play. Blanco eschews the rigid notions of gender of both mainstream and Ballroom cultures, drawing on those ideals while also offering an alternative that is noncompetitive and non-conforming.

Ballroom Rap as Genre

The artists I have explored here all engage in similar forms of what Bailey terms "performance labor" through which they participate in "individual and collective self-fashioning."[38] He writes that Ballroom "performance makes it possible to revise, negotiate, and reconstitute gender and sexual categories and norms, enabling Ballroom members to reconfigure gender and sexual roles and relations while constructing a more open minoritarian social sphere."[39] Rappers who incorporate aspects of Ballroom culture into their performances are similarly taking part in this performance labor, but they extend that work into the realm of hip hop. Additionally, through Ballroom references, be they lyrical, musical, or visual, these artists are also placing themselves within a Black queer cultural and musical lineage that has carried through urban LGBTQ communities of color

---

37. Stan Hawkins, *Queerness in Pop Music: Aesthetics, Gender Norms, and Temporality* (New York: Routledge, 2016), 209.

38. Bailey, *Butch Queens*, 32.

39. Bailey, *Butch Queens*, 17–18.

throughout the twentieth and twenty-first centuries in the United States, especially in New York City. Their references to this largely underground culture position them as the latest generation of Black queer cultural workers, who continuously challenge and rewrite the gender and sexuality options available to them.

Applying the genre label "Ballroom rap" to the work of openly queer or trans Black artists based in New York City positions their musical texts in relationship with each other in such a way that their multifaceted identities and musical styles are no longer collapsed into the contested category of "gay rap." Instead, this genre accounts for the shared cultural reference point that has led music journalists and listeners to already profile these artists in relation to each other, while also making visible the often unnoticed heritage of Black queer culture in the city over the past century and acknowledging that this culture is not monolithic and is constantly in flux. As Eric Drott notes, genres are groupings that must be "continually produced and reproduced."[40] The specific agents who perform genre-grouping acts are not necessarily artists themselves but rather listeners, critics, and scholars who wish to understand the relationships between certain musical texts and, for example, the social contexts or values that they might share. Thus, we can position an artist such as Mykki Blanco, who identifies more strongly with punk than rap, in conversation with other artists such as Leif, Zebra Katz, Azealia Banks, and Cakes da Killa and recognize the shared Black queer cultural work that they all do in their own diverse ways.[41]

Other agents besides artists can also identify and position contemporary rappers within a musical and cultural lineage in order to draw out common themes and strategies. In her groundbreaking musicological study of rap, Cheryl L. Keyes positions Black female rappers in a lineage with Black women blues singers of the early twentieth century, all of whom rearticulate and redefine Black female identity and use music as a site from which to

---

40. Drott, "End(s) of Genre," 10.

41. In a statement following the release of his mixtape *Gay Dog Food* (UNO, 2014), Blanco said, "You can choose to call me a gay rapper, you can choose to not even call me a rapper if you want to, it doesn't matter. I'm a punk, a creative punk and i'm [*sic*] going to continue to create and entertain without boundaries" (cited in Zoe Camp, "Mykki Blanco Releases *Gay Dog Food* Mixtape," *Pitchfork*, October 28, 2014, http://pitchfork.com/news/57225-mykki-blanco-releases-gay-dog-food-mixtape/). Articles that consider Blanco as part of the same cohort as other gay rappers in New York City include Clare Considine, "Zebra Katz, Mykki Blanco, and the Rise of Queer Rap"; Eric Shorey, "Queer Rap Is Not Queer Rap," *Pitchfork*, March 31, 2015, http://pitchfork.com/thepitch/712-queer-rap-is-not-queer-rap/; and Battan, "We Invented Swag."

"contest, protest, and affirm working-class ideologies of Black womanhood."[42] In so doing, she argues that women rappers in the late twentieth century did not emerge without precedent but instead are part of a continuum. In examining shared themes that both early blues women and late twentieth-century women rappers address in their music, Keyes demonstrates how women MCs find historical antecedents from which to draw inspiration and legitimization. Similarly, in his study of Black gay literary traditions of the 1980s and 1990s, Simon Dickel argues that Black gay writers often placed their work in conversation with earlier literature.[43] He notes that, like other marginalized groups, Black gay activists and artists sought legitimacy and self-empowerment through their references to the Harlem Renaissance and the protest era.[44] Ballroom rap, whether recognized by the artists, listeners, critics, or scholars, similarly places contemporary practices in conversation with historical traditions, legitimizing and calling attention to long-overlooked particularities of Black queer culture in New York City during the twentieth and twenty-first centuries.

Ballroom rappers also confront the idea that hip hop and Black queer cultural expressions are incompatible by demonstrating just how much they have in common. Rather than juxtaposing the two, they highlight the competitiveness—verbal (through lyrics), physical (through dance and gesture), and visual—that is a touchstone in both rap and Ballroom. Ballroom rappers also redefine hip hop's hardness and masculinity. Miles White writes that the rap's hardness is a means to perform privileged affective strategies: "The act of mean mugging in the performance of the hard masculine ideal in contemporary hip-hop adopts a privileged subjectivity that has historically been reserved for white males, a posture of confident masculinity in which one must project powerful emotions if one is to gain respect."[45] Ballroom rappers too access this hardness but through a gender-expansive framework that reflects their own gender system, demonstrating that this access is not available to only cisgender heterosexual men. One can be hard but also effeminate; one can be masculine but not male. Furthermore, this hardness stems not just from navigating and surviving a white supremacist world but

---

42. Cheryl L. Keyes, *Rap Music and Street Consciousness* (Urbana: University of Illinois Press, 2004), 187.

43. Simon Dickel, *Black/Gay: The Harlem Renaissance, the Protest Era, and Constructions of Black Gay Identity in the 1980s and 90s* (East Lansing: Michigan State University Press, 2011), 4.

44. Dickel, *Black/Gay*, 7.

45. Miles White, *From Jim Crow to Jay-Z: Race, Rap, and the Performance of Masculinity* (Urbana: University of Illinois Press, 2011), 18.

one that is also homo- and transphobic. Black queer rappers assert (or, perhaps more accurately, assume) their right to exist in hip hop, as well as their right to exist and fashion new worlds beyond the clubs and balls.

Black queer rappers based in New York City who incorporate aspects of Ballroom culture into their music engage in performance labor that articulates a Black queer identity that is specific if not to their city, then at least to northern urban centers in the United States. Artists working in other geographical areas engage in their own labor that connects them to their local lineages and articulates not only their Black queer identities but their regional identities as well. The enactment of these identities often involves the incorporation of musical and lyrical elements that are place-specific and that therefore serve as musical geographical markers. Their work does not constitute "gay rap" but rather one of many diverse subgenres that are produced and performed by openly queer and trans rappers.

Not only is the diversity of music being created by QTPOC (queer and trans people of color) rappers often ignored, but the fact that these artists have been and continue to be active is largely erased even, or perhaps especially, in narratives offered by other rappers. The very concept of "gay rap" is itself a response to the invisibility of these artists. Furthermore, when the role of queer rappers is seriously addressed, the narrative has focused on men. One group that has been largely erased from hip hop discourses is openly queer Black women, especially those with more masculine gender presentations. In the following chapter, I explore how queer women rappers such as Young M.A and Syd also fit into rap's queer lineage as women. They exist on a continuum of Black queer music-making practices but one that specifically articulates the intersections of race, gender, and sexuality for masculine-presenting queer women.

3 • "The Bro Code"

Black Queer Women and Female Masculinity in Rap

In 1996 rapper Queen Latifah gave us the quintessential Black butch character in her portrayal of Cleo in F. Gary Gray's bank heist film, *Set It Off.* Latifah's performance is one of the few that highlights Black female masculinity, particularly a queer one, in a largely positive way in pop culture.[1] In a film that focuses on the friendship of four Black women, Cleo's character is thoroughly integrated into the group, an imperfect but, as Jack Halberstam notes, "amazingly powerful representation of Black butchness."[2] While Cleo is not given the same level of complex and sympathetic backstory as her heterosexual best friends, Stony, Frankie, and T.T., she is nevertheless portrayed as unapologetically masculine and queer.

Although Latifah distanced herself at the time from her character's queerness (as she had long dodged rumors about her own queerness), the rapper's role in the film and her character's penchant for listening to gangsta rap cassettes (especially as she drives away in a freshly stolen vehicle) situate the film in hip hop culture.[3] Kara Keeling specifically situates *Set It Off* within the

---

1. For further discussion of Cleo's Black female masculinity, see Kara Keeling, "'Ghetto Heaven': *Set It Off* and the Valorization of Black Lesbian Butch-Femme Sociality," *Black Scholar* 33, no. 1 (2003): 33–46; and Judith Halberstam, *Female Masculinity* (Durham, NC: Duke University Press, 1998), 227–30. This book was written before Halberstam came out as trans and began publishing under the name Jack, so while I keep all citations true to the publication, I refer to him with he/him/his pronouns throughout this book.

2. Halberstam, *Female Masculinity*, 227.

3. Queen Latifah, in an interview with Danyel Smith, "Heads Ain't Ready for Queen Latifah's Next Move," *Vibe* (December 1996/January 1997), 98–102. Latifah has since been more open about her identity, most recently acknowledging her longtime partner in an acceptance speech for a BET Lifetime Achievement Award in June 2021.

genre of hip hop films that S. Craig Watkins refers to as "ghettocentric."[4] However, Keeling argues that Cleo challenges the sexism and homophobia often associated with or embedded in ghettocentricity that map narrowly perceived gender expression onto biological sex.[5] She writes, "Cleo's characterization seeks to expand ghettocentric black masculinity to include her, it also challenges the erotic economy that ghettocentric black masculinity currently facilitates. Cleo's ghettocentric butch masculinity opens onto both of these trajectories and keeps them in tension with each other without seeking a resolution of the two."[6] Cleo could have been a paradigm-shifting character in film as well as in hip hop in a broader sense—a significant representation of Black queer female masculinity that expands acceptable notions of Blackness, masculinity, queerness, and female identity in hip hop and popular culture discourses.

Twenty-five years later, Cleo remains such a significant cultural touchstone, a reference point for Black queer female masculinity, that in some ways she has overshadowed our understanding of contemporary rappers who fit that particular matrix of identities and gender expressions. She *is* that media representation of Black queer female masculinity, of the stud, of the Black butch. But this fictional character has become the main point of reference for all Black masculine women in hip hop; our discourses have not expanded to make space for Black queer female *masculinities*.

Hip hop discourses of authenticity are dominated by the construction of the typical rapper as a hypermasculine, Black, cisgender, and heterosexual man. Despite the diverse racial and gender identities of its founders and practitioners, as Imani Perry reminds us, hip hop generally, and rap in particular, "is an iteration of black language, black music, black style, and black youth culture."[7] As she points out, hip hop is also gendered male in that it provides a medium through which Black male identity is asserted but sometimes at the expense of Black women.[8] Several scholars have similarly focused on the expressions of Black male masculinity found in hip hop and how these expressions are consumed and understood by (primarily male) listeners of various races. For example, in *Thug Life: Race, Gender, and the Meaning of Hip-Hop*, Michael P. Jeffries examines how both Black

---

4. Keeling, "'Ghetto Heaven.'" Keeling refers to S. Craig Watkins, *Representing: Hip Hop Culture and the Production of Black Cinema* (Chicago: University of Chicago Press, 1998).

5. Keeling, "'Ghetto Heaven,'" 39.

6. Keeling, "'Ghetto Heaven,'" 39.

7. Imani Perry, *Prophets of the Hood: Politics and Poetics in Hip Hop* (Durham, NC: Duke University Press, 2004), 2.

8. Perry, *Prophets of the Hood*, 118.

and white men understand racial construction and authenticity in the genre.[9] He rightfully asserts that, regardless of the actual racial and gender diversity of hip hop practitioners, "most commercially successful American hip-hop has had a black male face, body, and voice," and that "the contest over cultural appropriation is explicitly concerned with the appropriation of black masculinity rather than simply blackness."[10] Thus, while it is easy to identify commercially successful artists who are not Black men, Perry and Jeffries confirm that hip hop is overall understood as a Black male masculine culture and that artists, especially rappers who are not Black men, must define themselves both in relation and opposition to that identity in order to be read as authentic performers in the genre.

Furthermore, as Miles White explains in his study of the performance of Black masculinity in rap, hip hop literacy is contingent upon reading and reinscribing meanings on Black (male) bodies even as hip hop culture has become a global phenomenon.[11] While the culture of hip hop is understood to be that of Black American men, it has been read, reconfigured, and reproduced globally and locally by members of many different communities. Although Black male masculinity is not a monolithic gender and racial expression shared by all Black American men, the codes that are embedded and reproduced in hip hop privilege certain expressions of Black masculinity that can be read as normative within this genre. Identities that fall outside of the configuration of Black, heterosexual, masculine male are always defined and redefined against that contextual norm.

In one of the first ethnographic studies of rap to incorporate Black women performers and listeners, Tricia Rose situates Black women rappers "as part of a dialogic process with male rappers (and others), rather than in complete opposition to them [in order to] consider the ways black women rappers work within and against dominant sexual and racial narratives in American culture."[12] As more research on women rappers appeared after Rose's study, there emerged a trend of scholars trying to understand this dialogic process by categorizing rappers according to their style of lyrical and physical gender expressions. For example, Cheryl L. Keyes classifies women rappers into four categories identified by an interpretive community: Queen

9. Michael Jeffries, *Thug Life: Race, Gender, and the Meaning of Hip-Hop* (Chicago: University of Chicago Press, 2011).

10. Jeffries, *Thug Life*, 9.

11. Miles White, *From Jim Crow to Jay-Z: Race, Rap, and the Performance of Masculinity* (Urbana: University of Illinois Press, 2011).

12. Tricia Rose, *Black Noise: Rap Music and Black Culture in Contemporary America* (Middletown, CT: Wesleyan University Press, 1994), 147.

Mother, Fly Girl, Sista with Attitude, and Lesbian (a category to which we will return in a moment).[13] Regina N. Bradley, drawing on Perry and Tracy Sharpley-Whiting, extends these archetypes to include the "badwoman" and "groupie" in her discussion of hip hop's gender politics.[14] Calling attention to the ways "hip-hop gender politics are often considered oppositional and frequently in a power struggle that intersects with race and class," she notes that "hip-hop masculinity is aggressive, dominant, and flattened while hip-hop femininity is submissive, (hyper)sexual, and silenced."[15] In her examples (which also include her own classification system for male rappers), she highlights the polarizing aspects of this dichotomy, simultaneously complicating hip hop's gender politics while still underscoring the desire to categorize rappers' gender expressions.

Fans, critics, and scholars alike use classification systems to understand a performer's work within the larger context of hip hop and to place multiple artists in conversation with each other, sometimes for comparison and sometimes as a point of competition. The problem is that while, as Keyes's work especially demonstrates, these categories can make visible the aesthetic values of hip hop's interpretive community, they can also be limiting in that they create boundaries that are then reinforced by that interpretive community. The Black woman rapper archetype "lesbian" is an illustrative example. In this (very short) section of her studies, Keyes offers only one example, Queen Pen, who was among the first rappers in the mainstream to openly identify as lesbian and to include lesbian themes in her music, especially in her song "Girlfriend." Keyes also emphasizes Queen Pen's femme appearance and contrasts this with her gestures, which she associates with "male hip-hop culture" rather than hip hop culture overall.[16] Keyes was one of the first scholars to include an openly queer Black woman rapper in her work and to account for some of the analytical frameworks necessary for understanding Black lesbian identity in the genre. However, because it includes only one example, one whose femme identity was emphasized, the category as presented is a limiting one that gives only a brief glimpse into what is really a myriad of Black queer women's experiences and expressions. Hip

---

13. Cheryl L. Keyes, "Empowering Self, Making Choices, Creating Spaces: Black Female Identity via Rap Music Performance," *Journal of American Folklore* 113, no. 449 (2000): 255–69; Keyes, *Rap Music and Street Consciousness* (Urbana: University of Illinois Press, 2002).

14. Regina N. Bradley, "Barbz and Kings: Explorations of Gender and Sexuality in Hip-Hop," in *The Cambridge Companion to Hip-Hop*, ed. Justin A. Williams (Cambridge, UK: Cambridge University Press, 2015), 181–91.

15. Bradley, "Barbz and Kings," 182.

16. Keyes, "Empowering Self," 264.

hop discourse thus has a very limited—and limiting—framework for understanding Black queer women artists.

Taking a more gender-expansive view requires interrogating the dichotomies of male/masculine and female/feminine that are not unique to hip hop but that hip hop discourses have largely upheld. One of the ways this conversation can expand is by incorporating a framework that accounts for female masculinity, especially a Black female masculinity in hip hop. Halberstam argues that "far from being an imitation of maleness, female masculinity actually affords us a glimpse of how masculinity is constructed as masculinity. In other words, female masculinities are framed as the rejected scraps of dominant masculinity in order that male masculinity may appear to be the real thing."[17] Masculinity is not a characteristic that only men have—a fact that, as Halberstam notes, should seem obvious and yet needs to be explicitly stated. Furthermore, female masculinity is not an imitation or emulation of male masculinity but rather its own form of expression that destabilizes fixed gender dichotomies. While Halberstam uses primarily white examples, he does note that race, class, and sexuality are intertwined with expressions and embodiments of masculinity and focuses on queer female masculinities. In his study of Filipino seamen, masculinity, and globalization, Kale Bantigue Fajardo adds to Halberstam's formulation that masculinities "refer to a heterogeneous spectrum of differently situated masculine racialized, classed, and geographically, historically, culturally, economically located and situated sex/gender formations and performances."[18] Like Halberstam, I am primarily concerned here with queer female masculinities, but like Fajardo, I emphasize the intersectional aspects of racialized masculinities specifically. Halberstam writes that "widespread indifference to female masculinity . . . has clearly ideological motivations and has sustained the complex social structures that wed masculinity to maleness and to power and domination."[19] In hip hop in the United States, an indifference to Black female masculinity is both a symptom and cause of ongoing marginalization of both women and LGBTQ+ rappers.

Black queer female masculinity, as it manifests in a culture that locates normalized masculinity in the white, middle-class, male body, can paradoxically be both hypervisible and invisible. Evelynn M. Hammonds illustrates the historical narrative of Black women's sexuality in the United States,

---

17. Halberstam, *Female Masculinity*, 1–2.

18. Kale Bantigue Fajardo, *Filipino Crosscurrents: Oceanographies of Seafaring, Masculinities, and Globalization* (Minneapolis: University of Minnesota Press, 2011), 6.

19. Halberstam, *Female Masculinity*, 2.

which has been largely predicated on combating negative stereotypes through a "politics of silence."[20] She writes, "Historically, black women have reacted to the repressive force of the hegemonic discourses on race and sex . . . with silence, secrecy, and a partially self-chosen invisibility."[21] Invisibility is a tactic to resist stereotypes of Black women as hypersexual and always available to [white] men, yet it also constitutes an erasure and silence. Hypervisibility, however, can create a hyperfocus on sexuality in a way that can inadvertently reinforce certain stereotypes. For Black queer women, this can lead to an expectation that one's sexual identity will constantly be performed for dominant groups in an acceptable manner. Drawing on the work of Hortense Spillers, Hammonds notes that "the historical narrative that dominates discussions of black female sexuality does not address even the possibility of a black lesbian sexuality or of a lesbian or queer subject."[22] For this reason, the risk of hypervisibility for Black queer women becomes greater, because they are articulating subject positions for which there is not yet a nuanced and complex understanding or recognition—they stand out. For Black queer women who are masculine of center, this is especially true and can lead to intense scrutiny and policing of gender and behavior. To engage in the politics of silence would be to remain invisible, but to speak out and name oneself would lead to a hypervisibility that brings its own dangers.

Two women rappers whose careers thus far highlight this paradox are Young M.A and Syd (formerly known as Syd Tha Kyd). Both successful in the commercial mainstream, Young M.A and Syd have very different musical styles, but they are both Black, queer, non-femme women rappers who must navigate the hypervisibility/invisibility paradox. Their musical expressions and the ways they have defined themselves in public, especially in response to homophobic comments made against them or in their professional circles, resist what Muñoz calls the "burden of liveness," or the mandate that "postcolonial, queer, and other minoritarian subjects . . . 'perform' for the amusement of a dominant power bloc."[23] As non-femme women artists, Young M.A and Syd do not fit into the previously established categories for women rappers, but they also do not assert their own category. This approach resists the "burden of liveness" and helps them navigate the hyper-

---

20. Evelynn M. Hammonds, "Toward a Genealogy of Black Female Sexuality: The Problematic of Silence," in *Feminist Genealogies, Colonial Legacies, Democratic Futures*, ed. J. Alexander and C. T. Mahanty (New York: Routledge, 1997), 93–104.

21. Hammonds, "Toward a Genealogy of Black Female Sexuality," 94.

22. Hammonds, "Toward a Genealogy of Black Female Sexuality," 101.

23. José Esteban Muñoz, *Disidentifications: Queers of Color and the Performance of Politics* (Minneapolis: University of Minnesota Press, 1999), 187.

visible/invisible paradox to which, as queer women of color, they are particularly susceptible.

It is important to note that Young M.A and Syd are far from the only women rappers to use masculine expressivity as way to access hip hop legibility. As I have written elsewhere, Nicki Minaj is a woman rapper who lyrically reproduces tropes of Black masculine rap authenticity in order to position herself as an authentic hip hop subject.[24] Shanté Paradigm Smalls similarly argues that in her raps, Jean Grae "deconstruct[s] heteronormative heterosexual relationships using the language, cadence, inflection, and tonality of some of her male counterparts."[25] Other artists, such as members of TLC and Salt 'n Pepa, have presented themselves at various times as tomboyish, a liminal and adolescent state that Halberstam argues is typically "associated with a 'natural' desire for the greater freedoms and mobilities enjoyed by boys."[26] All of these examples point to the dialogic positioning of (largely heterosexual) Black women in male-dominated rap in a way that challenges but does not necessarily disrupt the status quo. Their performances of masculinity are contextualized as either liminal (tomboys), undermined by a hyperfeminine gender presentation (Minaj), or an intentional and playful disruption of hip hop heteronormativity (Grae). Queer butch Black women rappers embody a masculinity that is neither temporary nor offset by femininity or heterosexuality. Their presence challenges hip hop's male masculinity and heteronormativity but in distinct ways that are worth examining more closely.

In the remainder of this chapter, I look first at Young M.A, highlighting a few musical examples that illustrate how she articulates a Black butch expression in the mainstream. She has always been open about being queer and raps about relationships with women, but she has received some unwanted attention as a result. I discuss rapper Kodak Black's inappropriate and homophobic comments directed at her over social media as well as Young M.A's response and the way she then moved away from identifying with the label "lesbian." Next, I discuss Syd's career trajectory, highlighting some of the parallels between her and Young M.A, especially in terms of navigating homophobia from male rappers. Syd has gone from the member of the rap collective Odd Future to forming her own subgroup, the Internet, to going

24. Lauron Kehrer, "Beyond Beyoncé: Intersections of Race, Gender, and Sexuality in Contemporary American Hip-Hop ca. 2010–2016" (PhD diss., University of Rochester, 2017).

25. Shanté Paradigm Smalls, "'The Rain Comes Down': Jean Grae and Hip Hop Heteronormativity," *American Behavioral Scientist* 55, no. 1 (2011): 86–95, esp. 86.

26. Halberstam, *Female Masculinity*, 6.

solo, all while being openly queer but similarly refusing to identify as a lesbian. I use the work and public positioning of these artists to argue for a framework that takes into account Black female masculinity in hip hop beyond *Set It Off*'s Cleo and how masculine-of-center Black women rappers carefully walk a line between being open about their sexualities but careful not to get categorized as musicians based on those identities.

Young M.A and the Bro Code

Young M.A first garnered attention with her song "Brooklyn Chiraq" (a freestyle over Nicki Minaj and G Herbo's "ChiRaq"), but it wasn't until her breakout single, "Ooouuu," was released in 2016 that she was really launched into hip hop's mainstream. Since then, the Brooklyn native has been featured in award shows and magazines, nominated for awards, and performed alongside artists such as Remy Ma and Beyoncé. Rather than waiting until she had already built a commercially successful career before publicly coming out, Young M.A has been open about her sexuality and articulated a queer subjecthood in her music from the beginning. Her first major hit epitomizes her lyrical style and thematic approach.

The track opens with M.A's slightly slurred and out of time speech as she professes that she's had too much Hennessy, the rapper's brown liquor of choice.[27] As she goes into the first verse, she mentions her friends and her crew, her willingness to be violent, and sexual encounters with women. She raps:

> I ride for my guys, that's the bro code (That's the bro code)
> Baby gave me head, that's a low blow (That's a low blow)
> Damn, she make me weak when she deep throat (When she deep
>   throat)
> I need a rich bitch, not a cheap ho (Not a cheap ho).

These are all lyrics typical for this genre of rap, but here they are explicitly queer, explicitly *butch*. Young M.A uses language one would expect from a male rapper and, in her reference to the bro code, aligns herself with her male crew members (the music video is available on YouTube: https://doi

---

27. In her own annotations for the lyrics on genius.com, Young M.A suggests she was drunk when she recorded the track, so "it feels authentic." https://genius.com/10188229, accessed June 25, 2020.

.org/10.3998/mpub.11306619.cmp.3). She also references sex with other women in terms taken right from the cisgender heterosexual male rapper's playbook:

> If that's your chick then why she textin' me? (Yo, why she textin')
> Why she keep callin' my phone speakin' sexually? (Speakin' ooh)
> Every time I'm out, why she stressin' me (Yo, why she stressin')
> You call her Stephanie? (You call her huh?) I call her Headphanie
> (Ooouuu)

But she also self-references using female pronouns: later in the song, she raps, "My brother told me, 'Fuck 'em, get that money sis!'" Performed in her signature low-timbre voice in her slow and relaxed flow, the track is actually fairly remarkable in its queer subtlety.

"Ooouuu" is very much a typical braggadocio rap of its time. On its inclusion in NPR's 200 Greatest Songs by 21st Century Women+ list, Mina Tavakoli describes the song as follows:

> a numbingly cold, New York-does-Atlanta banger about family, self-assurance, sex with women—ideas completely par for the course when it comes to most late 2010s rap chart-breakers. But its tricky beauty is largely in the double-take these themes can prompt in light of M.A.[sic]'s identity, and the track's near-seamless integration into the modern mainstream. In taking trap's parlance and fitting it directly onto her image, M.A—by her own intent—suddenly made being an openly out woman in hip-hop almost a point of indifference.[28]

Tavakoli's choice of words here is informative and revealing. She notes that Young M.A does not bend herself to fit hip hop's image, although admittedly many listeners might hear her as doing that. Rather, she takes "trap's parlance and [fits] it directly onto her image." Halberstam reminds us that female masculinity is not an imitation of male masculinity, even though it is often "framed as the rejected scraps of dominant masculinity in order that male masculinity may appear to be the real thing."[29] Young M.A's masculinity is not an imitation of hip hop masculinity but its own legitimate expression; as

---

28. Mina Tavakoli, "Young M.A., 'OOOUUU' (2016)," *The 200 Greatest Songs by 21st Century Women+*, *NPR.com*, July 30, 2018, https://www.npr.org/2018/07/09/627397206/turning-the-tables-the-200-greatest-songs-by-21st-century-women-part-6.

29. Halberstam, *Female Masculinity*, 1.

Tavakoli notes, she fits hip hop in her own image, not the other way around.

Young M.A's masculinity is not just performed through her appearance but also through her voice. Indeed, the first few times I heard "Ooouuu" on the radio without any visual images attached to the song, I thought I was listening to a cisgender male rapper. Young M.A's vocal performance exhibits a number of characteristics that Stephan Pennington has identified as elements of male-coded vocal performance, including lower pitch range; flat, monotone intonation with downward inflections; raspy timbre; dull articulatory attacks; use of volume rather than pitch for emphasis; and use of certain language (as discussed above).[30] Young M.A's flow as a rapper thus fits within the gendered expectations of the genre and is legible as normative in the sphere of hip hop sexual politics.

The lyrics of "Ooouuu" and their delivery are therefore subversive in their casualness. They are accentuated by call-and-response that Young M.A engages in with herself; she punctuates many lines with a follow-up, like parentheticals as notated here. For example, when she references the police, she makes a vocal siren sound after. She repeats important words like "I'm a boss." This is but one sonic characteristic that places Young M.A, like many other women rappers, in the lineage of women's blues traditions. Cheryl L. Keyes has discussed this relationship between women rappers and blues women, and her argument is worth quoting here at length:

> While one will find topics common to several black women's song traditions, including social commentary, political protest, and violence against women, there is a preponderance of prison and ghetto love songs among women blues and rap performers. Most of these songs illustrate the plight of being black and poor under a U.S. justice system that works in favor of the white and well-to-do. Using words uncommon in mainstream romantic pop or jazz songs, women of the blues affectionately refer to their male lovers as "Papa" or "Daddy," while women of rap refer to their male competitors or lovers as "sophisticated thugs" or "niggas." Songs about lesbian relationships are "mainstream" in the blues and rap traditions. Songs celebrating women loving women circulated in the classic blues repertory, for example, Ma

---

30. Stephan Pennington, "Transgender Passing Guides and the Vocal Performance of Gender and Sexuality," in *The Oxford Handbook of Music and Queerness*, ed. Fred Everett Maus and Sheila Whiteley (New York: Oxford University Press, published online January 2019), 6–8. https://doi.org/10.1093/oxfordhb/9780199793525.013.65.

Rainey's "Prove It On Me Blues." Similarly, rap music broke ground with a lesbian song by the female artist Queen Pen. . . . Finally, the classic blues singers defied mainstream attitudes about the full-figured black woman, who was often portrayed in patriarchal-controlled media as a mammy, an asexual being. Classic blues singers not only privileged the large-framed black woman, they embraced her as a sexually desirable and sexually active being. Such attitudes about being full-figured, fly, and seductive remain a fixture in hip-hop. Thus I firmly contend that the rise of female MCs in the late twentieth century represents an ongoing musical saga of black women's issues concerning male-female relationships, female sexuality, and black women's representations from a working-class point of view.[31]

I cite Keyes extensively here to demonstrate that the connections between women blues singers of the twentieth century and women rappers have already been established, but when it comes to queer, masculine women performers, there is a bit more at play. It is true that both genres express a particular Black working-class aesthetic, notably by using slang that one would not find in other genres of pop music and embracing sexuality and, at times, violence. I want to extend our understanding, however, of this shared Black working-class aesthetic to one that can also be queer. I disagree that lesbian themes have been "mainstream" in hip hop since the height of Queen Pen's career. Indeed, this is partly why Young M.A's success with "Ooouuu" is so remarkable: it brought lesbian sexuality, specifically a Black butch sexuality, into the mainstream, onto the airwaves, and into homes via televised performances. Keyes notes that blues singers and rappers also challenged patriarchal notions of full-figured Black women as asexual and non-desirable. Young M.A's success similarly challenges how butch Black women are often portrayed as non-desirable or stripped of their sexuality—the rapper makes space for the Black butch as both desirable and desiring subject.

Establishing herself in the rap mainstream, however, made her a target of harassment. In late February 2019 Kodak Black released the single "Pimpin Ain't Eazy," which mentions Young M.A in the chorus: "I be pullin' out straps on these fuck niggas / I go Young M.A on these dumb bitches / Like a dyke man, you niggas can't fuck with me." In the second verse he mentions her again, as well as two other women rappers and more references to having sex with a lesbian:

---

31. Keyes, *Rap Music and Street Consciousness*, 187–88.

Fuckin' DeJ Loaf like a stud . . .
Fuckin' on a dyke, I'm in love / I'm fuckin with a dyke, she the
 one . . .
Missy Elliott, come and sex me . . .
I'm fuckin' Young M.A, long as she got a coochie / Say she got the
 strap and the toolie, say she put the crack in her booty

The rhymes are bizarre, equating using a strap-on dildo with lesbian sex and expressing a desire to have sex with women he identifies as lesbian. The reference to DeJ Loaf has gone largely unmentioned in most media outlets' coverage of the song, but refers to a Detroit rapper who has spoken ambiguously about her dating life and has denied rumors about her sexuality for years.[32] There have long been rumors about Missy Elliott's sexuality, as well; in this track, Kodak Black obsesses over queer women rappers, especially those with more masculine gender presentations, both describing having sex *like* them ("I be pulling out the strap / Like I'm a dyke, or something") and wanting to have sex *with* them.

This attention, which some argue constitutes sexual harassment, was obviously unwelcome. It added to previous sexually suggestive comments Kodak Black had made about Young M.A, including a comment on a photo of her with Nicki Minaj posted on Instagram in which he wrote, "Both Of Y'all a Get It."[33] On March 17 Young M.A took to social media to respond to the harassment. In an Instagram Live video that is no longer available, she called Kodak Black and his followers who made similar comments or tagged her on social media "weird":

And y'all keep talking about this Kodak situation. Y'all niggas is weird, bro . . . and it be niggas on that shit. What's wrong with y'all? Is y'all niggas alright? Come on, bro. Like obviously the nigga's weird.[34]

Young M.A also said in a later live video that she was speaking mostly to people commenting on the YouTube video for the song and on social media:

32. In a 2017 profile DeJ Loaf stated, "I date whoever . . . I'm not into labels." Quoted in Clover Hope, "Quiet Storm: For Lifelong Loner DeJ Loaf, the Worldwide Stage Is an Ambitious Leap," *The Fader* (December/January 2017), https://www.thefader.com/magazine/107, accessed August 26, 2020.

33. Cited in Preezy, "Here's a Timeline of Kodak Black and Young M.A's Weird Beef," *XXL*, March 22, 2019, https://www.xxlmag.com/kodak-black-young-m-a-beef-timeline/.

34. Young M.A, quoted in Xavier Handy-Hamilton, "Kodak Black's Trolling Forces Young M.A to Respond," *Complex*, March 18, 2019, https://www.complex.com/music/2019/03/young-ma-responds-to-kodak-blacks-weird-comments.

In the live video . . . I'm literally talking about the people in the comments . . . and I'm like "Why y'all still on that? Get off that situation. Y'all dickeating." I know I'm a female stupid . . . but at the end of the day, that's not my preference. . . . That's why I said y'all weird.[35]

The rapper also stated that she would address Kodak Black about the situation in person at an event where they were both scheduled to perform. In a genre where diss tracks and social media responses happen quickly, the fact that Young M.A took her time before responding to the situation, and that she did so in such a measured way by not attacking the rapper or his fans and simply restating her own sexual orientation, shows the caution with which Black queer women must engage in these types of attacks so as not to invite further violence.

Kodak Black's response was to double-down, going on his own Instagram Live to ask "How are you a girl but don't want your pussy penetrated?"[36] This kind of harassment illustrates the particular intersections of misogyny and homophobia that Black lesbians face in general, but it is particularly revealing in terms of how butch women specifically are disrespected. Like much of the rhetoric in popular media around transgender people that focuses on intimacies of the body, this obsession with the mechanics of sex and genitalia are harmful to Black butch women in very specific ways. Not only does Kodak Black insist on sexualizing his colleague against her wishes, but he also expresses a complete disregard for Young M.A's identity. She insists that she only dates women, is only romantically and sexually attracted to women, and his interest in having sex as/with her is demeaning in that it denotes a complete disregard for her own bodily autonomy, her privacy, and the ways in which she wishes to be identified.

Kodak Black's response illustrates the real dangers of the hypervisible/invisible paradox for Black queer masculine women. On the one hand, Young M.A resists invisibility by being open about her sexuality, both in her music and in interviews. However, that openness has also made her a target for homophobic and misogynistic abuse. Kodak Black's attempts to undermine her queer identity rely on the conflation of gender identity, sexuality, and gender expression. As Anna Marie Smith argues, the desexualization of lesbians in the public and legal sphere also relies on this conflation to invisibilize lesbians, which conflates gender identity and expression, problematically

---

35. Young M.A, quoted in Handy-Hamilton, "Kodak Black's Trolling."

36. This Instagram Live video is no longer available but has been quoted in several articles, including Matthew Strauss, "Young M.A Responds to Kodak Black after He Raps Homophobic Lyrics about Her," *Pitchfork* March 18, 2019, https://pitchfork.com/news/young-ma-responds-to-kodak-black-after-he-raps-homophobic-lyrics-about-her/.

"equates femininity with absolutely passive behavior," and conflates gender identity with sexuality.[37] Furthermore, Smith argues that the conflation between gender identity, gender expression, and sexuality that positions all women as feminine and passive is intentional because it protects male interests:

> Patriarchal discourse protects the commodification of women by erasing the very possibility that women could be the subjects of our sexual practices. The naturalization of the idea that women are incapable of assertive sexual practices therefore plays a central role in patriarchal relations, for it legitimates the treatment of women as the sexual property of men.[38]

It is not just Young M.A's gender identity or sexuality that make her a target for Kodak Black; it is the naturalization of a gender and sexual binary in which Black queer masculine women cannot exist. By articulating that existence, Young M.A makes herself visible, but in a system in which her particular matrix of identities is Othered, she draws increased attention to her Otherness, making herself hypervisible.

Young M.A also tries to negotiate this hypervisibility by articulating a Black queer female identity in a way that could downplay that identity by not hyperfocusing on it. In an interview in September 2019, she responded to a question about her sexuality by saying she is not a lesbian; she is just Young M.A.[39] Several other media outlets picked up on her statement, to which she had added that she would not date dudes and that she loves women. Her resistance to the label "lesbian" is significant for a few reasons. One is that it helps her avoid the label "gay rapper." As noted in chapter 3, lumping artists together under this label pigeonholes them based on the idea of a shared identity with disregard to musical or thematic differences. In this same interview, Young M.A also eschewed the label "female rapper" for similar reasons, again insistent that she is "just" Young M.A.[40]

The rapper's resistance to both labels comes from the same place—a

---

37. Anna Marie Smith, "The Regulation of Lesbian Sexuality through Erasure: The Case of Jennifer Saunders," in *Lesbian Erotics*, ed. Karla Jay (New York: New York University Press, 1995), 171.

38. Smith, "Regulation of Lesbian Sexuality," 172.

39. Young M.A, "Young M.A Talks New Music & Says She's Not a Lesbian on Hollywood Unlocked [Uncensored]," YouTube, September 16, 2019, https://www.youtube.com/watch?v=ANLVMmN7O4g.

40. Young M.A, "Young M.A Talks New Music."

stated desire to avoid the limitations of being a female rapper or a gay rapper and expected to perform those identities and have her music heard in a particular way. This is a strategy she uses to push back against the industry's expectations and to resist the hypervisibility/invisibility paradox. Her insistence that she loves women and the ways she raps explicitly about relationships with other women ensures that as a queer person, that aspect of her identity cannot be made invisible or inaudible. She leaves no ambiguities on this matter, no way for her work to be understood outside of any queer context. And yet, the way she refuses to identify as a lesbian enables her to resist the exploitation of her identity into hypervisibility. Rather than situating her within a known category, or at least a category that most people think they know, she insists on her own freedom to just be. The very delicate balance that she achieves allows her queer identity to be seen while making it difficult for anyone to demand that she performs queerness on anyone else's terms but her own.

Although we have very few models for queer men rappers, we have even fewer for queer women. It is remarkable in some ways that Young M.A was able to build a mainstream career not as a precursor to coming out but on a foundation of being open about her queer identity from the beginning. She's not the only one.

"I'm the Only Person Like Me That I Know": Syd

Syd is not a rapper per se but has been a member of two rap collectives that have greatly pushed the development of hip hop in the past decade. She gained professional footholds as the main producer and DJ for Odd Future (full name: Odd Future Wolf Gang Kill Them All, or OFWGKTA), a rap collective cofounded and informally led by Tyler, The Creator. The collective was active from 2007 to 2015, although various members came and left during that time. As teenagers, the group members did some of their earliest recording in Syd's home studio in Los Angeles and used internet tools such as social media to grow their fan base. They also marketed their own clothing lines and had their own television show. Briana Younger, in a retrospective piece on the collective in *Pitchfork*, notes that the group "saw ahead to a time when accessibility, lifestyle branding, and 'content' are just as important as (if not more than) the music itself."[41] In 2011 Syd and fellow

---

41. Briana Younger, "Found Family: How Odd Future Changed Everything," *Pitchfork*, July 31, 2018, https://pitchfork.com/thepitch/found-family-how-odd-future-changed-everything/.

Odd Future member Matt Martians formed the Internet, a band whose style draws on hip hop, R&B, funk, electronic dance music, and jazz and takes its name in part from the virtual space in which the collective that the founding members belonged to had built their primary following. The role of the internet influenced Odd Future's whole aesthetic; as Younger notes, "Their very moral compass was connected to the world wide web, where trolling is the quickest way to build an audience."[42]

Syd played a crucial role in Odd Future's success, but the collective's image did not necessarily reflect an inclusive or even LGBTQ-friendly group. In her profile of the artist in a May 2017 article in the *Guardian*, Harriet Gibsone notes, "Syd was instrumental in their formation: she engineered their material and set up a fake PR firm to get blogs to notice the collective's explicit rap music."[43] As the group became increasingly popular, however, they also became notable for their unapologetically offensive lyrics, rife with homophobia and misogyny. While not necessarily unusual in some sub-genres of hip hop, by 2010 there had begun to be some pushback against casual use of the term "faggot" as a slur, especially in mainstream rap. Indeed, Odd Future, and especially Tyler, The Creator, was heavily criticized for its anti-LGBTQ language. For example, the group's scheduled performance at the Auckland, New Zealand, Big Day Out festival in 2011 was canceled thanks to pressure from local LGBTQ activists. Tyler, however, has consistently defended his use of the word "faggot," which appears not only in his lyrics but also in his tweets and, according to various interviewers, in casual conversation.[44] He told MTV, "Well, I have gay fans and they don't really take it offensive, so I don't know. If it offends you, it offends you."[45]

Syd was the only woman member of the Odd Future collective and, during the years when she was active with the group, the only openly queer member (Frank Ocean came out in 2012; Tyler, The Creator in 2017). However, she did not actively call attention to her difference. In her *New York Times Magazine* profile of Syd, Jenna Wortham describes her as "tomboyish,

---

42. Younger, "Found Family."

43. Harriet Gibsone, "Syd: 'The Backlash from the Gay Community Hurt My Feelings,'" *The Guardian*, May 30, 2017, https://www.theguardian.com/music/2017/may/30/syd-off-future-backlash-gay-community-hurt-my-feeling.

44. See, for example, Paul Lester, "Tyler the Creator in the UK: Forget Hip-Hop, We're the New Sex Pistols!" *The Guardian*, May 6, 2011, https://www.theguardian.com/music/2011/may/07/tyler-the-creator-odd-future.

45. Tyler, The Creator, quoted in Rob Markman, "Tyler, The Creator Defends His Use of *Other* F-Word," MTV.com, June 15, 2011, http://www.mtv.com/news/1665860/tyler-the-creator-defends-lyrics/.

in a muscle tee and a short haircut, she crackles with the manic energy that Odd Future shows were famous for. She was generally indistinguishable from the boys in the group."[46] Like Young M.A, Syd's masculine appearance is sometimes read as blending in; it is legible in a hip hop context. Unlike the flashy street style of the Brooklyn rapper, though, Syd's style reflects her own locality—West Coast skater—as evidenced in Odd Future's own clothing brand. Syd is similarly open about her interests in other women and refusal to date men but also resists labels for her sexuality, especially "gay." In an interview in 2012, she elaborated:

> To be honest, for the longest I never said I was gay, and that's the funniest part. . . . That's the funniest part, and I did that for a reason, just to keep everything open-minded and not close any doors for myself, you know? I feel like, you know, I'm not ignorant.
>
> I see a lot of females making music who are like me who are trying, but they try to use the gay thing too much. They try to take advantage of being gay and it's like, if it's really who you are, be who you are. So for me, it's been the same with being a female and being, you know, having whatever preference I have.[47]

"Having whatever preference I have" is a way of resisting potentially essentializing sexual categories, but she continues to make very explicit that her "preference" is for women: "[I] just try to make it about the music and nothing else. Nothing else, people got thrown off when 'Cocaine' was the first video, but I'm not about to be in a video kissing a dude, that's just not me, so it's the only way to go really."[48]

"Cocaine" was the first music video that Syd made with the Internet, and it was notable for its depiction of a lesbian couple that ends on a very bleak note. The video takes place at a carnival, where we see Syd walk in with her typical swagger. She sets her sights on a young femme woman who is laughing with a group of friends. The femme is holding a stuffed animal, suggesting

46. Jenna Wortham, "Syd Tha Kid & the Internet: How to Chart Your Own Path in a Post-Label Music Industry," *New York Times Magazine*, March 10, 2016, https://www.nytimes.com/interactive/2016/03/10/magazine/25-songs-that-tell-us-where-music-is-going.html?&_r=2#/syd-tha-kyd-the-internet-get-away.

47. Syd, quoted in Zanyra Thomas, "Odd Future's Syd the Kyd Talks Music, Identity, and the Internet," *Mass Appeal*, August 7, 2012, https://web.archive.org/web/20120922065011/http://massappeal.com/odd-futures-syd-the-kyd-talks-music-identity-and-the-internet-11146/.

48. Syd quoted in Thomas, "Odd Future's Syd the Kyd."

youth and innocence (the music video is available on YouTube: https://doi
.org/10.3998/mpub.11306619.cmp.4). Syd pulls the girl away from her
friends and they have a date at the carnival, going on rides, playing games,
and laughing together. The lyrics underscore Syd's character's nefarious
intentions: "I wanna, I wanna / Do you wanna do some cocaine?" Syd pulls
the girl into a dark corner out of sight and sets up what is presumably cocaine
for them to snort together. The aesthetics of the video then change to reflect
their experience under the influence, with other characters' cartoonish,
bugged-out eyes and trippy feel that seems more aligned with the high of a
psychedelic than cocaine. The girls make out, become more touchy-feely, and
the video narrative suggests that they are leading up to a night spent together.
Syd and the woman get into her truck, but just as Syd climbs in, she looks
over to see the woman passed out in the passenger seat, unable to be revived.
Rather than taking her to a safe place or making sure she is okay, Syd gets out
of the car, goes to the passenger side, and pulls the unconscious woman out.
The final scene shows the truck driving off, leaving the woman blacked out in
the street.

Syd faced backlash for the "Cocaine" video, particularly from LGBTQ
viewers who felt that it was a degrading portrayal of women and same-gender
relationships. Syd tried to explain her intent with the video on Tumblr, saying that she wanted the video to have an unhappy ending and to depict an
honest truth about drug use, not glamorize it.[49] The setting of the carnival is
a heavy-handed nod to the carnivalesque, the grotesqueness of drug use and
abuse. The lyrics taken at face value suggest "ignoring the consequence" of
using drugs. Syd's singing style is reminiscent of the seductive falsetto of
D'Angelo or Usher, with the music blending aspects of funk, R&B, and hip
hop; this is not the dark, hard hitting sound of southern trap or chopped and
screwed, or other genres associated with drug use, but much more playful.
Taken together, especially with the visual elements, the song is clearly one of
caution about the dangers of cocaine, not a sincere call to use it.

Syd told an interviewer that the "backlash [against 'Cocaine'] from the
gay community hurt my feelings."[50] With a notable lack of representation of
same-gender relationships in music videos, especially relationships between
two Black women, it is understandable that some would push back against
one of those few representations highlighting a clearly abusive and dysfunctional relationship. However, critics of the video clearly missed the point:
Syd and the Internet were not advocating for that kind of relationship but

49. Gibsone, "Syd: 'Backlash.'"
50. Syd quoted in Gibsone, "Syd: 'Backlash.'"

rather offering a critique of drug use through a fictional relationship that happened to be between two women, which was much more believable and effective than Syd portraying a heterosexual character on screen.

Like Young M.A, Syd articulates a sort of ambivalence about labels around her sexuality and, as in her response to criticism of the "Cocaine" video, has even distanced herself from any construction of LGBTQ community. In a 2019 interview with the *Guardian*, she explained to Tara Joshi:

> I don't feel like a part of the gay community. Like, I don't consider myself a lesbian. I consider myself a girl, a woman, a businesswoman. I don't really go to gay clubs. I just don't go out really. And I don't have any gay female friends—none that I hang out with on a regular basis. I'm the only person like me that I know.[51]

Not only does Syd express a disconnect from identity-based community, but she also eschews labels such as "lesbian." She stated in an interview with *LA Weekly*:

> I hate the word "lesbian." Or "pussy." Or even like, "thespian." They're just awkward words! If you know me you might hear me say the word "gay," or something. I'd much rather say gay than lesbian. Not only that, but I don't know if I'd kick it with a group of lesbians anyway.[52]

Again, we can understand some of the resistance to the term "lesbian" specifically due to the term's racial connotations; "lesbian" is often already constructed as a white identity, and dominantly white lesbian groups have historically perpetuated the racism of the larger culture rather than confronting or dismantling it. Syd does not articulate this specific reason, but her distancing from lesbians not just as an identity but as a group points to such a critique.[53]

---

51. Syd, quoted in Tara Joshi, "The Internet's Syd: 'I'm the Only Person Like Me That I Know,'" *The Guardian* April 13, 2019, https://www.theguardian.com/music/2019/apr/13/syd-the-internet-odd-future-interview-hive-mind.

52. Syd, quoted in Andrea Domanick, "Syd the Kyd on Odd Future, Her Sexuality, and Why She Hates the Word 'Lesbian,'" *LA Weekly*, January 12, 2012, https://www.laweekly.com/syd-the-kyd-on-odd-future-her-sexuality-and-why-she-hates-the-word-lesbian/.

53. For more on the white normality of LGBTQ identities, see Patricia Hill Collins, *Black Sexual Politics: African Americans, Gender, and the New Racism* (New York: Routledge, 2004). Bianca D. M. Wilson discusses lesbian gender identities and language among Black lesbians in her article "Black Lesbian Gender and Sexual Culture: Celebration and Resistance," *Culture, Health & Sexuality* 11, no. 3 (2009): 297–313.

We can also understand her reluctance within the context of a music industry that further limits the possibilities for expressing queer sexualities and non-normative genders. Syd's career overlaps with a period of change in this regard, where hip hop especially has started to grapple with homophobia and misogyny in its commercial iterations. Syd notes:

> We didn't make the ["Cocaine"] video to make a statement about Odd Future and homophobia. It was to showcase a song by the Internet. But over the years I've come across so many dyke singers, dyke rappers, people with real heart and passion, and it's a shame that not one of them has made it. And I get it, the world is just now starting to become open about homosexuality. I can't really say I've contributed to that, and I'm grateful to the people who have set a path for me to be who I am today. And I guess in that sense I want to return the favor.[54]

Embodying any form of gender or sexual difference necessitates a hyperawareness of how that difference might impact one's career. Syd's earliest approach, like that of many other artists, was to not make it a big deal so as not to bring a hyperfocus on that aspect of herself to the exclusion of attention to her musicality. The danger of that approach, especially for a DJ, is erasure.

Although some might view the "Cocaine" video as a way of Syd coming out publicly, Syd never really had a public coming-out moment because she was always already out as an artist. This is significant because it demonstrates that it is possible to build a career in hip hop while being openly queer, but it also means she did not get the same kind of publicly voiced support that her male colleagues did when they outed themselves. Fellow Odd Future member Frank Ocean is a perfect example. When Ocean came out, he received a lot of support from the hip hop industry. From Tyler, The Creator's supportive tweet to hip hop mogul Russell Simmons, who wrote, "I am profoundly moved by the courage and honesty of Frank Ocean," many artists treated the occasion as the first coming out of any hip hop artist.[55] Even though Syd and Frank Ocean were both Odd Future members, only Ocean received this kind of outpouring and support for his LGBTQ identity.[56]

---

54. Syd, quoted in Domanick, "Syd the Kyd on Odd Future."

55. Russell Simmons, "The Courage of Frank Ocean Just Changed the Game!," *Globalgrind*, July 4, 2012, https://globalgrind.com/1857832/russell-simmons-letter-to-frank-ocean-gay-bi-sexual-comes-out-photos/.

56. Tyler, The Creator also seemingly came out in 2017 with the release of his album *Flower Boy*, but given his past homophobic lyrics, many journalists and fans met this admission with confusion rather than adoration. See, for example, Benjamin Lee, "Is Tyler, the Creator Coming Out as a Gay Man or Just a Queer-Baiting Provocateur?," *The Guardian*, July 25,

And yet, during her time in the Odd Future collective, Syd was often called upon to answer questions regarding her colleague's homophobia especially. She regularly argued that Tyler, The Creator was not homophobic nor were other members of the collective, but you can also hear in her responses a growing frustration with the question. For example, in an interview with the *Huffington Post*, Alex Chapman asked, "This video [for 'Cocaine'] follows a lot of scrutiny toward Odd Future for being anti-gay. Do you think this will silence any of the group's harsher critics?"[57] To which Syd replied, "Well, apparently it hasn't, but whatever. Some people just need something to be mad about."[58]

The language that Syd used in this and other interviews is important because it reflects that desire to avoid the hypervisibility/invisibility paradox, or rather, to carefully navigate it. She does not closet herself, but she does not apologize for her collaborator's homophobia; to position herself in opposition would further call attention to her own difference and potentially place her at odds with her hip hop colleagues. As Hammonds argues, the historical narrative of Black women's sexualities that sustained a politics of silence and exclusion of queer identities has also positioned those identities as threatening:

> If we accept the existence of the "politics of silence" as an historical legacy shared by all black women, then certain expressions of black female sexuality will be rendered as dangerous, *for individuals and for the collectivity*. It follows, then, that the culture of dissemblance makes it acceptable for some heterosexual black women to cast black lesbians as proverbial traitors to the race. And this, in turn, explains why black lesbians—whose "deviant" sexuality is framed within an already existing deviant sexuality—have been wary of embracing that status of "traitor," and the potential loss of community such an embrace engenders.[59]

2017, https://www.theguardian.com/music/2017/jul/25/tyler-the-creator-flower-boy-gay-man-or-queer-baiting-provocateur.

57. Alex Chapman, "The Internet's Syd and Matt Talk 'Cocaine' and Homophobia," *Huffington Post*, November 29, 2011, https://www.huffpost.com/entry/the-internet-interview_b_1118724?guccounter=1&guce_referrer=aHR0cHM6Ly93d3cuZ29vZ2xlLmNvbS8&guce_referrer_sig=AQAAAAnk3uRwwoqE1V0qPxMangyt0PRII2eCOeBUkIQMeBeb1ki9rnbg37b7F0gx-R7SaxdAsD7YrrfVl_0yjxbOEwNbmuAFPnlGwfwu0tgdQBmZ-IrWVUfwtq2wOTxslHm81lY46WRviazkdICtoZx8e_abXZ7eWIrT1q3gWJ2wYbBA.

58. Syd, quoted in Chapman, "The Internet's Syd and Matt Talk 'Cocaine' and Homophobia."

59. Hammonds, "Toward a Genealogy of Black Female Sexuality," 101–102. Emphasis mine.

Syd, like Young M.A, does not embrace an explicitly lesbian or queer identity that would align her with an LGBTQ community and potentially alienate her from a Black community or her own hip hop community in part because, as I have explored elsewhere, those communities are often seen as incompatible.[60] Syd was the exception, not the rule, and during her time with Odd Future and the Internet, she was careful to be open enough about her sexuality to be considered "out" but refused to implicate her collaborators in her own oppression. As C. Riley Snorton notes, Syd also resists a "politics of pride," a "variation on the 'politics of respectability,' which articulate a normative structure for how queers should behave in and for their publics."[61] She resists invisibility as well as normativity but also resists putting herself so far out there as to risk her tenuous place as the only woman in the group.

That is, until she embarked on her solo career. While Syd has continued to suggest that Tyler, The Creator and other members of Odd Future are not homophobic, she does recognize that aspects of their behavior and their language were problematic and the role she might have played in excusing their behavior. Gibsone writes:

> In hindsight, Syd wonders whether she, the crew's only female, was their "get out of jail" card when accusations of homophobia were raised. When she left, she says, "Tyler [The Creator, Odd Future's front man] got mad at me at first. It was like: 'Dang, why do you guys need me that bad?' Then it made me think that maybe it's so they could say certain things. And use me as an excuse." She is quick to confirm that her former crew are not homophobic, something she follows with a short, sharp "Hah!"[62]

Even as Syd acknowledges her concerns about how her presence as a queer woman in the collective might have been used as a defense for homophobic behavior, she continues to protect her former bandmates by saying they are not homophobic, even if she undermines that statement with a "hah!" Yet again there is a balancing act between pushing back against the sort of hypervisibility that could have allowed Syd to be used as a defense for other peo-

---

60. See, for example, Lauron Kehrer, "A Love Song for All of Us?: Macklemore's 'Same Love' and the Myth of Black Homophobia," *Journal of the Society for American Music* 12, no. 4 (2018): 425–48.

61. C. Riley Snorton, "On the Question of 'Who's Out in Hip Hop,'" *Souls: A Critical Journal of Black Politics, Culture, and Society* 16, nos. 3–4 (2014), 289.

62. Gibsone, "Syd: 'The Backlash From the Gay Community Hurt My Feelings.'"

ple's homophobia and not pushing back so hard as to be seen as confrontational or aggressive, characteristics that are often stereotypically applied to Black women. It is an impossible situation, and her language reflects that.

Since the release of her first solo album, *Fin* (2017), Syd has opened up about her experiences with depression and connected it with some of the pressures of dealing with real or perceived homophobia in Odd Future:

> In the beginning it was tough, especially being part of a group that everybody thought was homophobic. Then, years later, everybody's gay! People wanted to talk to me about it the most. Like, you have an issue with Tyler's lyrics, but you want to talk to me about it? Talk to him about it! I started to resent it.[63]

In her *New York Times Magazine* write-up, Wortham documents Syd's increasing depression while on tour with the group, related in part to having to deal with the "hypermasculinity and caustic sense of humor" of the other members of the group as well as pressure from the LGBTQ community to distance herself from the group. Syd noted:

> The gay community hated me for being part of Odd Future. They thought Odd Future was homophobic because they tend to use homophobic slang, and they were like, "How can you work for and support homophobes?" But they *aren't* homophobic; they just don't really care whether you're offended or not.[64]

The dual stress of touring with a group of men who were (by her own accounts) insensitive to challenges she was facing and who in many ways attempted to use her as a shield from criticisms of homophobia, combined with the pressure from the LGBTQ groups who argued that she was supporting homophobia, was too much to navigate. Eventually, Syd unofficially left the group to focus on her work with the Internet and then officially left to focus on her solo work. She notes that at the news of her departure, the other Odd Future members "weren't happy about it. I was their get-out-of-jail-free card. It's easy to say they aren't homophobic because Syd is there."[65] But in addition to the musical opportunities afforded her through these

---

63. Syd, quoted in Joshi, "Internet's Syd."
64. Syd, quoted in Wortham, "Syd Tha Kid & the Internet."
65. Syd, quoted in Wortham, "Syd Tha Kid & the Internet."

decisions, it is clear that there were mental health concerns as well—concerns specific to her experiences as the group's only openly queer member (at the time) and the group's only woman.

Joshi notes that during her time with Odd Future, Syd was "simultaneously anonymous and highly scrutinized."[66] Unlike other artists I've discussed in this book, Syd is not a rapper, and during the early years of her career she was behind the decks, working as a DJ and producer. In some ways this made her even more invisible than the rappers. And yet, her identity, especially within Odd Future, made her hypervisible, as she was held up as a counterexample to or excuse for the rappers' homophobic and misogynistic lyrics. Embarking on a solo career has allowed her to literally speak (or sing) her own words and no longer be used as a prop. In Syd's words, "Feeling invisible definitely makes you want to become visible sometimes, [but] not by going out and saying something outlandish or doing anything crazy. It makes you want to be great."[67]

Black Queer Women and the Burden of Liveness

While Young M.A and Syd are very different artists musically and lyrically, there are some similarities in their career trajectories. They both navigate hip hop, a genre in which a particular Black male masculinity is normalized, as masculine-of-center Black queer women. Often their approach reads as just one of the guys. Their Black female masculinity is legible when it is contextualized within hip hop's Black (male) masculinity—in some ways, they conform to expectations. Aligning themselves with other men also prevents them from being perceived as a threat. While Young M.A, for example, raps about sleeping with women who are romantically or sexually involved with other men, she also aligns herself with a group of men who are part of her crew, her ride-or-dies. While Syd acts out a dysfunctional romantic relationship between two women in a music video, she also refuses to identify as a feminist.[68]

Syd's and Young M.A's self-distancing from identity labels like "lesbian" can further mark conformity. It is important to note that neither artist is closeted; they have both been open about their desires for women from the onset of their careers. And yet, declarations such as "I don't like labels" or

66. Joshi, "Internet's Syd."
67. Syd, quoted in Gibsone, "Syd: 'Backlash.'"
68. Thomas, "Odd Future's Syd the Kyd."

"I'm just me" can function as a downplaying of their queer identity. Many Black masculine queer women refuse to identify with that label "lesbian" because it can have white racial connotations. There are other terms, however, that could be used to signal queer identity, and these rappers do not refer to themselves with those, either, instead resisting any labels. It is not an erasure but a strategy that invites the critic and listener to focus less on identity and more on the music.

Of course, these identities are themselves embedded in and articulated through the music, but to call the work of queer rappers "gay rap," as we saw in chapter 2, does a disservice to both the artists and the music. It also contributes to the hypervisibility of LGBTQ artists of color: they are seen but only in a particular way. They are also then expected to be constantly performing their identities for an audience that largely consists of people who identify differently from them and are most often in a more dominant social group. José Muñoz describes this problem as the "burden of liveness" and notes that this burden is placed on queer women of color especially:[69]

> Some performances are structured through historically embedded cultural mandates that the body of color, the queer body, the poor body, the woman's body perform his or her existence for elite eyes. This performance is positioned within the dominant culture as a substitute for historical and political representation. Thus, performing beyond the channels of liveness and entering larger historical narratives seems especially important.[70]

Black women rappers, especially Black queer women rappers, are expected to perform their identities not for the benefit of other Black queer women but for others in positions of privilege over them.

How Young M.A and Syd present themselves, especially in interviews, is one way they resist the burden of liveness and push back against expectations that they perform their identities in particular ways. They carefully position themselves to avoid both the invisibility that Black queer women already experience but that is particularly the case in mainstream hip hop, and the problematic hypervisibility that can come with positioning oneself as an openly queer rapper, especially as an openly queer woman rapper. They may be more or less successful at avoiding this paradox at any given moment, but the trajectory of their careers so far suggests that it is possible to resist being

---

69. Muñoz, *Disidentifications*, 188.
70. Muñoz, *Disidentifications*, 188.

classified as either a "gay rapper" or "female rapper" and still have a mainstream career as a Black queer woman in hip hop. Even though it is important to name the specific ways in which Black queer masculine women experience marginality in the genre, their enactment of resistance—resistance to classification, resistance to normative sexualities, resistance to the responsibility of activism, as well as resistance to the burden of liveness—opens up new possibilities for others to resist, including women, LGBTQ artists, and others who might be marginalized otherwise.

It matters that Young M.A and Syd are both examples of hip hop artists who have careers in the genre's mainstream and that they never had to "come out" as queer. When a male rapper or hip hop artist comes out as gay or queer, it represents a significant challenge to hip hop's status quo and thus garners a lot of attention. The reactions to Frank Ocean and Lil Nas X's public disclosures are representative examples. However, there has not yet been a male hip hop artist who achieved that level of mainstream success while being openly queer from the beginning of their career. Both Ocean and Lil Nas X had built a wide fanbase and had commercial success before coming out, and it is difficult to speculate that they may have had the same careers if they had been open about their sexualities from the beginning. Women artists are already perceived as challenging hip hop's norms, both in terms of gender and sexuality, and their success in the mainstream is already marked as unusual. The fact that Young M.A and Syd have been open about their sexualities from the outset should be in and of itself meaningful, as it marks a sea change in how LGBTQ artists can navigate mainstream hip hop. The fact that they continue to resist specific language to self-identify and the way music journalists have framed their success show how their intersectional identities have still not been normalized, but they are creating important precedents for ways of being in hip hop.

When discourses about hip hop position both LGBTQ artists and women as something Other, or outside, that needs to be categorized in order to be understood, they create a very limited and limiting view of what the genre is. This is especially limiting for Black queer women and even more so for those whose gender expression is masculine-of-center rather than femme. The language and frameworks for understanding and interpreting performances by artists like Syd and Young M.A as Black queer female masculine performances have not been widely applied to hip hop studies. Doing so will help us understand LGBTQ and hip hop communities not as distinct groups with some overlap but rather as deeply embedded within each other.

The pressure that openly LGBTQ artists face to be political, to identify strongly with labels like "lesbian," and to overtly articulate and perform those identities, is palpable. I have positioned both Young M.A and Syd in conversation here not to make an argument about a shared butch or masculine-of-center aesthetic but to demonstrate how they face similar pressures and similarly navigate those pressures in their public self-fashioning. Indeed, their distinct visual and musical styles are highly localized: Young M.A is a fan of street wear with flashy accessories, including jewel-encrusted grills, and she invokes her Afro-Latinx Caribbean heritage especially in her occasional use of Spanish, while Syd's style more closely reflects that of West Coast skater kids.[71] I point here not to a shared strategy based on common identity but an attempt to illuminate individual responses to a shared problem. Rather than categorizing women rappers based on similarities in appearance or lyrical approach, or how they might be compared to that fictional representation of Black queer female masculinity represented in *Set It Off*'s Cleo, we should shift our attention to the discourses that necessitate such categorizations in the first place.

The ways that we categorize rappers, especially QTPOC rappers, can shape how we hear (or don't hear) them in their own music. In the following chapter, I consider the specifically Black queer performances of New Orleans bounce, sometimes called "sissy bounce," as it emerges from a local scene onto a national stage. Drake, Beyoncé, Missy Elliott, Diplo, and other mainstream, non–New Orleans artists have recently incorporated musical elements of bounce into their own chart-topping work. However, New Orleans artists themselves have not yet achieved the same commercial success. Furthermore, national artists' use of elements from this hyper-local hip hop style as sonic flavoring often problematically reduces bounce rappers, especially Black queer rappers, to disembodied vocal samples. Through an examination of recent tracks by Drake, I raise questions about ethical sampling and collaboration practices in hip hop and ask, What is gained, and what is lost, when a local genre finds a national audience but its queer artists do not?

---

71. Young M.A's father is Jamaican and her mother is Puerto Rican.

4 • "Nice For What"

New Orleans Bounce and Disembodied Queer Voices in the Mainstream

It's Friday night, October 19, 2018, and my wife, some friends, and I arrive later than planned to the packed 9:30 Club in Washington, DC. While this venue has a rich history, primarily as a place where punk artists and other local groups performed legendary shows, we are here for the Head Bangas Tour, headlined by New Orleans funk group Tank and the Bangas. This is not entirely accurate; while I am looking forward to seeing the Bangas, we are all really here to see the second act, bounce rapper Big Freedia. Annoyed with our friends who delayed our arrival and made us miss the first act, my wife and I are listening attentively in the lobby when we hear from inside the club that unmistakable voice of the Queen Diva herself. As soon as we show our tickets, we promptly leave our friends behind, run hand in hand through the corridor along the side of the venue, push our way through the packed floor to get as close to the stage as we can, and get to work. Big Freedia has commanded us to shake.

Big Freedia has been steadily building her national profile for the past fifteen years, but that profile has been boosted by a few appearances on mainstream artists' tracks, specifically Beyoncé's "Formation" (2016), Drake's "Nice For What" (2018), and, more recently, Kesha's "Raising Hell" (2019). During this DC performance, she referenced these features in a medley of songs, moving from "Formation" to Adele's "Hello" (2015, which has been made into several bounce remixes), and concluding with her extemporized versions of both Drake's "Nice For What" and "In My Feelings" (2018).

In this medley, Freedia highlights some of the ways that bounce has musically engaged with the mainstream and vice versa. She performs her own original work that was sampled in these songs and offers something of a bounce remix to other portions. She also draws audience participation, banking on the fact that the majority of the audience will know most, if not all, of the words to each commercial hit.

However, after paying homage to these songs, Big Freedia motions to the DJ to cut off the music and closes the segment by saying, "Fuck all that radio shit. Bitch, I'm the Queen of Josephine, ya heard me?" Notably, in both this performance and one I attended in Richmond, Virginia, in August 2018, she moves from this medley directly into a showcase for audience members who want to shake (dance) on stage, an element of bounce shows that originated in New Orleans. Freedia therefore draws a clear distinction between bounce's mainstream presence and the local and diasporic modes of performance that continue to exist outside of that mainstream.

We can interpret Freedia's rhetorical distancing as a response to the ways these commercial iterations (or perhaps appropriations) of bounce engage artists like Big Freedia on a national stage but erase their queerness in the process. Drake follows Beyoncé, Missy Elliott, Diplo, and other national artists who have incorporated musical elements of bounce, especially those created by queer and trans bounce musicians, into their own work. However, these LGBTQ New Orleans artists themselves have not yet achieved the same prominence.

Queer and trans rappers face barriers to entering the commercial mainstream that their heterosexual counterparts do not. As such, aside from a few examples (including those discussed in chapter 3), there are very few openly queer and trans artists in the genre who have obtained a high level of commercial success. Furthermore, while queer artists and influencers have been shaping the sound of hip hop, they do not benefit from the same level of representation or visibility as straight artists. The recent proliferation of songs by mainstream artists that use samples from New Orleans bounce is an illustrative example. For over the past decade, queer and trans rappers have been the dominant force in New Orleans bounce, a dance-centric hip hop genre specific to this city. It is in part because of their personal and professional networks that bounce found audiences outside of New Orleans, finding its way into national artists' songs. However, the queer artists sampled in these and other examples, including the openly queer and gender nonconforming Big Freedia, are rarely given much visibility as collaborators; they seldom appear in music videos, for example, and instead become purely audible samples in which their queer identities are erased.

In this chapter I examine how national artists' use of elements from this hyper-local hip hop style as sonic flavoring often problematically reduces bounce rappers, especially queer rappers, to disembodied vocal samples. This approach typically either obscures the music's New Orleans roots or exoticizes the city but always erases the queer people and communities that make it. I briefly trace the queer roots of bounce outside of New Orleans and offer some examples as case studies of how bounce has been sampled, demonstrating that recent releases by Drake and others raise questions about ethical sampling and collaboration practices in hip hop.

The Rise of "Sissy Bounce"

"Sissy bounce" is the term that was coined by local music journalist Alison Fensterstock to refer to the critical mass of "sissy rappers," or openly gay or trans rappers most prominent in the bounce scene in the post-Katrina era. The term draws on the language of bounce rappers themselves, such as influential artist Sissy Nobby, who self-identify as gay and reclaim a once pejorative term to openly express their sexual and gender identities through their performances. While the term is somewhat contested (as I discuss below), it is helpful for thinking through the ways bounce has not only made space for queer and trans rappers but has also centralized them and their experiences.

Sissy bounce may seem like a surprising development for hip hop, which, as we've seen throughout this book, historically has struggled with representing identities outside of the hypermasculine, cisgender, heterosexual male model that has become the most easily recognizable rapper image today. It is much less surprising, though, if we consider this development as part of New Orleans's much longer history of Black queer performance. As Bettina Love writes:

> Beyond the Crescent City's elastic sound of fusing African, French, and Spanish music, historically New Orleans is home to some of the most gender-bending public celebration traditions. . . . The Big Easy is a site of performance, play, and pleasure, with Black bodies as the main attraction using Black cultural forms of expression that embody a Black radical imagination, and sometimes ratchetness (i.e., intentionally not conforming to respectability politics and gender norms), to disrupt and respond to oppression.[1]

---

1. Bettina Love, "A Ratchet Lens: Black Queer Youth, Agency, Hip Hop, and the Black Ratchet Imagination," in *Mouths of Rain: An Anthology of Black Lesbian Thought*, ed. Briona Simone Jones (New York: New Press, 2021), 236–37.

This history overlaps with Carnival and masking traditions, as well as a history of drag performance. For example, in his oral history of Black queer New Orleans, Alix Chapman points to Bobby Marchan, a gay singer and promoter who began his career as a female impersonator, as a central figure who ties together New Orleans Black queer history and its musical history.[2] Marchan was one of several queer performers who frequented the Dew Drop Inn, an important venue in the history of rhythm and blues and for New Orleans's Black queer community during much of the twentieth century. The Dew Drop Inn was also a site for Little Richard's queer performance of "Tutti Frutti," before the promise of commercial success necessitated lyrical modification.[3] As Fensterstock notes:

> Gay performers have been celebrated forever in New Orleans black culture. Not to mention that in New Orleans there's the tradition of masking, mummers, carnival, all the weird identity inversion. There's just something in the culture that's a lot more lax about gender identity and fanciness.[4]

Queer and trans bounce rappers, as Chapman argues, are part of this Black queer lineage of New Orleans. Their role in bounce, however, necessitates overlap with local rap traditions.

New Orleans bounce music first emerged in the early 1990s and quickly took over the local rap scene. Bounce scholar Matt Miller writes that this style was particularly popular in part because it spoke to the specific location of New Orleans's housing projects and impoverished neighborhoods and was influenced by other local vernacular music traditions, including the parades of "social aid and pleasure" clubs and the rise of brass bands.[5] He traces the "emergence of bounce as a distinctive local subgenre" to MC T. Tucker and DJ Irv's 1991 song, "Where Dey At," and other tracks that relied heavily on the Showboys' 1986 recording, "Drag Rap" (referring to the televi-

---

2. Alix Chapman, "The Punk Show: Queering Heritage in the Black Diaspora," *Cultural Dynamics* 26, no. 3 (2014): 327–45.

3. See, for example, Ashon Crawley, "He Was an Architect: Little Richard and Blackqueer Grief," *NPR.com*, December 22, 2020, https://www.npr.org/2020/12/22/948963753/little-richard-black-queer-grief-he-was-an-architect.

4. Alison Fensterstock, quoted in Jonathan Dee, "New Orleans's Gender-Bending Rap," *New York Times*, July 22, 2010, http://www.nytimes.com/2010/07/25/magazine/25bounce-t.html?pagewanted=all&_r=0.

5. Matt Miller, *Bounce: Rap Music and Local Identity in New Orleans* (Amherst: University of Massachusetts Press, 2012), 6.

sion show *Dragnet*, not the act of dressing or performing in drag).[6] He notes that the use of this recording generated a style that became distinctive to New Orleans:

> In this period, the preferences of New Orleans audiences—which included polyrhythmic layering of musical elements, tempi between 95 and 105 b.p.m. [beats per minute], vocal performances in cellular structures, an emphasis on collective experience based in call-and-response rather than individual narrative—were, to an important extent, distinct from those associated with national, mainstream audiences. Artists or companies in New Orleans who ignored these preferences did so at their peril; engagement with audiences at the grassroots level of nightclubs and block parties was a crucial first step for aspiring artists, producers, and label owners, regardless of their personal artistic aspirations, and bounce was quickly becoming central to the expectations of local audiences.[7]

As Miller points out, the popularity of the Showboys' "Drag Rap," a song often referred to in New Orleans as "Triggerman" or "Triggaman" after one of its New York City–based co-producers, Phillip "Triggerman" Price, reflects how the early New Orleans rap scene was reliant on trends from New York City in its earliest days.[8] The Roland 808–produced "Drag Rap" or "Triggaman" beat became the skeleton of the newly emerging sample-based genre.

To this day, bounce music is built over only a handful of beats. In the early 1990s, producers combined the "Drag Rap" beat with Cameron Paul's "Brown's Beat," a drum break taken from "Rock the Beat," a 1987 track by Derek B, to create the iconic bounce sound referred to as "dat beat." According to Sissy Nobby, contemporary bounce beats are primarily built on five main samples: (1) the "Drag Rap"/"Triggerman" beat; (2) "Brown's Beat"; (3) the "Roll Call" beat (produced by DJ Dickie but based on a Mannie Fresh beat that is based on a beat used by bounce rapper Cheeky Blakk); (4) Big Freedia's "Na" beat, which is a looped sample of her singing "Na"; and (5), more recently, what he calls the DJ Doug beat.[9] Other beats are added, and some artists have moved away from relying on preexisting samples, but the

---

6. Miller, *Bounce*, 75.

7. Miller, *Bounce*, 75–76.

8. Miller, *Bounce*, 78.

9. Sissy Nobby, interview with Holly Hobbs, New Orleans, July 11, 2014, NOLA Hiphop Archives, http://digitallibrary.tulane.edu/islandora/object/tulane%3A28446.

majority of bounce tracks are made with beats based on the "Drag Rap"/"Triggerman" and "Brown's Beat" combination.

In the years following the release of "Where Dey At," bounce music persisted as a local favorite but was largely ignored by major labels and national rap markets, in part because it was so place-specific and oriented toward New Orleans audiences. In the late 1990s, New Orleans rappers who were breaking into mainstream markets, such as Lil Wayne, shifted their sound away from bounce to appeal more widely to national audiences.[10] By the early 2000s, the culture was still a part of the soundscape of the city, but according to Rusty Lazer, a DJ who has worked with numerous bounce artists, including Big Freedia, the scene had somewhat stagnated.[11] Sissy rappers had started to gain footholds in the scene, but they were more the exception than the rule.[12] There were successful and prominent queer and trans artists, such as Katey Red, who got her start performing in 1998 at a nightclub near the Melpomene housing projects, where she was raised, but they were far from a dominating force.[13] However, the rise of sissy bounce can be linked directly to the impact of Hurricane Katrina, as sissy rappers played a prominent role in the city's recovery.

On August 29, 2005, Hurricane Katrina passed southeast of the city of New Orleans, missing the city but making landfall in the nearby St. Bernard and Plaquemines parishes. As has since been well documented, it was not so much the storm itself but the preventable failures of human-made levees and the subsequent flooding of large portions of the city that caused the most damage. The lasting destruction created by these floods had a disproportionate impact on Black and low-income communities.[14] In addition to those who evacuated before the storm, many others were forced to leave in the aftermath of Katrina, resulting in a displacement of a large amount of the city's population. This created a New Orleans diaspora in other parts of the country, including cities such as Houston, Dallas, Atlanta, and Baton Rouge.[15] Many displaced citizens, particularly those who lacked resources to

---

10. See Miller, *Bounce.*

11. Rusty Lazer, interview with the author, June 8, 2016.

12. Rusty Lazer, interview.

13. Dee, "New Orleans's Gender-Bending Rap." DJ Rusty Lazer told me it was DJ Jubilee who first identified Katey Red as a talented rapper and created her first opportunity to perform in front of an audience.

14. See, for example, Jean Ait Belkhir and Christiane Charlemaine's intersectional analysis of the storm's disproportionate impact in "Race, Gender, and Class Lessons from Hurricane Katrina," *Race Gender & Class* 14, no. 1–2 (2007): 120–52.

15. Laura Bliss, "10 Years Later, There's So Much We Don't Know about Where Katrina Survivors Ended Up," *City Lab*, August 25, 2015, http://www.citylab.com/politics/2015/08

rebuild, never returned to the city, creating a significant shift in New Orleans's demographics.[16]

Despite the horrors of the storm and the recovery period, Hurricane Katrina in many ways helped bounce, as it created the conditions that allowed the genre to attain even more popularity both within and outside the city. This boost occurred for three reasons: First, the newly formed New Orleans diaspora created a demand for bounce outside of the city, as many of the displaced were homesick for their regional music. Second, this displacement also encouraged bounce artists to embrace the use of digital tools, such as social media websites and download platforms, to share bounce music, giving the genre a reach that stretched beyond the city limits. Third, the storm left a musical vacuum within the city, as many clubs shut down and musicians fled. Bounce artists, specifically sissy rappers, filled that void and were among the very first musicians to return and bring live music performance back to the city.

The experiences of one of those New Orleans residents who was displaced by the storm, bounce artist Ha Sizzle, exemplify this change. In the summer of 2005, the rapper, then preparing for his senior year of high school, recorded what would become three of his biggest hits: "She Rode That Dick Like a Soldier," "Bounce It Biggity Bounce It," and "Buckle Your Knees." He relocated to Texas in anticipation of the storm and finished school at North Dallas High. There, he was surprised when he discovered one day that a classmate had downloaded "Bounce It Biggity Bounce It" as her cell phone ring tone, and he realized that the track, which had been produced by DJ Lil Man, was a hit among New Orleans bounce fans in the new diaspora. After recovering from the shock of hearing his own music being played outside his hometown, he responded by connecting to potential audiences and other artists through social media:

> Immediately I get on MySpace and I'm with it finding out everything that was taking place. I made a MySpace. So many different people,

---

/10-years-later-theres-still-a-lot-we-dont-know-about-where-katrina-survivors-ended-up/40 1216/. Part of this article draws on research conducted by the RAND Corporation as part of its Displaced New Orleans Residents Survey (DNORS) project.

16. Elizabeth Fussell, "Constructing New Orleans, Constructing Race: A Population History of New Orleans," *Journal of American History* 94, no. 3 (2007): 846–55. Fussell notes that the perception that New Orleans became "older, whiter, and more affluent" was largely supported by population data. She further argues that a larger proportion of white residents had returned to the city than Black residents largely because of the pre-existing income and housing disparities that existed (and persist) along racial lines.

the main person was my DJ, Lil Man, he hit me up, he was in Houston, Texas [and] he was like, man where you at? You're the biggest thing poppin'. You have the hottest bounce song that's out, ever. And when Katrina came, I can say from fifty states to overseas, "She Rode That Dick Like a Soldier" and "Bounce It Biggity Bounce It" was being played.[17]

Upon discovering that there was a displaced audience for his music, Ha Sizzle reconnected with his DJ and began performing outside of New Orleans:

I was young, I was lost . . . I didn't know what to do. I didn't know who to call, I didn't know how to do this, I didn't know how to do that, I had no management, no promoter, none of that. So, I'm just like, I don't know what to do. But then my DJ—thank god for DJ Lil Man--he wound up getting everyone the right contact information on me and I moved from Dallas, went to Houston and went to perform everywhere down south, and I just went to traveling, performing little songs and it was just everything.[18]

While touring in the South, Ha Sizzle found homesick audiences who had visceral reactions to hearing live bounce music performed again:

I actually seen people cry and tell me "I really love that song," like, "this song really brought me back." So many people was hurt because of Katrina and lost so much. Bounce music wasn't everywhere no more. New Orleans bounce music is the culture. We hear this every day out, no matter if we played trap music, country music, western music, R&B music, bounce music gonna be somewhere in there. Once that took place it's like, everyone just went to falling in love with the music even more, with bounce music. People who never even heard bounce music. And I must say Katrina was a big eye-opener, and it opened up the door to bounce music. . . . I was kinda proud more than anything because it brought back the smile and the joy of the culture.[19]

The demand for bounce music grew among the diaspora outside of New Orleans, and the genre also gained new listeners, inspiring artists and fans

---

17. Ha Sizzle, interview with the author, New Orleans, June 17, 2016.
18. Ha Sizzle interview.
19. Ha Sizzle interview.

alike to find new ways of making the music more easily accessible. As digital downloads and CD sales outside of New Orleans increased, one DJ got the idea to create a YouTube channel dedicated to bounce music. From this one channel, listeners outside of New Orleans could hear their favorite artists, old and new songs. Ha Sizzle explains:

> They had people listen to bounce all over. A lot of local DJs went to sell their bounce music from online to selling CDs at the clubs, and everyone just went to buying them. We was getting them FedEx, UPS, everyone was just getting the bounce music no matter if it was old or new, people just wanted to hear it. And then my best friend—Magnolia Schooly was his name, God rest his soul, he passed away in 2013—he took upon himself and put all bounce music on YouTube, and he had the most views and subscribers, with over a million people that was following him and listening to music. Bounce music, New Orleans bounce music. He had every artist. And it was not to get paid, it was not to make money off no one else's music. It was because of the loss that a lot of people had in the city of the music. He decided to put it on YouTube and just put it out to everyone. And he did that.[20]

New Orleans's displaced citizens actively sought out the sounds that most reminded them of home, and an unintended but positive consequence of the newly formed diaspora was the inroads bounce artists began to make outside of their native city. Rapper Keno notes that because of Katrina, bounce music actually became stronger in many ways: "It's like that's all we had left as a unit was bounce music."[21]

Many residents were slow to return to New Orleans. The earliest return-ees came home to a lack of services, and this extended to musical communities.[22] By most accounts, bounce artists were among the first musicians to return to the city and begin performing again. Sissy Nobby, who returned to New Orleans at the end of September 2005, claims to have been the very first artist to begin performing in the city after Katrina. As he explained to inter-viewer Holly Hobbs, he wanted to come back "because I was getting home-sick because of bounce music, honestly. . . . I came back maybe, in the end of

---

20. Ha Sizzle interview.

21. Keno, interview with the author, New Orleans, June 14, 2016.

22. See, for example, Elizabeth Fussell, Narayan Sastry, and Mark VanLandingham, "Race, Socioeconomic Status, and Return Migration to New Orleans after Hurricane Katrina," *Population and Environment* 31, no. 1/3 (2010): 39.

September. They still had our lights off and the streets were still smelling some type of way and stuff, but I came back."[23] He found that because so few performers had returned as quickly as he had, a plethora of opportunities were available:

It was a lot of work, there was a lot of businesses open, I had jobs. Clubs were trying to get back, they called whoever they could get. I think that's what really helped me a lot, that I came back to the city first and these clubs was like, we need a hype person we need someone to do this and this and that. So that really helped me out a lot to get these clubs. While all these other artists that normally be in the clubs was like, they're trying to capitalize Houston, I came back home.[24]

He recalled his first post-Katrina performance, which took place at a teen club on the West Bank, as being a positive homecoming of sorts: "By the time dancing teens come in and stuff, it felt like home again. It felt like home again. I'm like, 'Yas! Glad to be back.' It felt good. It was just a good vibe, a good feeling."[25]

Bounce music was instrumental in bringing small moments of pleasure to a mourning city. In 2005, 5th Ward Weebie released his song "Fuck Katrina" as a way to inject some humor into what he called a "terrible, horrible situation."[26] He later recalled:

I'm also a victim of Katrina. [I] lost my history, lost a lot during that time, misplaced family members, all that. We went through all that. People in New Orleans, we have big spirits when it comes down to going through something. That's why we second line after funerals. We're sad, we cry, that's in the dirt, but then it's, pick your head back up, life move on. Let's celebrate that, they're going to a better place, or whatever the case may be. ["Fuck Katrina"] just was one of those situations just like that. Like, man, we went through a lot, man, it's time to, let's pick our spirits back up. Let's get some humor about the situation. It was like a healing to the soul for a lot of people, is to be able to laugh at that. To be like, "yeah, that's the truth!" . . . And people started

---

23. Sissy Nobby interview.

24. Sissy Nobby interview.

25. Sissy Nobby interview.

26. 5th Ward Weebie, interview with Holly Hobbs, New Orleans, 2014, NOLA Hiphop Archives, http://digitallibrary.tulane.edu/islandora/object/tulane%3A28432.

getting right back to normal life. And I was glad that I was able to do that and that I was part of that.[27]

As Weebie suggests, the song was widely popular in part because it reflected a New Orleans tradition of turning tragedy into a celebration for those who continue living.[28] Keno agrees that "Fuck Katrina" helped mark bounce as an important soundtrack to the recovery process by bringing people throughout the city, not just those who listened to bounce before the storm, to the few clubs that were open:

> ["Fuck Katrina"] was a bounce song about Katrina but the whole city knew it. It just brought bounce that's from the club scenes [to everyone] . . . after Katrina because that's all we had. There wasn't many clubs over there; they only had a few but everybody flocked to them. And that's how we felt at home again, despite the tragedy.[29]

Weebie, like other bounce artists, draws a distinct connection between the city's tradition of funeral second lines and the work of bounce in New Orleans residents' grieving process post-Katrina. As anthropologist Helen A. Regis notes, the term "second line" has come to have multiple but connected meanings:

> It refers to the dance steps, which are performed by [social and pleasure] club members and their followers during parades. It also refers to a distinctive syncopated rhythm that is said to have originated in the streets of New Orleans. More importantly, second line means the followers, or joiners, who fall in behind the "first line," composed of the brass band and the social club, which typically sponsors the parade. . . . The distinctive interaction between the club members, musicians, and second liners produces a dynamic participatory event in which there is no distinction between audience and performer. . . . When jazz funerals elicit mass participation, they too are second lines.[30]

---

27. 5th Ward Weebie interview.

28. The song was even featured on the HBO show *Treme*, a series that offered a fictionalized account of the years immediately following the storm. *Treme*, season 1, episode 4, directed by Anthony Hemingway (New York: HBO Entertainment, 2010).

29. Keno interview.

30. Helen A. Regis, "Blackness and the Politics of Memory in the New Orleans Second Line," *American Ethnologist* 28, no. 4 (2001): 755.

As Regis explains, the key component of the second line is the element of participation; everyone is expected to engage in dancing, regardless of the solemnity of the event. Joel Dinerstein similarly notes that in a second line, "everyone is supposed to dance or, at the very least, roll wid it: as a phrase, this refers both to the physiological movement—a sort of half-crouched, bent-over, rolling dance-walk—and the philosophical import of maintaining one's spiritual balance in the face of social and economic pressures."[31] Second lines, then, offer opportunities for enacting kinetic community responses to grief, especially in the context of jazz funerals. While outsiders to the city may consider joyful expressions to be inappropriate responses to somber occasions, to native New Orleanians these expressions embody a sense of celebration for those left behind to continue living. They are a much-needed respite in a world full of racial and class disparities.

In this cultural context, bounce, with its up-tempo beats and sense of humor and fun, was the perfect musical style to help mitigate grief. Ha Sizzle emphasizes what he calls the joyful nature of bounce as its key feature and the main reason for its popularity, particularly in the wake of Katrina. He notes that "bounce music . . . can take you from being sad to happy. . . . In New Orleans you have people who pass away out there, and we second line, and we have DJs throw block parties; they become nothing but bounce music, and we shake [dance]."[32] Rusty Lazer also notes that "after Katrina it was the immediacy of [Big Freedia's] return that really led to the positional dominance of gay rappers, I would say. The fact [is] that these were the artists who came back and locked in immediately and went to work on making people happy, who really, really needed it."[33]

Sissy rappers were not, however, the only bounce rappers to return to the city. As Nobby notes, DJ Jubilee also returned fairly quickly.[34] So why did sissy rappers become the dominant force in bounce after the storm? One reason may lie in the kinship networks that queer and trans artists formed among themselves. In addition to being part of a bounce community, these artists were also members of New Orleans's LGBTQ community. As I argue in chapter 3, nonbiological kinship networks play an important role in many Black queer communities. Much like the house system of the Ballroom scene, many sissy bounce artists belong (or at one time belonged) within a hierarchical family structure in which more seasoned performers and older mem-

---

31. Joel Dinerstein, "Second Lining Post-Katrina: Learning Community from the Prince of Wales Social Aid and Pleasure Club," *American Quarterly* 61, no. 3 (2009): 618.

32. Ha Sizzle interview.

33. Rusty Lazer interview.

34. Sissy Nobby interview.

bers of the community act as "gay mothers" or, less often, "gay fathers" to younger, less experienced members. For example, Sissy Nobby is Big Freedia's gay daughter, indicating that Freedia has served in some ways as a mother figure or mentor to Nobby. Not all members of this network are bounce artists; for example, in her memoir Big Freedia mentions that Mark Tavia, a "sissy" from her neighborhood, became her gay mom when she was a teenager.[35] The kinship network does, however, include artists, and their connections often move from the personal to the professional and back again.

Keno identified Sissy Nobby as his gay mom and Ha Sizzle as his gay dad and noted that both helped him navigate the LGBTQ community.[36] When he was outed to his family as gay by some peers, they were not very supportive, and Keno ended up moving in with Nobby and staying with him for a year. He recalls:

> [Nobby] really taught me just about the gay world, period. And it was like a bunch of us in Nobby's house, me and like five of my gay brothers. And Nobby took care of all of us. . . . I will say no matter what happens between us, I'mma always have that love for him, I'll never disrespect him like, in public or anything. Yeah, we might get into it from time to time, but I never actually take it there. I just have too much love and respect for him.[37]

Keno notes that his personal relationship to Nobby differed from his professional one in that there was an added element of competition, but he also acknowledges that he learned from the more experienced gay rapper, who also gave him opportunities early on in his career:

> Nobby really taught me how to hustle, how to get out there and grind with my music. 'Cause I went to a lot of shows with him, his shows. Well, I can honestly say he kinda like was a mentor to me. Because he let me perform, open up for him a lot, and Freedia did also.[38]

---

35. Big Freedia and Nicole Balin, *Big Freedia: God Save the Queen Diva!* (New York: Gallery Books, 2015), 13.

36. Keno interview. While Keno identified Ha Sizzle as his "gay dad," Sizzle himself does not necessarily identify as gay. He prefers not to label himself or his sexuality, and he emphasizes in conversation and on social media posts that he has biological children with a female partner, which could easily mark him as heterosexual.

37. Keno interview.

38. Keno interview.

It is worth noting that when I first asked both Keno and Ha Sizzle about mentors in bounce, both claimed they did not have any, although they did have artists they looked up to and respected. It was later in the conversations, in the context of the LGBTQ community, that both acknowledged that figures such as Sissy Nobby served as mentors to them. It is possible that the familial ties between these community members trump their professional ones, leading Keno and Ha Sizzle to view Nobby as a kinship figure first and foremost and a professional mentor secondarily. This approach, like that taken by children who distance themselves from their parents in order to assert their own independence, also indicates the younger rappers' desire to make their own unique marks on bounce music.

As in any biologically based family, members of queer kinship networks do not always agree with each other or even get along. As Rusty Lazer notes, the system in New Orleans can cause headaches for promoters, who must carefully navigate the social relationships between kinship members:

> [In bounce] all the family things apply, and it's real. And it also means that sometimes when I'm a person who's looking at it as a businessperson from outside just being like, so, hey, I got this show, so and so's not available but they want an opening act, can we just go and bring this person? And then [an artist might be] like, I don't talk to him. You know? Like, dammit there's shit that I gotta consider. But that's also why I live in New Orleans, because real talk counts. If you have a real talk situation, let's real talk it, and if you can't be around them, don't be around them. It's a small town, you don't have to be around everybody.[39]

Rusty Lazer identifies ways the kinship network can make it difficult to program certain artists together, but the opposite, as Keno demonstrates, is also true; gay mothers and gay fathers can help bring new artists into the scene by offering them opportunities as well.

Hurricane Katrina and the human-made structural and policy failures that followed devastated the city of New Orleans, but the storm also opened up new opportunities for bounce artists, and sissy rappers in particular, that led to a flourishing of the genre in its wake. The New Orleans diaspora helped spread bounce to other communities outside of the city and led to the increased use of digital means of disseminating the music. Bounce artists were among the first musicians to return to the city, and they engaged in

---

39. Rusty Lazer interview.

much-needed entertainment to sustain the recovery process and help the residents of the city process their grief.

It was the queer and trans rappers associated with so-called sissy bounce specifically that helped propel style beyond the Crescent City. Like the Black queer networks discussed in relation to disco in chapter 2 and Ballroom rap in chapter 3, the social and familial networks among these rappers not only facilitated business and performance opportunities but also influenced the aesthetics of the subgenre. It was the willingness of some of these artists to perform in spaces that were unusual for bounce artists but associated with LGBTQ listeners that also helped this expand this reach of influence. Big Freedia's successful touring and television appearances are the most explicit example, but other artists such as Keno and Ha Sizzle also contributed to the sounds that were being heard and later incorporated by mainstream artists. I emphasize queer and trans identities here not to essentialize these artists but to make clear the significant influence these artists had not just on the local level but on a national, if not global, scale.

Resisting "Sissy Bounce"

Although "sissy bounce" is easy shorthand that centers the identities of queer and trans performers, not all queer and trans bounce artists appreciate being included under this umbrella term. Resistance to the sissy bounce label also comes from artists' desires not to see themselves or their work pigeonholed as another form of "gay rap." They do not want to be limited to performing just for LGBTQ audiences or feel that the topics about which they rap are limited because they are expected to speak to only queer or trans experiences. This resistance reflects how integrated queer and trans rappers are in the overall bounce scene; aside from very few naysayers like Partners-N-Crime (PNC)'s Mr. Meana, who has suggested that queer artists are overshadowing bounce's (presumably heterosexual) legacy, sissy artists have been widely welcomed and continue to be the most visible artists in the genre.[40] Even Mr. Meana's concerns were not explicitly with the presence or even success of queer rappers but that the scene is "oversaturated with their style of bounce" and overshadowing the work of heterosexual

---

40. Alison Fensterstock, "Sissy Strut: Gay Rappers Carry the Torch for Bounce, but Not All Local Rappers Are Comfortable with That," *Gambit*, August 12, 2008, http://www.bestofneworleans.com/gambit/sissy-strut/Content?oid=1250945, accessed July 23, 2016.

artists such as himself.[41] Some have suggested that this open acceptance of queer and trans rappers is unique to New Orleans, such as Miller, who said in 2008, "If there's going to be a town where gay rappers are going to break out, New Orleans would pretty much be the only place in the world that could happen."[42] Regardless of whether or not that is actually the case (and clearly other American cities, especially New York City, have their own clusters of openly queer or trans rappers making national and international inroads), it does speak to the fundamental importance of appreciative local communities (such as those found in New Orleans) for queer and trans rappers as they build professional networks and fan bases. The idea for some is that if their local communities are accepting, there is no need to distinguish themselves from their heterosexual and cisgender counterparts, and that their identities are just part of who they are as performers. Thus, many sissy bounce rappers have insisted that they do not perform sissy bounce; they are simply bounce artists like their heterosexual counterparts.

So-called sissy rappers are not the only performers in the contemporary bounce scene, but they are by far the current dominant force. And yet, many bounce artists still resist the label "sissy bounce" to describe themselves and their music. Big Freedia told *Time* magazine that there is really no such thing as sissy bounce:

> We don't separate it here in New Orleans at all. It's just bounce music. Just because I'm a gay artist, they don't have to put it in a category or label it. We have a lot of straight artists here, and they are offended by the term sissy bounce. We never did separate it here at home, and we don't plan on it.[43]

This resistance could be a strategy to negotiate a few issues with being openly queer or trans in bounce in particular but also in hip hop more generally. One of them is that queer and trans bounce artists want to avoid being further ghettoized within an already small, primarily local genre and expected to constantly perform their sexual and gender identities. Many artists have songs that are explicitly queer ("homo songs"), especially Big Freedia and Sissy Nobby, but others don't. Some have lyrics that reflect the same sexual

41. Fensterstock, "Sissy Strut."

42. Matt Miller, cited in Fensterstock, "Sissy Strut."

43. Big Freedia, cited in Nolan Feeney, "Twerk? Yaka? Duffy? Buku? Big Freedia's Guide to Bounce Music Slang," *Time*, June 17, 2014, http://time.com/2890212/big-freedia-just-be-free-bounce-music-slang/.

fluidity that dancers often embody, but others rap about completely different topics altogether. Ha Sizzle explains:

> I never ever qualify myself as like they say the sissy music because I'm the type of person I feel that music is music. Just because a person grows up being gay, straight, bisexual, anything does not mean that people can just go ahead and give them the title, oh, since you're gay you doing sissy music. No! No, no, no, no. I could be gay, I could be straight, I could be bisexual, I could be transgender, I'm doing music. Okay? So I always was the person to follow my mind, I never ever laid behind other people or be a follower always just a leader. . . . I never was the type of person to be like everyone else. If you have someone saying that they like to eat pussy, or they like to suck dick, I never was the person to go right behind them and say oh this what I like 'cause they said it. No, I give it to them, I say I like to pet puppies. And then after that everyone would start saying, oh my god I like to pet puppies too!⁴⁴

While Ha Sizzle identifies openly queer and trans artists as the biggest influences on his early career and his interest in bounce, he distances himself from the idea that they constitute a separate category of bounce music, preferring instead to forge what he views as his own path.

A second issue is that many contemporary bounce artists have mainstream aspirations, and they understand that the hip hop industry outside of New Orleans is different from their local scene in that it is more judgmental of any kind of difference. For example, the manager of one openly gay rapper I interviewed informed me that because the rapper was a month away from dropping a single with a major national artist, he would not be discussing sissy bounce or anything related to that because they did not want to jeopardize their collaborative relationship with the mainstream artist. The rapper disagreed with his manager's decision and spoke to me openly about his experiences, but the manager's reluctance is indicative of the level of homophobia that persists in the music industry, which has led some openly queer artists not necessarily to closet themselves but to downplay their queer identities so as not to risk missing opportunities on a national level.

Some rappers, such as Keno, use a positive, resilient attitude to carefully navigate the tension that can result from being an openly queer artist from New Orleans who seeks collaborations with nationally recognized artists:

---

44. Ha Sizzle interview.

It's 2016, like, get over it. It is what it is. . . . We're not out here down bad—oh I'm gonna mess with you, mess with you, mess with you. We're just living. I don't mess with anybody right now. I just want to focus on my music.[45]

He pushes against the idea that hip hop is not ready for queer rap artists and that he must remain closeted in order to have mainstream success. He also noted that Big Freedia had broken down a lot of barriers for queer artists and that the world outside of New Orleans was becoming generally more accepting of LGBTQ people, including performers. He was also keen to point out that there are most likely many more queer people in hip hop; gay rappers are not necessarily new, but their openness and increased visibility is.

Ha Sizzle takes a similar approach. He, too, feels that the music should be the most important aspect of any artist, regardless of how they identify. He explains it as follows:

I'm a grown man. I have a daughter. I refuse to be stereotyped, or be that person that people try to make a clown out of because they don't have nothing else better to do with themselves and they don't want to see your music advance to where it's at. That's why I'm so proud and so happy for Big Freedia. Okay? I'm super excited for Fly Boi Keno. Super excited. Sissy Nobby. I'm excited for the things that these— Nicky da B, God rest his soul—things that all these people are getting to accomplish and do with their music. To say that we are the people who are stereotyped each and every day. People want the image. Oh, you can't do this 'cause you look this certain way. You can't do this, you can't do that. Well, music is music. Just let the music speak for itself. That's all I want. If people let the music speak for itself, I'd be big right now.[46]

Ha Sizzle's response speaks to how integrated queer and trans artists are in the New Orleans bounce scene generally. Except for a few folks who want to "bash gays," as he put it, most bounce fans have no qualms about the queer and trans identities of the most prominent contemporary rappers.[47] Many are thrilled about the national profile Big Freedia has developed through her reality show, and everyone is incredibly proud of her success. Even Mannie

45. Keno interview.
46. Ha Sizzle interview.
47. Ha Sizzle interview.

Fresh, an influential New Orleans rapper and former in-house producer for Cash Money Records, has stated that gay rappers have been around the city "forever" and that in the local culture it is not a big deal:

> We got gay gangsters in New Orleans, dude. It's deep. But that's just the whole thing about New Orleans. We cool, nothing bothers us. We're a city where if you mind yours, we cool. Our hip hop scene . . . bounce is just crazy, that's a part of New Orleans. But we got another side of it as well. For some reason, there's a lot of gay artists that do bounce music right now. But it don't bother nobody in the city because it's just a flavorful city. We just embrace everything, we not trippin'.[48]

Fresh continues to explain that the label "sissy bounce" is not a term that the artists themselves created, nor one that he would use to describe the prevalence of queer and trans rappers in the city:

> That's a label that somebody put on it. But there's some dudes I wouldn't say that to. I wouldn't say that's sissy bounce of some of them. Some of them dudes [are] like real hardcore killers! To me, I'm gonna respect everybody. Whatever is going on with you, that's your space, and you have the right to have individuality.[49]

Like Ha Sizzle, Mannie Fresh argues that queer and trans bounce artists' identities do not matter as long as they are talented musicians who put out good music. He even suggested that there could be a nationally recognized rap star who was openly gay—if only this person had enough talent.

Although statements like Mannie Fresh's indicate that attitudes toward openly gay rappers, and openly queer and trans people in general, have shifted, they also promote the idea that the music industry is a meritocracy where one's level of success depends solely on their inherent talent and ability as well as a willingness to work hard. It relies on a sort of sexuality-blind approach that ignores the fact that queer and trans artists do have experiences that are different from those of other rappers and that those experiences can have an impact on their ability to achieve mainstream success. The

---

48. Mannie Fresh, interview for VladTV, "Mannie Fresh Speaks on Gay Tolerance in the N.O. Rap Scene," YouTube, April 5, 2013, https://www.youtube.com/watch?v=MlqpiQB CP98.

49. Mannie Fresh interview.

existence of queer kinship networks within the bounce scene suggests that these artists have more difficulties navigating social life and their careers and that these networks were created to help mitigate those struggles. While the networks themselves do provide opportunities for their members, as illustrated above in the aftermath of Katrina, their necessity also demonstrates continuing challenges and barriers for openly queer and trans rappers.

Big Freedia's story is both exceptional and illustrative. Having built up her local following in the years leading up to Katrina, Freedia writes in her memoir that she was in demand among audiences in Texas after the storm.[50] In 2009 she began working with Rusty Lazer, who booked her at gigs with queer-friendly punk bands in places like New York City that drew, among others, a LGBTQ audience, and he eventually arranged her first international gigs. Lazer describes Freedia's willingness to perform in new contexts as key to her growing success:

> Somebody like Freedia is willing to go out on the road and like play for people who, she looks out at the room and it doesn't look like her, it looks like a mixture of things she may have seen before or not seen before in some cases. Like some nights we played punk shows, some nights we played . . . we played in like downtown Toronto at one point, for a festival. And it's like, businesspeople walking by at like 2:00 in the afternoon! We're not 2:00 in the afternoon [music] unless you live in New Orleans. We do that at 2:00 in the afternoon here, but nobody else is doing that. And we looked ridiculous, people were staring at us and shaking their heads, and I didn't even feel for them. I'm like, I'm sorry, I'm sorry we have to like bring you this 3:00 a.m. thing right now. That's the kind of challenge that you love as a musician, and Freedia, because of her being willing to break through that wall, you get to have these challenges, and you can either relish them or you can see them as a burden. I think Freedia relishes those challenges.[51]

Freedia's willingness to perform outside of New Orleans and parts of the South that had audiences already familiar with bounce allowed her to find new audiences, some of which were predicated more on shared LGBTQ identities and cultures than on musical style and genre. Big Freedia's television show, *Big Freedia: Queen of Bounce* (later renamed *Big Freedia Bounces Back*), which aired for six seasons on Fuse from 2013 to 2017, further infil-

---

50. Big Freedia, *Big Freedia: God Save the Queen Diva!*
51. Rusty Lazer interview.

trated national media with the sounds and stories of queer and trans bounce artists. And in the years since then, she has continued touring, as my opening vignette illustrates. While a number of aforementioned artists were able to expand their careers beyond New Orleans, Big Freedia has gained the largest visibility and, in turn, brought bounce culture to those who might otherwise never experience it firsthand.

Whether we choose to call it sissy bounce or not, queer and trans rappers are at this current moment bounce's ambassadors both within and outside New Orleans. In part because of their personal and professional connections through their kinship networks, and because of their role in spreading bounce in the post-Katrina New Orleans diaspora, queer and trans rappers became not only some of the most visible figures in bounce but also the point of contact between national artists and the previously hyper-local genre. It was the performances and recordings of queer and trans artists primarily that influenced mainstream artists to begin incorporating aspects of bounce into their own work.

Bounce in the Mainstream

With the increased popularity of bounce, aided by its infectious dance beat, it makes sense that national artists would begin to incorporate aspects of the genre in their own music. The producer Diplo has featured queer bounce artists, particularly the late Nicky da B and Keno (formerly Fly Boi Keno) on the moderately successful tracks "Express Yourself" and "Beats Knockin'," respectively. The combination of electronic dance music (EDM) and bounce has been particularly successful, with Keno choosing to brand his own style as EBM, or electronic bounce music. The rapper was also recently featured on a track with the nationally known, Atlanta-based rapper Lil Jon.

When queer bounce artists are featured on tracks by mainstream artists, however, they are not always properly credited. As I've written elsewhere, Beyoncé's 2016 surprise hit "Formation" is a clear example. While Big Freedia was an acknowledged collaborator on the track, the late bounce artist Messy Mya was not; in fact, in 2017 Messy Mya's estate sued Beyoncé for $20 million and credit "as a writer, composer, producer, and performer" on the track.[52] Additionally, the "Formation" video uses footage from a 2012 docu-

---

52. Legal Entertainment, "Beyoncé Sued for $20 Million by the Estate of Messy Mya over 'Formation,'" *Forbes*, February 7, 2017, https://www.forbes.com/sites/legalentertainment/20

mentary short about New Orleans bounce called *That B.E.A.T.* While Beyoncé's team clarified that they received permission from the owner of the footage to use it in the music video, the director, producer, and artists, including a young Black gay dancer, were not involved in the decision-making process, nor were they compensated.[53] One of my informants was reluctant to speak about the situation on record but did try to express to me the disappointment many of the artists experienced when the single was released:

> It's not something that's worth casting aspersions on anybody. I don't actually blame anyone. I think this is just the expedience of the industry at large. And so it's not like, oh Beyoncé's supposed to be perfect because she's famous! Or because she represents for Black women or whatever. She doesn't have to be perfect; she can't get everything right. I don't really care. But I do know that the dancer in question called me the morning after the video came out and was crying and was sad. When I went to bed I was like, when he sees this I wonder if he's gonna call me and be happy or sad. And I went to bed and I woke up and he called me and he was crying. I secretly hoped you would just be happy, because I knew there's nothing we can do about it and he was like, I do too. If someone had just asked me, I would've given the right to use it away for free.[54]

The New Orleans artists involved do not have the financial or legal means to fight a major celebrity like Beyoncé for compensation or recognition. As my source noted, it took their original work out of context and assigned control of the narrative away from the creators of their own work and to Beyoncé and her team. While the artists featured in *That B.E.A.T.* would have most likely said yes to appear in what has become an iconic video from the legendary singer, they were never even given the opportunity to decide for themselves.

Others use the intellectual work of bounce artists more subtly. Missy Elliott's 2016 single "Pep Rally" references the marching band traditions that

17/02/07/beyonce-sued-for-20-million-by-the-estate-of-anthony-barre-messy-mya-over-for mation/#2cbdb80d5b02, accessed February 11, 2017.

53. Myles Tanzer and Michelle Kim, "Beyoncé Clarifies Dispute over 'Formation' Video Footage," *The Fader*, February 7, 2016, http://www.thefader.com/2016/02/07/beyonce-for mation-video-documentary-footage-credit.

54. Anonymous source, interview with the author, June 2016. For more on the use of bounce in "Formation," see Lauron Kehrer, "Who Slays? Queer Resonances in Beyoncé's *Lemonade*," *Popular Music and Society* 42, no. 1 (2019): 82–98.

permeate the city but also features lyrics that sound eerily similar to bounce artist Ha Sizzle's "Bounce It Biggity Bounce It" (Ha Sizzle's "Bounce it, biggity bounce it, biggity bounce it, biggity bounce it" becomes Elliott's "Bounce, biggity bounce, biggity-biggity bounce, bounce") and what sounds like a sample vocal from Big Freedia at the very end of the track.[55] Despite the vocal similarities, Sizzle is not credited on the track, although he noticed the resemblances right away:

> I truly love Missy Elliott's "Pep Rally." When I first heard it, first [thing] that came to my head was, mmm, Missy Elliott must've been listening to some of my music. And once I heard it again and a lot of other people, artists heard it everyone went to calling me, "Man Missy Elliott must've listened to your music 'cause she sound like your style of bounce music." And then the confirmation came that she does listen to bounce music, once I spoke with one of her friends. And her friends is like, "Yes 'cause she always listening to this and that and she put on [bounce] music. . . ." But just by hearing that, I was like, well, at least she heard. At least she's hearing me.[56]

Ha Sizzle was reluctant to speak negatively about both Missy Elliott and the track, instead framing the release as a compliment to his own work and as a good thing for his blossoming career and bounce music more generally. However, it is clear that, as with Beyoncé, the national star was drawing on the local scene without explicitly crediting its primarily queer and trans artists.

Ha Sizzle was given full credit for his contribution to "Child's Play," a track from rapper Drake's 2016 album, *Views*. The song samples Sizzle's "She Rode That Dick Like a Soldier," which he notes was in heavy rotation in Houston after it was released in 2005.[57] In the original, Sizzle raps, "She rode that dick like a soldier / She rode it like a soldier / She rode it like a Calliope soldier." He repeats these lines three more times, replacing "Calliope" with "Magnolia," "jungle," and finally "Melpomene," referencing the city's housing projects that played a major role in bounce's development. Ha Sizzle frequently names specific neighborhoods, projects, and other locations in his songs and shows, an act he refers to as "roll call," as a way to invite listeners to

---

55. New Orleans native K. Keon Foley-Griffin, also known as Keon the Connect, performs the hook and chorus on the track.

56. Ha Sizzle interview.

57. Ha Sizzle interview.

respond and feel represented. While we might be tempted to assume that the gender pronouns used here automatically reference women twerking, we should be skeptical of fixed gendered meanings. Ha Sizzle is, as mentioned above, resistant to being singled out as queer. Nevertheless, we might also consider the pronouns' usage for gender nonconforming or effeminate gay men—the "she" riding the dick might be a man, the gender more commonly associated with soldiers. A queer reading of this song could resonate with listeners (and dancers) who have a reference point for the multiple gender possibilities for "she."

This is the section of "She Rode That Dick" that is sampled in "Child's Play," starting at the two-minute mark. It plays softly in the mix while over it, Drake intones "Bounce that shit like woah" twice, and then, as Ha Sizzle raps in the background, "Rode that dick like a soldier / she rode it like a soldier / she rode it like a [pause] yeah, yeah / I got it / yeah." Drake strips the sample of its New Orleans specificity by refusing to name those places, transforming the local reference to one that is more universal. Furthermore, the context of the song negates the queer possibilities of the sample. Ha Sizzle's lyrics, which are less overtly queer than, for example, those of Big Freedia, can be more easily redeployed here. The heterosexual possibilities of the gender pronoun "she" allow the sample to operate on a track that is seemingly normative and straight. In the mainstream context, markers of New Orleans's specificity and queer possibility in "She Rode That Dick" can be heard only by listeners already attuned to those signifiers from Ha Sizzle's performance. At the same time, this sample reflects the influence that queer bounce artists have on mainstream artists. Ha Sizzle told me that Drake's management team asked him to get permission to sample the track, credited him as a writer, and, at the time of our interview, both parties were in talks about bringing him on tour as an opening act. It seems, however, that those plans never came to fruition.

In April 2018, Drake released "Nice For What," a single built on a sample of Lauryn Hill's "Ex-Factor" that includes vocals by Big Freedia and 5th Ward Weebie, as well as other bounce music elements. This bounce flavor, which can be attributed to the work of New Orleans–based producer BlaqNmilD, contributed to the track's commercial success; "Nice For What" entered the *Billboard* Hot 100 chart at number one. However, even Drake, who has officially credited bounce artists, fails to translate their contributions into visibility. Big Freedia is notably absent from the music video for "Nice For What," which features a roster of cameos by celebrity women. The video includes appearances by: Olivia Wilde, Misty Copeland, Issa Rae, Rashida Jones, Tracee Ellis Ross, Tiffany Haddish, Yara Shahidi, Zoe Saldana, Letitia

Wright, Syd, and others. These cameos, combined with lyrics such as "I've been peepin' what you bringin' to the table / Workin' hard, girl, everything paid for / First-last, phone bill, car note, cable / With your phone out, gotta hit them angles," suggest that Drake meant "Nice For What" to be a nod toward women's empowerment. The exclusion of images of Big Freedia, whose vocals are so recognizable on the track but whose appearance challenges notions of male and female, suggests that this empowerment is limited. While one could argue that the inclusion of Syd opens space for queer and gender non-normative identities, as I discuss in the previous chapter, Syd's gender presentation makes her more legible as a woman artist in hip hop, not less. Big Freedia's feminine appearance and gay male identity presents more of a challenge to hip hop's normative framings and, apparently, to Drake's heterosexuality.

The Queen of Bounce does make a very brief appearance in the video for Drake's follow-up single, "In My Feelings," which was filmed in New Orleans. According to Freedia, however, she had to facilitate that appearance by contacting the Canadian rapper when she found he was shooting in her hometown: "I decided to hit him up myself and was like, 'Why you didn't let me know you were in New Orleans?' . . . And he was like, 'I just got here. Why don't you come through? We're shooting a video tonight. I want you to get a few cameos.' So I did that."[58] Even though the Black, queer, gender nonconforming rapper did make it into the "In My Feelings" video, the cameos are incredibly brief shots of Freedia holding a mic at 4:29 and flipping her hair at 5:10, both moments that pass in the blink of an eye (the music video is available on YouTube: https://doi.org/10.3998/mpub.11306619.cmp.5).

Myles Johnson writes of Drake's use of Big Freedia's voice but not her image, "Mainstream culture [has seemingly made] a phantom or ghost out of a living person."[59] Indeed, while we might hear queer and trans bounce artists sampled on the radio, very rarely do we get to see them; they become disembodied vocal samples, further marginalized within hip hop's mainstream. Queer and trans artists have been driving the recent developments in bounce that have made the local genre attractive to national artists and audiences, but they have not been centered in the national conversation, contributing to the invisibility of queer and trans identities in hip hop.

In his recent article on ghosting, a sampling practice in which a beat is

58. Wandera Hussein, "Big Freedia Reportedly Contacted Drake First to Be in 'In My Feelings' Video," *The Fader*, August 6, 2018, https://www.thefader.com/2018/08/06/big-freedia-call-drake-in-my-feelings.

59. Myles E. Johnson, "The Ghost of Big Freedia," *Vice*, April 18, 2018, https://noisey.vice.com/en_us/article/59j4xn/big-freedia-drake-beyonce-essay.

built around a preexisting sample but the sample itself is later removed to avoid litigation, Elliott H. Powell argues that this practice often "establishes queer spatiotemporal interfaces between bodies, technology, and the social formations of race, gender, and sexuality."[60] He argues that

> ghosting, as an intermundane collapsing of spatiotemporal dimensions, points to how a focus on the ear rather than the eye, on audibility rather than visuality, creates space for queer temporalities' musical iterations and manifestations; ghosting makes audible the possibilities of queer sonic temporalities.[61]

In Drake's recent bounce-inflected songs, as well as the other examples I've given, however, the samples of queer artists are explicit, not implicit, as they might be using a ghosting technique. Drake uses samples from bounce artists outright—with permission, sometimes compensation, and usually with credit. Following Powell, we can understand those samples to establish spatiotemporal relationships that are queer and place-specific (recalling New Orleans), but those relationships are negated when the queer sources of samples are excluded from, or minimized within, the visual images associated with the musical text. If, as Powell suggests, sampling practices create queer possibilities, the use of samples by openly queer artists, or queer samples, moves us from the realm of the possible into the realm of the actual. The heterosexual rapper's response, the lack of visibility to accompany this audibility, can be read as a distancing technique, an effort to negate the queer spatiotemporal relationships that using such samples might invoke. Drake distances himself from the queer images, and thus potentially queer associations, even as he engages with queer sounds.

Conclusion

Artists like Big Freedia are put in a tricky position when it comes to pushing back against this invisibilizing force. If they complain too much, they might ruin the possibility of future collaborations with mainstream artists. If they don't complain at all, they remain open to exploitation. This is not to say

---

60. Elliott H. Powell, "The Ghosts Got You: Exploring the Queer (After) Lives of Sample-Based Hip-Hop," in *The Oxford Handbook of Hip Hop Music*, ed. Justin D. Burton and Jason Lee Oakes (Oxford University Press, published online August 2018), 1.

61. Powell, "Ghosts Got You," 6.

they don't push back at all; indeed, LGBTQ artists often resist exploitation, but they often do so through Black queer modes of critique such as throwing shade. One of the most lasting definitions of "shade" comes from the documentary *Paris Is Burning*, in which legendary Ballroom participant Dorian Corey explains, "Shade is, 'I don't tell you you're ugly, but I don't have to tell you because you know you're ugly.' And that's shade."[62] Shade is subtle; it allows for critique ("you're ugly") with plausible deniability ("I don't tell you you're ugly"). For example, after the release of Drake's "Nice For What" single and video, Freedia said in an interview with *The Fader*:

> We're steady moving forward to get the bounce culture even further out there and, as you can see, other artists are recognizing our music and our talent down here in New Orleans. One day we might get our category at these awards or on the charts. I've worked tremendously hard to make things happen for New Orleans culture. I just want us to get the proper recognition and the proper credit that we deserve.[63]

This mode of critique protects Freedia's future interests by not necessarily naming Drake explicitly but challenging the lack of visibility the mainstream artist provided. These critiques might only be legible to certain listeners, but they are certainly present.

Ideally, bounce artists, especially queer and trans bounce rappers, will be able to transition into the mainstream without losing both their New Orleans flavor and their openness about their identities and will be given full credit for their work. One example of a more equitable approach might be Big Freedia's recent collaborations with pop star Kesha. In October 2019, Kesha released the lead single for her album *High Road*, "Raising Hell," which featured the bounce rapper and included some of bounce's musical elements. While the rapper does not appear visually in the music video, in which Kesha portrays a blonde televangelist who kills her abusive husband, Big Freedia's vocals and musical influence can be clearly heard throughout. What makes this collaborative relationship different from those previously discussed is the fact that a few months later, in February 2020, Kesha was a featured artist on Big Freedia's single "Chasing Rainbows" and appeared prominently in the song's video. Additionally, when Kesha announced her 2020 High Road

---

62. Dorian Cory in *Paris Is Burning*, directed by Jennie Livingston (Miramax Films, 1990).

63. Big Freedia, quoted by Ben Dandridge-Lemco, "Big Freedia Explains How She Got on Drake's New Bounce-Inflected Song," *The Fader*, April 9, 2018, https://www.thefader.com/2018/04/09/big-freedia-drake-nice-for-what-interview.

Tour, Big Freedia was slated to be a special guest (not just an opening act) at twenty-two out of twenty-six performances.[64] Unfortunately, the tour was canceled due to COVID-19, but the promotion for the tour emphasized Big Freedia's participation. It is worth noting that Kesha is a pop singer; perhaps mainstream pop's increasing acceptance of openly queer artists in the past decade has made more equal partnerships easier to achieve in that genre than in hip hop.

Conversations around hip hop can get mired in the idea of white appropriation (and rightfully so). The processes by which white artists engage with Black music styles and gain cultural capital as well as financial capital without facing the same challenges of systemic racism that the Black artists do has been well documented.[65] But there are other kinds of appropriation—for example, appropriation of queer cultural works in which the queer aspects are downplayed or even erased. In the instances of bounce in the mainstream, we see heterosexual Black artists appropriate Black queer music in a way that similarly erases queer origins and meanings and, even if there is financial or creative credit given, does not give cultural capital to those artists who must navigate homophobia and transphobia not only in the music industry but in their own lives as well. It is the need for both financial and cultural capital for LGBTQ artists that makes questions of sampling and collaboration especially fraught and therefore the opportunities for appropriation particularly acute.

This is also why Big Freedia's insistence on bringing bounce to the masses outside of New Orleans is so significant. In addition to the stop on the Head Bangas Tour with which I opened this chapter, I have to date seen Big Freedia perform in Richmond, Virginia, and Boston, Massachusetts, each with different opening acts. While the dancers and set list might also change, Freedia consistently brings a high-energy performance, takes time to share the spotlight with local dancers pulled from the audience, and engulfs the club in a sense of joy for the duration of her set. She also reminds the audience that no matter whose song she might appear in on the radio, she is still invested in New Orleans and bounce culture.

In March 2020, like most of the world, New Orleans shut down in

---

64. Claire Shaffer, "Kesha Announces 'High Road' North American Tour," *Rolling Stone*, January 7, 2020, https://www.rollingstone.com/music/music-news/kesha-high-road-tour-93 4536/.

65. See Tricia Rose, *The Hip Hop Wars: What We Talk about When We Talk about Hip Hop—And Why It Matters* (New York: Basic Civitas Books, 2008); and Bakari Kitwana, *Why White Kids Love Hip Hop: Wankstas, Wiggers, Wannabes, and the New Reality of Race in America* (New York: Basic Civitas Books, 2006) for just two examples.

response to the emerging COVID-19 pandemic. For local musicians, whose livelihood depends largely on performing for live audiences in small, packed venues and crowded festivals, the pandemic brought new challenges. As gigs were canceled, some artists, such as Big Freedia and Ha Sizzle, turned to virtual options. Freedia began live-streaming Sunday brunches and backyard performances, engaging with her audiences around the country who were similarly stuck at home. Unlike the wake of Hurricane Katrina, during which performers could travel to places unaffected by the storm and perform, there was nowhere to go during the pandemic but online. Like their response to that disaster, though, bounce artists were resilient and found ways to share their music with eager listeners.

On Saturday, April 10, 2021, more than one year after the beginning of the pandemic, I received a text from a friend living in New Orleans. The text included a video clip from an outdoor venue. When I pressed play, I was regaled by the familiar sounds of "Rent," a song from Freedia's 2018 EP, *3rd Ward Bounce*. The accompanying text read, "First show since pandemic!!" With the increased availability of vaccines and the gradual loosening of restrictions, live music gatherings were yet again returning to the city—and who better to provide the soundtrack, yet again, than queer bounce artists? While it was hard to tell demographics of a largely masked audience in a cell phone video, it appears that the crowd was diverse in terms of race, gender, and age. What they shared in common was movement; there did not seem to be any still bodies in the audience, and I immediately thought of the role of dance after the disaster of 2005. While the pandemic was clearly not over, there appeared to be a sense of healing in being able to gather in community and dance to sounds of bounce's breakout star. Regardless of Big Freedia's work outside the city, New Orleans is clearly still her home, and the pandemic did not stifle the joy that emanates from a bounce performance.

The successes and mainstream popularity of Big Freedia, as well as those of openly queer and trans artists from other parts of the United States, such as New York City, suggest that the country is ready for an openly gay rap superstar. Many artists, queer and straight, believe that sexual orientation should be a nonissue in hip hop generally, as it seemingly is in New Orleans. Certainly, Mannie Fresh believes so:

> It can happen [a nationally-recognized gay rap star] if it's based on your talent. Because a lot of people come to New Orleans and it's just like what you said, they can't believe the whole culture of the city. They like, well, y'all got your own little thing going on, y'all living in

your own little bubble. The crazy thing is, you gotta take like a Frank Ocean. Well, Frank Ocean said what he said [and came out as queer], yeah, it took guts, but in New Orleans it wasn't a big deal because it was like, well, shit, that's been around here for forever. Nobody in New Orleans was trippin'. That was just like, wow, all right. You should'a been said.[66]

However, mainstream artists like Drake may incorporate queer artists and their work into their own music but typically render their queerness invisible and inaudible through a lack of context and appropriate acknowledgment. The complexities of authorship and recognition in the context of bounce thus illuminate the particular intersections of being Black and queer or trans generally but also in hip hop specifically. Queer and trans bounce artists push back against discourses that position hip hop as inherently homophobic, but their reception outside of New Orleans suggests that mainstream hip hop still has a long way to go toward fully recognizing and embracing their contributions. As Big Freedia noted of her appearance in Drake's "In My Feelings" video, "I think that other artists out there should feel the same way, that no matter what your background is—no matter if you're a gay artist—that we can be able to be there just as anyone else."[67]

---

66. Mannie Fresh interview.
67. Hussein, "Big Freedia Reportedly Contacted Drake."

Outro

"Call Me By Your Name"

Demarginalizing Queer Hip Hop

Rap seemed to finally get its mainstream openly gay superstar in 2019, when rapper Lil Nas X came out on social media. His swift rise to fame following the success of (and controversies over) his country trap hit, "Old Town Road" showed no signs of slowing even with his disclosure. Indeed, Lil Nas X hit a milestone in May 2021 when he made a guest appearance on the season's final episode of *Saturday Night Live*, where he performed his two most recent releases, "MONTERO (Call Me By Your Name)" and "SUN GOES DOWN," both with explicitly gay themes, and appeared in a parody song about Pride month celebrations. Not only was there an openly gay Black rapper featured on the late-night show, but his performances highlighted his queer identity.

Lil Nas X released the single and music video for "MONTERO (Call Me By Your Name)" on March 26, 2021. The title of the song is a nod to the 2017 queer coming-of-age film *Call Me by Your Name*, based on the 2007 novel by André Aciman. The song, with its flamenco-influenced instrumentals, had been previewed a few days before in a Super Bowl ad for Logitech. In the ad's voice-over, Lil Nas X lists instances when he has defied logic in his career, including the lines "Logic said cowboys can't wear pink" and "Logic believes I couldn't come out on top or ever." When the music video and song officially dropped, it was clear that, as in the commercial, Lil Nas X's queerness was a central focus.

In the video for "MONTERO," the rapper plays various characters in a computer-animated retelling of the biblical fall of man. Christian imagery abounds as Lil Nas X depicts the temptation of the serpent as a same-sex sexual encounter, the main character's trial and death by stoning for submitting to the temptation, and his choice to descend to hell on a stripper's pole rather than ascend to heaven. Once in hell, he performs a lap dance in thigh-high stiletto-heeled boots for Satan before ending the song by breaking Satan's neck and placing his horns on his own head (the music video is available on YouTube: https://doi.org/10.3998/mpub.11306619.cmp.6).

The visuals of the "MONTERO" video are powerful because they encapsulate many of the religious-based arguments that have long been used against LGBTQ people. Lil Nas X uses the medium to push back against those arguments and present a message of self-acceptance. The lyrics encompass queer acceptance, but, unlike songs like Macklemore and Ryan Lewis's "Same Love," they resist homonormalizing narratives about respectable gay coupling.[1] The song opens with a booty call, and in the pre-chorus Lil Nas X rap/sings:

Cocaine and drinkin' with your friends
You live in the dark, boy, I cannot pretend
I'm not fazed, only here to sin
If Eve ain't in your garden, you know that you can

These lyrics are indicative of a messy queer relationship but one that is messy without shame. Lil Nas X flips the script on Christian anti-gay rhetoric and turns it into a catchy hit that also refuses a respectable gay politics.

Like Frank Ocean, with whom I opened this book, Lil Nas X published a note on social media along with the release of "MONTERO" that addressed his queer identity and a particular male lover who inspired the song. Unlike Ocean's letter, though, which was couched in opaque language that took a bit of deciphering, Lil Nas X's letter, addressed to his fourteen-year-old self, is quite clear:

dear 14 year old montero,

i wrote a song with our name in it. it's about a guy i met last summer. i know we promised to never come out publicly, i know we promised to never be "that" type of gay person, i know we promised to die with the secret, but this will open doors for many other queer people to simply exist. you see this is very scary for me, people will be angry, they will say i'm pushing an agenda. but the truth is, i am. the agenda to make people stay the fuck out of other people's lives and stop dictating who they should be. sending you love from the future.[2]

---

1. "SUN GOES DOWN" similarly addresses themes of self-acceptance.

2. Lil Nas X, "dear 14 year old montero," Twitter, March 26, 2021, https://twitter.com/LilNasX/status/1375297562396139520.

Like Ocean, Lil Nas X came out through social media and his music after having already built a career in the mainstream. Lil Nas X, though, has made his approach much more explicit. The differences between these two disclosures reflect the changing legal and social landscape for LGBTQ artists in the nine years between them. While Lil Nas X expressed fear about publicly coming out and certainly faced some backlash from a number of conservatives, his popularity has only continued to grow with each new queer release.

"MONTERO (Call Me By Your Name)" and "SUN GOES DOWN" are not the only songs in Lil Nas X's oeuvre to explicitly address queer themes, but their recent releases and their pairing on the *Saturday Night Live* performance are indicative of the landscape that has changed for openly queer and trans rappers from when I started writing this book. While queer and trans rappers were once largely relegated to underground scenes or always just on the cusp of mainstream success, there are now multiple openly queer rappers garnering mainstream attention, although none quite as much as Lil Nas X (yet). Furthermore, with more direct but playful language and social media messaging, Lil Nas X invites us to center his queer identity while also resisting homonormalizing and respectability discourses around that identity. For example, in the run-up to the release of *MONTERO*, his first full-length album, Lil Nas X unveiled fictional pregnancy photos of himself complete with a baby bump, positioning the album as his "industry baby." On the day the album came out, he also released a short video depicting him in the hospital giving birth to the album. At one point, one of the two doctors in the delivery room says, "I can see the baby!" to which the other responds, "DaBaby?" Lil Nas X then exclaims, "Let's go!" and the three momentarily break into the choreography from "BOP," rapper DaBaby's 2019 hit.[3] This moment is a subtle jab at DaBaby, who has been criticized for his homophobic onstage comments at the Rolling Loud Miami music festival in July 2021, but the criticism is subsumed into the larger celebration (and promotion) of *MONTERO*. Lil Nas X thus deftly uses social media to respond to homophobic criticism, but more importantly, he uses it to promote his own work, which forces us to center queerness in hip hop rather than view it only from the margins. He also invites us to reconsider the positioning of hip hop as antithetical to queerness.

Perhaps nowhere is Lil Nas X's engagement with homoeroticism through hip hop more evident than in "INDUSTRY BABY," which, at the time of this writing, holds the number one position on the *Billboard* Hot 100 chart.[4]

---

3. The music video for "BOP" was co-choreographed by DaniLeigh and Coach Cherry.
4. The Hot 100 chart for the week of October 23, 2021.

Released on July 23, 2021, the video depicts Lil Nas X's imprisonment in and subsequent escape from the fictional Montero State Prison.[5] Drawing on tropes of prisons as queer spaces in which sexual encounters between men are normalized, the "INDUSTRY BABY" video shows the rapper surrounded by Black gay men, including those dancing in a blurred-out naked shower scene. The song also includes a feature by Jack Harlow, a white heterosexual rapper who uses his verse to remind listeners that he is definitely not gay, a stance clearly supported by his appearance in the video with a female guard, which functions as a sort of heterosexual interlude in an otherwise queer work. On the one hand, the song and video present an unapologetically queer eroticism; on the other hand, Harlow's presence on the track leverages a successful heterosexual artist to make the track more palatable to non-queer audiences. The explicitly queer aesthetic of "INDUSTRY BABY" is tempered with a nod to heterosexuality, showing that while both can coexist in rap, there is still anxiety about potentially alienating straight audiences. Nevertheless, having such an overtly queer hip hop song top the *Billboard* charts is meaningful and marks a shift in the reception of queer rappers.

Lil Nas X also pushes against, or perhaps queers, the boundaries of genre. Indeed, this genre blurring was a source of controversy before the rapper publicly disclosed his queer sexuality. In December 2018 he released "Old Town Road," which became popular on online platforms such as Sound-Cloud and YouTube but really took off as a meme on TikTok. By the end of February 2019, the song was number one on Spotify's Viral 50 playlist, topped the iTunes country music chart, and, once Lil Nas X secured a major label deal, debuted at number eighty-three on the *Billboard* Hot 100 and number nineteen on the *Billboard* Hot Country Songs chart. After this initial success, though, *Billboard* quietly removed the song from the country charts. In a statement provided to *Rolling Stone* magazine, *Billboard* stated:

> Upon further review, it was determined that "Old Town Road" by Lil Nas X does not currently merit inclusion on *Billboard*'s country charts. When determining genres, a few factors are examined, but first and foremost is musical composition. While "Old Town Road" incorporates references to country and cowboy imagery, it does not embrace enough elements of today's country music to chart in its current version.[6]

---

5. A day after the video's release, Lil Nas X announced that he had joined forces with the Bail Project, a nonprofit working to end cash bail, to create the Bail X Fund. He used the attention that his video garnered to leverage donations for the fund and call attention to the disproportionate impact that cash bail has on Black communities.

6. *Billboard* magazine statement cited in Elisa Leight, "Lil Nas X's 'Old Town Road' Was

"Old Town Road" relies heavily on a banjo sampled from Nine Inch Nails's "34 Ghosts IV" and combines these musical and lyrical tropes common in country music with a trap beat. Lil Nas X has called it "country trap," and he is not the first to work in this genre (Young Thug released a mixtape in 2018, *Beautiful Thugger Girls*, that incorporates country stylings), nor is he the first to bring hip hop aesthetics to country (Jason Aldean's "Dirt Road Anthem" and Brad Paisley and LL Cool J's "Accidental Racist" come to mind). Yet, even after the release of a remix version of the song featuring country star Billy Ray Cyrus in April 2019, the song was still not added back to the country charts, a move that many considered to be motivated by racial discrimination more than any musical discussion. Regardless of the reasoning behind *Billboard*'s decision, Lil Nas X has leaned into this blurring of genres, stating in an interview with *Time* magazine, "It's not one [genre], it's not the other. It's both. It should be on both [charts]."[7]

In retrospect, outside of the debates about musical style, it is easier to see the elements of "Old Town Road" that perhaps the folks at *Billboard* found parodic of country music as examples of queer camp instead. Lil Nas X raps in the end of the second verse, "Bull ridin' and boobies / Cowboy hat from Gucci / Wrangler on my booty." While he gestures toward heterosexual relationships ("Cheated on my baby / You can go and ask her"), the use of "boobies" suggests an adolescent playfulness more than an assertive heterosexual masculinity, as does the self-referential use of "booty." The flashy cowboy outfits he and Cyrus wear in the second half of the song's music video similarly suggest a queer camp aesthetic (the music video is available on YouTube: https://doi.org/10.3998/mpub.11306619.cmp.7). The images of the song and video recall the history of both Black cowboys and gay rodeos, a history that country trap seems particularly well-suited to represent. As he noted years later in the Logitech commercial, "Logic said cowboys can't wear pink." In a sense, even before he was officially out, Lil Nas X has been challenging the heteronormativity of multiple genres while actively queer world-making.

Lil Nas X's recent live cover of Dolly Parton's "Jolene" further illustrates the ways he queers genre. In the performance for BBC Radio One's Live Lounge that Ann Powers called "the logical end of the arc that began with 'Old Town Road,'" Lil Nas X sets aside his rapping in place of a more sub-

a Country Hit. Then Country Changed Its Mind," *Rolling Stone*, March 26, 2019, https://www.rollingstone.com/music/music-features/lil-nas-x-old-town-road-810844/.

7. Lil Nas X, quoted in Andrew R. Chow, "Lil Nas X Talks 'Old Town Road' and the *Billboard* Controversy," *Time*, April 5, 2019, https://time.com/5561466/lil-nas-x-old-town-road-billboard/.

dued sung utterances murmured into a silver glittering microphone.[8] While the queer potential of "Jolene" has been established by Nadine Hubbs, typically the song evokes an entanglement between two or more women.[9] Here, Lil Nas X suggests another kind of queer entanglement, one in which he is fighting Jolene (who could be a woman or someone of another gender) for *his man*. Parton, herself an icon of gay culture, tweeted her own approval of the performance, saying it was "really good."[10] Not only does this performance solidify Lil Nas X's queer approach, but it also allows us to look retroactively at his earliest successes such as "Old Town Road" and consider his engagements with country music and country trap as a queering of these genres as well. If hip hop proved too challenging to enter as an openly gay man, Lil Nas X used other approaches to find his way into a rapidly changing industry and, once there, has continued to push for change.

In his description of the sonic-spatial construction of the hip hop room at the Black gay club, Jeffrey McCune situates the relationship between hip hop and queerness:

> The dynamic duo, hip-hop and queer space . . . are incongruous at surface level, but a deeper examination can explain this coupling. Historically, hip-hop culture and music have gone against the grain of traditional American music and style—often critiquing dominant structures and modifying other musical forms. Likewise, queerness has also disrupted normative tales of sexuality, restructuring the perceived composition of our society and generally challenging normative sociosexual rules and regulations. Together, they seem to make a "fabulous" pair. These two world-making apparatuses disrupt norms, interrogate new ground, and encourage exploration outside the domains of normativity. Ultimately, the relationship between hip-hop and black queer expression is a sort of meeting of two queers. Thus, hip-hop music's use as a medium for homoerotic engagements is not odd, but almost anticipatory.[11]

8. Ann Powers, "Lil Nas X, 'Jolene,'" *NPR.org*, September 21, 2021, https://www.npr.org/sections/now-playing/2021/09/21/1039353679/lil-nas-x-jolene.

9. Nadine Hubbs, "'Jolene,' Genre, and the Everyday Homoerotics of Country Music: Dolly Parton's Loving Address of the Other Woman," *Women & Music: A Journal of Gender and Culture* 19 (2015): 71–75.

10. Dolly Parton, "I was so excited . . ." Twitter, September 29, 2021, https://twitter.com/DollyParton/status/1443335105318211586, accessed October 21, 2021.

11. Jeffrey Q. McCune, Jr., *Sexual Discretion: Black Masculinity and the Politics of Passing* (Chicago: University of Chicago Press, 2014), 79.

McCune further notes that the use of hip hop in a queer space is related to the ways "young postmodern black queer subjects" adapt and adopt Black cultural practices for their own use. Rather than being incongruous, he argues, "Hip-hop is as much a part of queer world-making as queer world-making is a part of the history of hip-hop."[12] As he continues to build an oeuvre of self-referencing work, Lil Nas X is participating in this queer world-making in multiple ways. However, he is not the first nor the only one.

What I hope to have demonstrated in this book is that hip hop does not necessarily need to be appropriated to be understood as queer—the relationships between queerness and hip hop are not just spatial but also historical and musical. I have traced these connections between Black queer expressions and hip hop to the earliest emergences of the genre and provided frameworks for understanding the contemporary expressions of Black queer and trans artists. Lil Nas X and the other artists discussed in this book challenge the existing discourses that position hip hop and queerness as opposites. They are also part of a longer lineage of Black queer music practices. While Lil Nas X is innovating and his visibility unprecedented, he is not an anomaly—he is the result of decades of queer involvement in hip hop.

Demarginalizing queer expressions in hip hop does not devalue the contributions of artists like Lil Nas X but rather allows us to position his performance in a way that makes it legible as hip hop. This centering also expands our understanding of performances by non-queer performers; women who defy gender expectations, such as Megan Thee Stallion and Rapsody, for example, become legible within a framework that decentralizes limiting expectations of cisnormative heterosexual masculinity. And we can do this beyond hip hop as well. What other queer expressions in popular music have been diminished for the sake of neat narratives?

The media coverage of New York City–based Black queer rappers, the increasing influence of queer and trans New Orleans bounce artists on the work of mainstream performers, and the large-scale commercial success of Lil Nas X all suggest that queer hip hop artists are experiencing a moment of unprecedented visibility. This visibility, however, has not yet translated into a radical repositioning of normative rapper identities. I hope that by reframing this moment as one rooted in rap's history we can reshape those narratives. I also hope that reframing our conversations helps to open the possibility for artists to identify as LGBTQ openly as they build their careers. Perhaps then we can bring hip hop's queer past, present, and future fully out of the closet.

---

12. McCune, *Sexual Discretion*, 80.

Bibliography

Amico, Stephen. "'I Want Muscles': House Music, Homosexuality and Masculine Signification." *Popular Music* 20, no. 3 (2001): 359–78.

Bailey, Marlon M. *Butch Queens Up in Pumps: Gender, Performance, and Ballroom Culture in Detroit.* Ann Arbor: University of Michigan Press, 2016.

Bailey, Moya. "Homolatent Masculinity & Hip Hop Culture." *Palimpsest: A Journal on Women, Gender, and the Black International* 2, no. 2 (2013): 187–99.

Battan, Carrie. "We Invented Swag: NYC's Queer Rap." *Pitchfork*, March 21, 2012, http://pitchfork.com/features/articles/8793-we-invented-swag/.

Belkhir, Jean Ait, and Christiane Charlemaine. "Race, Gender, and Class Lessons from Hurricane Katrina." *Race Gender & Class* 14, no. 1–2 (2007): 120–52.

Big Freedia and Nicole Balin. *Big Freedia: God Save the Queen Diva!* New York: Gallery Books, 2015.

Bliss, Laura. "10 Years Later, There's So Much We Don't Know about Where Katrina Survivors Ended Up." *City Lab*, August 25, 2015, http://www.citylab.com/politics/2015/08/10-years-later-theres-still-a-lot-we-dont-know-about-where-katrina-survivors-ended-up/401216/.

Bouie, Jamelle. "Blacks Don't Have a Corporal Punishment Problem." *Slate*, September 19, 2014, http://www.slate.com/articles/news_and_politics/politics/2014/09/blacks_and_corporal_punishment_why_we_invent_black_pathologies.single.html.

Bradley, Regina N. "Barbz and Kings: Explorations of Gender and Sexuality in Hip-Hop." In *The Cambridge Companion to Hip-Hop*, edited by Justin A. Williams, 181–91. Cambridge, UK: Cambridge University Press, 2015.

Buckland, Fiona. *Impossible Dance: Club Culture and Queer World-Making.* Middletown, CT: Wesleyan University Press, 2002.

Bychawski, Adam. "Snoop Lion Says He Doesn't Know Whether Homosexuality Will Ever Be Seen as 'Acceptable' in Rap Music." *Nme*, April 6, 2013, http://www.nme.com/news/snoop-dogg/69594. Accessed September 30, 2016.

Camp, Zoe. "Mykki Blanco Releases *Gay Dog Food* Mixtape." *Pitchfork*, October 28, 2014, http://pitchfork.com/news/57225-mykki-blanco-releases-gay-dog-food-mixtape/.

Chapman, Alex. "The Internet's Syd and Matt Talk 'Cocaine' and Homophobia." *Huff-*

ington Post, November 29, 2011, https://www.huffpost.com/entry/the-internet-inter
view_b_1118724?guccounter=1&guce_referrer=aHR0cHM6Ly93d3cuZ29vZ2xl
LmNvbS8&guce_referrer_sig=AQAAAAnk3uRwwoqE1V0qPxMangyt0PRII2e
COeBUkIQMeBeb1ki9rnbg37b7F0gx-R7SaxdAsD7YrrfVl_0yjxbOEwNbmuAF
PnlGwfwu0tgdQBmZ-IrWVUfwtq2wOTxslHm81lY46WRviazkdICtoZx8e_ab
XZ7eWIrT1q3gWJ2wYbBA.

Chapman, Alix. "The Punk Show: Queering Heritage in the Black Diaspora." *Cultural Dynamics* 26, no. 3 (2014): 327–45.

Charnas, Dan. *The Big Payback: The History of the Business of Hip-Hop*. New York: New American Library, 2010.

Chow, Andrew R. "Lil Nas X Talks 'Old Town Road' and the *Billboard* Controversy." *Time*, April 5, 2019, https://time.com/5561466/lil-nas-x-old-town-road-billboard/.

Christgau, Robert. "Customer Guide Reviews: Macklemore & Ryan Lewis." *Robertchristgau.com*, http://www.robertchristgau.com/get_artist.php?name=macklemore.

Clay, Andreana. "'Like an Old Soul Record': Black Feminism, Queer Sexuality, and the Hip-Hop Generation." *Meridians* 8, no. 1 (2008): 53–73.

Collins, Patricia Hill. *Black Sexual Politics: African Americans, Gender, and the New Racism*. New York: Routledge, 2004.

Connelly, Joel. "Same-Sex Marriage Leads in Washington, Passes in Maryland, Maine." *Seattle PI*, November 6, 2012, http://blog.seattlepi.com/seattlepolitics/2012/11/06/same-sex-marriage-leads-in-washington-maryland-and-maine/.

Considine, Clare. "Zebra Katz, Mykki Blanco, and the Rise of Queer Rap." *The Guardian*, June 8, 2012, http://www.theguardian.com/music/2012/jun/09/zebra-katz-rise-of-gay-rappers.

Crawley, Ashon. "He Was an Architect: Little Richard and Blackqueer Grief." *NPR.org*, December 22, 2020, https://www.npr.org/2020/12/22/948963753/little-richard-black-queer-grief-he-was-an-architect.

Cunningham, Michael. "The Slap of Love." *Open City Magazine*, No. 6 (1996), 175–96.

Currid, Brian. "'We Are Family': House Music and Queer Performativity." In *Cruising the Performative: Interventions into the Representation of Ethnicity, Nationality, and Sexuality*, edited by Sue-Ellen Case, Philip Brett, and Susan Leigh Foster, 165–96. Bloomington: Indiana University Press, 1995.

Dandridge-Lemco, Ben. "Big Freedia Explains How She Got on Drake's New Bounce-Inflected Song." *The Fader*, April 9, 2018, https://www.thefader.com/2018/04/09/big-freedia-drake-nice-for-what-interview.

Dee, Jonathan. "New Orleans's Gender-Bending Rap." *New York Times*, July 22, 2010, http://www.nytimes.com/2010/07/25/magazine/25bounce-t.html?pagewanted=all&_r=0.

Dickel, Simon. *Black/Gay: The Harlem Renaissance, the Protest Era, and Constructions of Black Gay Identity in the 1980s and 90s*. East Lansing: Michigan State University Press, 2011.

Dinerstein, Joel. "Second Lining Post-Katrina: Learning Community from the Prince of Wales Social Aid and Pleasure Club." *American Quarterly* 61, no. 3 (2009): 615–37.

Domanick, Andrea. "Syd the Kyd on Odd Future, Her Sexuality, and Why She Hates the Word 'Lesbian.'" *LA Weekly*, January 12, 2012, https://www.laweekly.com/syd-the-kyd-on-odd-future-her-sexuality-and-why-she-hates-the-word-lesbian/.

Drott, Eric. "The End(s) of Genre." *Journal of Music Theory* 57, no. 1 (2013): 1–45.

Echols, Alice. *Hot Stuff: Disco and the Remaking of American Culture.* New York: W. W. Norton, 2010.

Egan, Patrick J., and Kenneth Sherrill. *California's Proposition 8: What Happened, and What Does the Future Hold?* San Francisco: National Gay and Lesbian Task Force, 2009.

Ewoodzie, Joseph C., Jr. *Break Beats in the Bronx: Rediscovering Hip-Hop's Early Years.* Chapel Hill: University of North Carolina Press, 2017.

Fajardo, Kale Bantigue. *Filipino Crosscurrents: Oceanographies of Seafaring, Masculinities, and Globalization.* Minneapolis: University of Minnesota Press, 2011.

Feeney, Nolan. "Twerk? Yaka? Duffy? Buku? Big Freedia's Guide to Bounce Music Slang." *Time*, June 17, 2014, http://time.com/2890212/big-freedia-just-be-free-bou nce-music-slang/.

Fensterstock, Alison. "Sissy Strut: Gay Rappers Carry the Torch for Bounce, but Not All Local Rappers Are Comfortable with That." *Gambit*, August 12, 2008, http://www .bestofneworleans.com/gambit/sissy-strut/Content?oid=1250945. Accessed July 23, 2016.

Fikentscher, Kai. *"You Better Work!": Underground Dance Music in New York City.* Hanover, CT: Wesleyan University Press, 2000.

Frank, Gillian. "Discophobia: Antigay Prejudice and the 1979 Backlash against Disco." *Journal of the History of Sexuality* 16, no. 2 (2007): 276–306.

Fussell, Elizabeth. "Constructing New Orleans, Constructing Race: A Population History of New Orleans." *Journal of American History* 94, no. 3 (2007): 846–55.

Fussell, Elizabeth, Narayan Sastry, and Mark VanLandingham. "Race, Socioeconomic Status, and Return Migration to New Orleans after Hurricane Katrina." *Population and Environment* 31, no. 1/3 (2010): 20–42.

Garber, Eric. "A Spectacle of Color: The Lesbian and Gay Subculture of Jazz Age Harlem." In *Hidden from History: Reclaiming the Gay and Lesbian Past*, edited by Martin Duberman, Martha Vicinus, and George Chauncey Jr., 318–31. New York: Meridian, 1990.

Gibsone, Harriet. "Syd: 'The Backlash from the Gay Community Hurt My Feelings.'" *The Guardian*, May 30, 2017, https://www.theguardian.com/music/2017/may/30/syd-off-future-backlash-gay-community-hurt-my-feeling.

Green, Jesse. "Paris Has Burned." *New York Times*, April 18, 1993.

Halberstam, Judith. *Female Masculinity.* Durham, NC: Duke University Press, 1998.

Hammonds, Evelynn M. "Toward a Genealogy of Black Female Sexuality: The Problematic of Silence." In *Feminist Genealogies, Colonial Legacies, Democratic Futures*, edited by J. Alexander and C. T. Mahanty, 93–104. New York: Routledge, 1997.

hampton, dream. "Thank You, Frank Ocean." *Life + Times*, July 4, 2012, http://lifeandti mes.com/thank-you-frank-ocean.

Handy-Hamilton, Xavier. "Kodak Black's Trolling Forces Young M.A to Respond." *Complex*, March 18, 2019, https://www.complex.com/music/2019/03/young-ma-re sponds-to-kodak-blacks-weird-comments.

Hart, Benji. "Vogue Is Not for You: Deciding Whom We Give Our Art To." *Radfag*, May 31, 2015, https://radfag.com/2015/05/31/vogue-is-not-for-you-deciding-whom-we -give-our-art-to/.

Hawkins, Stan. *Queerness in Pop Music: Aesthetics, Gender Norms, and Temporality.* New York: Routledge, 2016.

"A History of Rappers Standing Up for Gay Rights." *Complex*, May 15, 2012, http://www.complex.com/music/2012/05/history-rappers-not-being-homophobic/.

Hope, Clover. "Quiet Storm: For Lifelong Loner Dej Loaf, the Worldwide Stage Is an Ambitious Leap." *The Fader* (December/January 2017), https://www.thefader.com/magazine/107. Accessed August 26, 2020.

Hubbs, Nadine. "'I Will Survive': Musical Mappings of Queer Social Space in a Disco Anthem." *Popular Music* 26, no. 2 (2007): 231–44.

Hubbs, Nadine. "'Jolene,' Genre, and the Everyday Homoerotics of Country Music: Dolly Parton's Loving Address of the Other Woman." *Women & Music: A Journal of Gender and Culture* 19 (2015): 71–75.

Hubbs, Nadine. *The Queer Composition of America's Sound: Gay Modernists, American Music, and National Identity*. Berkeley: University of California Press, 2004.

Hughes, Walter. "In the Empire of the Beat: Discipline and Disco." In *Microphone Fiends: Youth Music & Youth Culture*, edited by Andrew Ross and Tricia Rose, 147–57. New York: Routledge, 1994.

Hussein, Wandera. "Big Freedia Reportedly Contacted Drake First to Be in 'In My Feelings' Video." *The Fader*, August 6, 2018, https://www.thefader.com/2018/08/06/big-freedia-call-drake-in-my-feelings.

Jeffries, Michael. *Thug Life: Race, Gender, and the Meaning of Hip-Hop*. Chicago: University of Chicago Press, 2011.

Johnson, Myles E. "The Ghost of Big Freedia." *Vice*, April 18, 2018, https://noisey.vice.com/en_us/article/59j4xn/big-freedia-drake-beyonce-essay.

Jones, Alisha Lola. *Flaming?: The Peculiar Theopolitics of Fire and Desire in Black Male Gospel Performance*. New York: Oxford University Press, 2020.

Joshi, Tara. "The Internet's Syd: 'I'm the Only Person Like Me That I Know.'" *The Guardian*, April 13, 2019, https://www.theguardian.com/music/2019/apr/13/syd-the-internet-odd-future-interview-hive-mind.

Juzwiak, Rich. "Rapper Le1f's *Letterman* Terrific Performance Was Also Important." *Gawker*, March 14, 2014, http://gawker.com/rapper-le1fs-letterman-terrific-performance-was-also-i-1543798565.

Kajikawa, Loren. *Sounding Race in Rap Songs*. Oakland: University of California Press, 2015.

Keeling, Kara. "'Ghetto Heaven': *Set It Off* and the Valorization of Black Lesbian Butch-Femme Sociality." *Black Scholar* 33, no. 1 (2003): 33–46.

Kehrer, Lauron. "Beyond Beyoncé: Intersections of Race, Gender, and Sexuality in Contemporary American Hip-Hop ca. 2010–2016." PhD diss., University of Rochester, 2017.

Kehrer, Lauron. "A Love Song for All of Us?: Macklemore's 'Same Love' and the Myth of Black Homophobia." *Journal of the Society for American Music* 12, no. 4 (2018): 425–48.

Kehrer, Lauron. "Who Slays? Queer Resonances in Beyoncé's *Lemonade*." *Popular Music and Society* 42, no. 1 (2019): 82–98.

Keyes, Cheryl L. "Empowering Self, Making Choices, Creating Spaces: Black Female Identity via Rap Music Performance." *Journal of American Folklore* 113, no. 449 (2000): 255–69.

Keyes, Cheryl L. *Rap Music and Street Consciousness*. Urbana: University of Illinois Press, 2004.

Kitwana, Bakari. *Why White Kids Love Hip-Hop: Wankstas, Wiggers, Wannabes, and the New Reality of Race in America.* New York: Basic Civitas Books, 2005.

Lawrence, Tim. *Love Saves the Day: A History of American Dance Music.* Durham, NC: Duke University Press, 2003.

Lee, Benjamin. "Is Tyler, the Creator Coming Out as a Gay Man or Just a Queer-Baiting Provocateur?" *The Guardian,* July 25, 2017, https://www.theguardian.com/music/20 17/jul/25/tyler-the-creator-flower-boy-gay-man-or-queer-baiting-provocateur.

Legal Entertainment. "Beyoncé Sued for $20 Million by the Estate of Messy Mya over 'Formation.'" *Forbes,* February 7, 2017, https://www.forbes.com/sites/legalentertain ment/2017/02/07/beyonce-sued-for-20-million-by-the-estate-of-anthony-barre -messy-mya-over-formation/#2cbdb80d5b02.

Leight, Elisa. "Lil Nas X's 'Old Town Road' Was a Country Hit. Then Country Changed Its Mind." *Rolling Stone,* March 26, 2019, https://www.rollingstone.com/music/mus ic-features/lil-nas-x-old-town-road-810844/.

Lester, Paul. "Tyler the Creator in the UK: Forget Hip-Hop, We're the New Sex Pistols!" *The Guardian,* May 6, 2011, https://www.theguardian.com/music/2011/may/07/ty ler-the-creator-odd-future.

Love, Bettina. "A Ratchet Lens: Black Queer Youth, Agency, Hip Hop, and the Black Ratchet Imagination." In *Mouths of Rain: An Anthology of Black Lesbian Thought,* edited by Briona Simone Jones, 226–48. New York: New Press, 2021.

Manjoo, Farhad. "Props to Obama: Did He Help Push California's Gay-Marriage Ban over the Top?" *Slate,* November 5, 2008, http://www.slate.com/articles/news_and _politics/politics/2008/11/props_to_obama.html.

Markman, Rob. "Tyler, The Creator Defends His Use of *Other* F-Word." MTV.com, June 15, 2011, http://www.mtv.com/news/1665860/tyler-the-creator-defends-lyrics/.

McCune, Jeffrey Q. Jr. *Sexual Discretion: Black Masculinity and the Politics of Passing.* Chicago: University of Chicago Press, 2014.

McDonald, Natalie Hope. "America's Next Top Gay Rapper? Leif Responds to Homophobia in Hip Hop. Plus: Watch His Latest Music Video." *Philadelphia,* July 24, 2012, http://www.phillymag.com/g-philly/2012/07/24/gay-rapper/.

McKinley, James C., Jr. "Stars Align for a Gay Marriage Anthem." *New York Times,* June 30, 2013, http://www.nytimes.com/2013/07/01/arts/music/stars-align-for-a-gay -marriage-anthem.html?_r=0.

McKinley, Jesse, and Kirk Johnson. "Mormons Tipped Scale in Ban on Gay Marriage." *New York Times,* November 14, 2008, http://www.nytimes.com/2008/11/15/us/po litics/15marriage.html?pagewanted=all&_r=0.

McNally, James. "Azealia Banks's '212': Black Female Identity and the White Gaze in Contemporary Hip-Hop." *Journal of the Society for American Music* 10, no. 1 (2016): 54–81.

Miller, Matt. *Bounce: Rap Music and Local Identity in New Orleans.* Amherst: University of Massachusetts Press, 2012.

Mincher, Chris. "Macklemore & Lewis' 'Same Love' Is More Than a Pro–Gay Marriage Anthem." *AV Club,* January 24, 2014, http://www.avclub.com/article/macklemore -amp-lewis-same-love-is-more-than-a-pro--200929.

Miyakawa, Felicia M. *Five Percenter Rap: God Hop's Music, Message, and Black Muslim Mission.* Bloomington: Indiana University Press, 2005.

Muñoz, José Esteban. *Disidentifications: Queers of Color and the Performance of Politics.* Minneapolis: University of Minnesota Press, 1999.

Naramore, Leanne. "Hip-Hop's Macklemore x Ryan Lewis Release Beautiful Video for 'Same Love.'" *HRC.org*, October 3, 2012, http://www.hrc.org/blog/entry/hip-hops -macklemore-x-ryan-lewis-release-beautiful-video-for-same-love. Accessed April 2, 2015.

Neal, Mark Anthony. "Trafficking in Monikers: Jay-Z's 'Queer' Flow." *Palimpsest: A Journal on Women, Gender, and the Black International* 2, no. 2 (2013): 156–61.

Nika, Colleen. "Q&A: Azealia Banks on Why the C-Word Is 'Feminine.'" *Rolling Stone*, September 10, 2012, http://www.rollingstone.com/music/blogs/thread-count/azeal ia-banks-on-why-the-c-word-is-feminine-20120910. Accessed September 10, 2016.

Nilles, Billy. "Why Lil Nas X's Last Year Is Such a Big Deal." *Eonline.com*, January 25, 2020, https://www.eonline.com/news/1060868/why-lil-nas-x-breaking-billboard -records-is-such-a-big-deal.

Nyong'o, Tavia. "Queer Hip Hop and Its Dark Precursors." *Palimpsest: A Journal on Women, Gender, and the Black International* 2, no. 2 (2013): 144–46.

Pennington, Stephan. "Transgender Passing Guides and the Vocal Performance of Gender and Sexuality." In *The Oxford Handbook of Music and Queerness*, edited by Fred Everett Maus and Sheila Whiteley. New York: Oxford University Press. Published online January 2019. https://doi.org/10.1093/oxfordhb/9780199793525.013.65.

Perry, Imani. *Prophets of the Hood: Politics and Poetics in Hip Hop.* Durham, NC: Duke University Press, 2004.

Perry, Imani. "Untitled." *Palimpsest: A Journal on Women, Gender, and the Black International* 2, no. 2 (2013): 166–67.

Peterson, Jessie. "Zebra Katz's 'Tear the House Up' Music Video: Look by Look." MTV. com, June 3, 2014, http://www.mtv.com/news/2520801/zebra-katzs-tear-the-house -up-music-video-look-by-look/.

Powell, Elliott H. "The Ghosts Got You: Exploring the Queer (After) Lives of Sample-Based Hip-Hop." In *The Oxford Handbook of Hip Hop Music*, edited by Justin D. Burton and Jason Lee Oakes. New York: Oxford University Press. Published online August 2018. https://doi.org/10.1093/oxfordhb/9780190281090.013.29.

Powell, Elliott H. "Unmastered: The Queer Black Aesthetics of Unfinished Recordings." *Black Scholar* 49, no. 1 (2019): 28–39.

Powers, Ann. "Lil Nas X, 'Jolene.'" *NPR.org*, September 21, 2021, https://www.npr.org /sections/now-playing/2021/09/21/1039353679/lil-nas-x-jolene.

Preezy. "Here's a Timeline of Kodak Black and Young M.A's Weird Beef." *XXL*, March 22, 2019, https://www.xxlmag.com/kodak-black-young-m-a-beef-timeline/.

Regis, Helen A. "Blackness and the Politics of Memory in the New Orleans Second Line." *American Ethnologist* 28, no. 4 (2001): 752–77.

Rodríguez, Richard T. "Hip Hop Spice Boyz." *Palimpsest: A Journal on Women, Gender, and the Black International* 2, no. 2 (2013): 140–43.

Rose, Tricia. *Black Noise: Rap Music and Black Culture in Contemporary America.* Middletown, CT: Wesleyan University Press, 1994.

Rose, Tricia. *The Hip Hop Wars: What We Talk about When We Talk about Hip Hop— And Why It Matters.* New York: Basic Civitas, 2008.

Salkind, Micah E. *Do You Remember House?: Chicago's Queer of Color Undergrounds.* New York: Oxford University Press, 2019.

Savage, Dan. "Black Homophobia," *The Stranger*, November 5, 2008, http://slog.thestra nger.com/2008/11/black_homophobia. Accessed April 22, 2015.

Schloss, Joseph G. *Making Beats: The Art of Sample-Based Hip-Hop*. Middletown, CT: Wesleyan University Press, 2004.

Shaffer, Claire. "Kesha Announces 'High Road' North American Tour." *Rolling Stone*, January 7, 2020, https://www.rollingstone.com/music/music-news/kesha-high-ro ad-tour-934536/.

Sharpley-Whiting, T. Denean, and Tiffany Ruby Patterson-Myers, eds. *Palimpsest: A Journal on Women, Gender, and the Black International* 2, no. 2 (2013).

Shorey, Eric. "Queer Rap Is Not Queer Rap." *Pitchfork*, March 31, 2015, http://pitchfork .com/thepitch/712-queer-rap-is-not-queer-rap/.

Simmons, Russell. "The Courage of Frank Ocean Just Changed the Game!" *Globalgrind*, July 2012, http://globalgrind.com/1857832/russell-simmons-letter-to-frank-ocean -gay-bi-sexual-comes-out-photos/.

Smalls, Shanté Paradigm. "Queer Hip Hop: A Brief Historiography." In *The Oxford Handbook of Music and Queerness*, edited by Fred Everett Maus and Sheila Whiteley. Published online September 2018. https://doi.org/10.1093/oxfordhb/9780199793525.013 .103.

Smalls, Shanté Paradigm. "'The Rain Comes Down': Jean Grae and Hip Hop Heteronormativity." *American Behavioral Scientist* 55, no. 1 (2011): 86–95.

Smith, Anna Marie. "The Regulation of Lesbian Sexuality through Erasure: The Case of Jennifer Saunders." In *Lesbian Erotics*, edited by Karla Jay, 164–79. New York: New York University Press, 1995.

Smith, Danyel. "Heads Ain't Ready for Queen Latifah's Next Move." *Vibe* (December 1996/January 1997), 98–102.

Snorton, C. Riley. "On the Question of 'Who's Out in Hip Hop.'" *Souls: A Critical Journal of Black Politics, Culture, and Society* 16, nos. 3–4 (2014): 283–302.

Strauss, Matthew. "Young M.A Responds to Kodak Black after He Raps Homophobic Lyrics about Her." *Pitchfork*, March 18, 2019, https://pitchfork.com/news/young-ma -responds-to-kodak-black-after-he-raps-homophobic-lyrics-about-her/.

Sullivan, Andrew. "The Grim Truth." *The Atlantic*, November 5, 2008, http://andrewsul livan.theatlantic.com/the_daily_dish/2008/11/the-grim-truth.html.

Sullivan, Mecca Jamilah. "Fat Mutha: Hip Hop's Queer Corpulent Poetics." *Palimpsest: A Journal on Women, Gender, and the Black International* 2, no. 2 (2013): 200–213.

Tanzer, Myles, and Michelle Kim. "Beyoncé Clarifies Dispute over 'Formation' Video Footage." *The Fader*, February 7, 2016, http://www.thefader.com/2016/02/07/beyo nce-formation-video-documentary-footage-credit.

Tavakoli, Mina. "Young M.A, 'OOOUUU' (2016)." In *The 200 Greatest Songs by 21st Century Women+. NPR.org*, July 30, 2018, https://www.npr.org/2018/07/09/62739 7206/turning-the-tables-the-200-greatest-songs-by-21st-century-songs-women-part-6.

Thomas, Anthony. "The House the Kids Built: The Gay Black Imprint on American Dance Music." In *Out in Culture: Gay, Lesbian, and Queer Essays on Popular Culture*, edited by C. K. Creekmur and A. Doty, 437–46. Durham, NC: Duke University Press, 1995.

Thomas, Zanyra. "Odd Future's Syd the Kyd Talks Music, Identity, and the Internet." *Mass Appeal*, August 7, 2012, https://web.archive.org/web/20120922065011/htt p://massappeal.com/odd-futures-syd-the-kyd-talks-music-identity-and-the-intern et-11146/.

Vick, Karl, and Ashley Surdin. "Most of California's Black Voters Backed Gay Marriage Ban." *Washington Post*, November 7, 2008, http://www.washingtonpost.com/wp-dyn/content/article/2008/11/06/AR2008110603880.html.

Walcott, Rinaldo. "Boyfriends with Clits and Girlfriends with Dicks: Hip Hop's Queer Future." *Palimpsest: A Journal on Women, Gender, and the Black International* 2, no. 2 (2013): 168–73.

Watkins, S. Craig. *Representing: Hip Hop Culture and the Production of Black Cinema.* Chicago: University of Chicago Press, 1998.

Weisbard, Eric. *Top 40 Democracy: The Rival Mainstreams of American Music.* Chicago: University of Chicago Press, 2014.

White, Miles. *From Jim Crow to Jay-Z: Race, Rap, and the Performance of Masculinity.* Urbana: University of Illinois Press, 2011.

Wilson, Bianca D. M. "Black Lesbian Gender and Sexual Culture: Celebration and Resistance." *Culture, Health & Sexuality* 11, no. 3 (2009): 297–313.

Wilson, Mark D. "Post-Pomo Hip-Hop Homos: Hip-Hop Art, Gay Rappers, and Social Change." *Social Justice* 34, no. 1 (107) (2007): 117–40.

Wortham, Jenna. "Syd Tha Kid & the Internet: How to Chart Your Own Path in a Post-Label Music Industry." *New York Times*, March 10, 2016, https://www.nytimes.com/interactive/2016/03/10/magazine/25-songs-that-tell-us-where-music-is-going.html?&_r=2#/syd-tha-kyd-the-internet-get-away.

Younger, Briana. "Found Family: How Odd Future Changed Everything." *Pitchfork*, July 31, 2018, https://pitchfork.com/thepitch/found-family-how-odd-future-changed-everything/.

Media

"Azealia Banks Goes Off on TI, Iggy + Black Music Being Smudged Out." YouTube video, 47:30. From an interview conducted by Ebro Darden, Laura Stylez, and Peter Rosenberg. Posted by HOT 97, December 18, 2014, https://www.youtube.com/watch?v=uFDS-VEEl6w. Accessed September 10, 2016.

Beyoncé. "Formation." Music video. Directed by Melina Matsoukas. Parkwood, 2016.

Big Freedia. "Chasing Rainbows." Music video. Directed by Jonah Lincoln Best and Lagan Sebert. East West Records, 2020.

Blanco, Mykki. "Coke White, Starlight." Music video. Directed by Tristan Patterson. Dogfood Music Group, 2015.

Blanco, Mykki. "High School Never Ends." Music video. Directed by Matt Lambert. IK7/Dogfood, 2016.

Blanco, Mykki. "She Gutta." Music video. Directed by Jude MC. UNO NYC, 2014.

Blanco, Mykki. "Wavvy." Music video. Directed by Francesco Carrozzini. UNO NYC, 2012.

Bucano, Rocky. "True story . . ." Facebook, November 15, 2020, https://www.facebook.com/1304512998/posts/10219362243949207/?d=n.

DaBaby. "BOP on Broadway (Hip Hop Musical)." Music video. Directed by Reel Goats. Interscope, 2019.

Drake. "In My Feelings." Music video. Directed by Karena Evans. Young Money/Cash Money, 2018.

Drake. "Nice For What." Music video. Directed by Karena Evans. Young Money/Cash Money, 2018.

Gray, F. Gary, dir. *Set It Off*. Streaming film. Peak Films, 1996.

The Internet, "Cocaine." Music video. Directed by Matt Alonzo. Odd Future, 2011.

Kesha. "Raising Hell." Music video. Directed by Luke Gilford. RCA/Kemosabe, 2019.

Late Show with David Letterman. "Bryan Cranston/Melissa Rauch/Leif." Season 21, episode 43. CBS, March 13, 2014.

Leif. "Koi." Music video. Directed by Simon Ward. Terrible Records, 2015.

Leif. "Soda." Music video. Directed by Sam Jones. Boysnoize Records, 2012.

Lil Nas X. "dear 14 year old montero." Twitter, March 26, 2021, https://twitter.com/Lil NasX/status/1375297562396139520.

Lil Nas X. "Defy Logic/Logitech/Big Game Commercial." YouTube video, 1:00. Posted by Logitech, February 2, 2021, https://www.youtube.com/watch?v=3dBl1iwqqbw. Accessed October 25, 2021.

Lil Nas X. "Lil Nas X Gives Birth." YouTube video, 1:39. Directed by Adrian Per. Posted September 17, 2021, https://www.youtube.com/watch?v=v7C0OVhvofI. Accessed October 25, 2021.

Lil Nas X. "Lil Nas X—Jolene (Dolly Parton Cover) in the Live Lounge." YouTube video, 2:28. Posted by BBCRadio1VEVO, September 21, 2021, https://www.youtube .com/watch?v=RWjnC8HSRdU. Accessed October 25, 2021.

Lil Nas X. "MONTERO (Call Me By Your Name)." Music video. Directed by Tanu Muino and Lil Nas X. Columbia, 2021.

Lil Nas X. "Old Town Road." Music video. Directed by Calmatic. Columbia, 2019.

Lil Nas X and Jack Harlow. "INDUSTRY BABY." Music video. Directed by Christian Breslauer. Columbia, 2021.

Livingston, Jennie, dir. *Paris Is Burning*. Film/DVD. Miramax, 1990.

Madonna. "Vogue." Music video. Directed by David Fincher. Warner Bros., 1990.

Mannie Fresh. "Mannie Fresh Speaks on Gay Tolerance in the N.O. Rap Scene." YouTube video, 2:45. Posted by VladTV, April 5, 2013, https://www.youtube.com/watch?v= MlqpiQBCP98. Accessed October 24, 2021.

Ocean, Frank. "thank you's." tumblr.com, July 4, 2012, http://frankocean.tumblr.com /post/26473798723.

Parton, Dolly. "I was so excited . . ." Twitter, September 29, 2021, https://twitter.com/Do llyParton/status/1443335105318211586. Accessed October 21, 2021.

POSE. Television series. FX, 2018–2021.

Saturday Night Live. "Anya Taylor-Joy/Lil Nas X." Season 46, episode 20. NBC, May 22, 2021.

Smith, Troy L. "From the D.J. Quick of Queens, New York Series: Part 1." Facebook, July 10, 2015, https://www.facebook.com/troylsmith21/posts/10206308633131191.

That B.E.A.T. Documentary short. Directed by Abteen Bagheri. 2013.

Treme. Television series. HBO, 2010–2013.

Tyler, The Creator. "My Big Brother Finally Fucking Did That." Twitter, July 4, 2012, https://twitter.com/tylerthecreator/status/220409501487079424. Accessed September 30, 2016.

Wills, Leila. "2 Can Y'all Get Funky." *Trapped in a Culture* Podcast, January 2020, streaming audio, 15:07, https://trappedinaculture.com/podcast. Accessed May 29, 2021.

Young M.A. "Ooouuu." Music video. Directed by a piece by guy and Young M.A. M.A Music, 2016.

Young M.A. "Ooouuu." Verified annotation on *Genius.com*, 2016, https://genius.com /10188229.

"Young M.A. Talks New Music & Says She's Not a Lesbian on Hollywood Unlocked [Uncensored]." YouTube video, 57:55. Posted by Hollywood Unlocked, September 16, 2019, https://www.youtube.com/watch?v=ANLVMmN7O4g.

Zebra Katz x Hervé. "Tear the House Up." Music video. Directed by Ghost+Cow [Brandon LaGanke and John Carlucci]. Mad Decent, 2014.

Interviews

Anonymous. Interview with the author. Personal interview. New Orleans, June 8, 2016.

5th Ward Weebie. Interview with Holly Hobbs. Video. New Orleans, 2014. NOLA Hiphop Archives. Accessed July 25, 2016. http://digitallibrary.tulane.edu/islandora /object/tulane%3A28432.

Ha Sizzle. Interview with the author. Personal interview. New Orleans, June 17, 2016.

Keno. Interview with the author. Personal interview. New Orleans, June 14, 2016.

Rusty Lazer. Interview with the author. Personal interview. New Orleans, June 8, 2016.

Sissy Nobby. Interview with Holly Hobbs. Video. New Orleans, July 11, 2014. NOLA Hiphop Archives, Accessed August 4, 2016. http://digitallibrary.tulane.edu/islando ra/object/tulane%3A28446.

Discography

5th Ward Weebie. "Fuck Katrina (The Katrina Song)." FattBoy Entertainment. MP3 single, 2015 (originally released 2005).

Banks, Azealia. *1991*. Interscope Records. MP3 EP, 2012.

Banks, Azealia. *Broke with Expensive Taste*. Azealia Banks/Prospect Park. MP3 album, 2014.

Beyoncé. *Lemonade*. Parkwood Entertainment/Columbia Records. Digital video album, 2016.

Big Freedia. *3rd Ward Bounce*. East West Records. MP3 EP, 2018.

Big Freedia. *Hitz Vol. 1 (1999–2010)*. Big Freedia. MP3 album, 2010.

Big Freedia. *Just Be Free*. Queen Diva Music. MP3 album, 2014.

Black, Kodak. "Pimpin Ain't Eazy." *Bill Israel*. Dollaz N Dealz/Sniper Gang/Atlantic. Streaming album, 2020.

Blanco, Mykki. *Gay Dog Food*. UNO NYC. MP3 album, 2014.

Blanco, Mykki, and Brenmar. "Wavvy." UNO NYC. MP3 single, 2012.

Bloody & Leif. *Liquid*. Boysnoize Records. MP3 EP, 2012.

Cakes da Killa. *The Eulogy*. Mishka NYC. MP3 mixtape, 2013.

Cakes da Killa. *Hunger Pangs*. Mishka NYC. MP3 mixtape, 2014.

Cakes da Killa. *I Run This Club*. Hot Mom USA. MP3 EP, 2013.

Chic. "Good Times." Atlantic. Vinyl single, 1979.

De La Soul. "Kicked Out the House." *De La Soul Is Dead*. Tommy Boy. CD album, 1991.

Derek B. "Rock the Beat." Profile Records. 1987.

Diplo. "Express Yourself (featuring Nicky da B)." Mad Decent. MP3 single, 2012.

DJ Jubilee. "Stop, Pause (Do the Jubilee All)." Take Fo' Records. Vinyl album, 1993.

DJ Jubilee. *Walk with It*. The New Take Fo' Records. Vinyl and CD album, 2000.

Drake. "Child's Play." *Views*. Young Money. MP3 album, 2016.

Drake. "Nice For What." *Scorpion*. Young Money. MP3 album, 2018.

Elliott, Missy. "Pep Rally." Atlantic. MP3 single, 2016.

First Choice. "Let No Man Put Asunder." Salsoul. Vinyl single, 1983.

Ha Sizzle. *The Voice of Bounce, Vol. 1*. The Sizzles Entertainment. MP3 album, 2016.

The Impressions. *People Get Ready*. ABC-Paramount. Vinyl LP, 1965.

The Internet. "Cocaine." *Purple Naked Ladies*. Odd Future Records. Digital album, 2011.

Jungle Brothers. "I'll House You." *Straight Out the Jungle*. Warlock Records. Vinyl LP, 1988.

Katz, Zebra. *Ima Read* (feat. Njena Reddd Foxxx). Mad Decent. MP3 EP, 2012.

Katz, Zebra, and Hervé. *Tear the House Up*. Mad Decent. MP3 EP, 2014.

Latifah, Queen. "Come Into My House." *All Hail the Queen*. Tommy Boy. Vinyl LP, 1989.

Leif. *Hey*. Terrible Records. MP3 EP, 2014.

Leif. *Riot Boi*. Terrible Records. MP3 EP, 2015.

Lil Jon, Kronic, and Onderkoffer. "Bad Bitches (featuring Keno)." Sup Girl Records. MP3 single, 2016.

Lil Nas X. "MONTERO (Call Me By Your Name)." Columbia Records. MP3 single, 2021.

Lil Nas X. "Old Town Road." *7 EP*. Columbia Records. MP3 EP, 2019.

Lil Nas X. "SUN GOES DOWN." Columbia Records. MP3 single, 2021.

Macklemore and Ryan Lewis. *The Heist*. Macklemore, LLC. MP3 album, 2012.

Madonna. "Vogue." Sire/Warner Bros. Cassette and CD single, 1990.

Masters at Work. "Blood Vibes/The Ha Dance." Cutting Records. Vinyl single, 1991.

MC T. Tucker and DJ Irv. "Where Dey At?" Charlot Records. Cassette single, 1991.

MFSB. *Love Is the Message*. Philadelphia International Records. Vinyl album, 1973.

Ocean, Frank. *Channel Orange*. Island Def Jam Music Group. MP3 album, 2012.

Red, Katey. *Melpomene Block Party*. Take Fo' Records. CD album, 1999.

Red, Katey. *Y2 Katey: The Millennium Sissy*. Take Fo' Records. CD album, 2000.

Ross, Diana. "Love Hangover." Motown. Vinyl single, 1976.

The Showboys. "Drag Rap." Profile Records. Vinyl single, 1986.

Skrillex and Diplo. "Beats Knockin (featuring Fly Boi Keno)." *Skrillex and Diplo Present Jack Ü*. Atlantic. MP3 single, 2015.

Sugarhill Gang. "Rapper's Delight." Sugar Hill. Vinyl single, 1979.

Summer, Donna. "MacArthur Park." Casablanca. Vinyl single, 1978.

Sylvester. "You Make Me Feel (Mighty Real)." Fantasy Records. Vinyl single, 1978.

Sylvester. "Dance (Disco Heat)." Fantasy Records. Vinyl single, 1978.

Vanity 6. "Nasty Girl." Warner Bros. Vinyl single, 1982.

Various artists. *Mykki Blanco Presents C-ORE*. Dogfood Music Group. MP3 album, 2015.

Young M.A. "Ooouuu." M.A Music. MP3 and streaming single, 2016.

Index

"1 Bad Bitch" (Katz), 57
3rd Ward Bounce (Big Freedia), 122
5th Ward Weebie, 103–4, 117
"34 Ghosts IV" (Nine Inch Nails), 128
"212" (Banks), 58
1991 (Banks), 58

A$AP Rocky, 43
"Accidental Racist" (Paisley and LL Cool J), 128
Aciman, André, 124
Afrika "Baby Bam," 3
Age of Consent, 40
Aldean, Jason, 128
Amico, Stephen, 30
appropriation, 46, 69, 95–96, 121–23, 130
Atlanta, Georgia, 99
audiences, 94–95, 98, 113, 122
authenticity, 16–17, 68–69, 73

Bailey, Marlon M., 46–48, 56, 61, 63
Baker, Houston A., Jr., 33
Ballroom culture: Ballroom rap and, 15, 51–53; drag and, 61; fashion and, 60; gender and, 47–48; house music and, 37–38, 45, 48–50; houses and, 46–47; musical references in, 56–60; performance labor and, 65; queer rap and, 5, 44–45; reading and, 54–55; realness and, 61–62; self-fashioning and, 63
Ballroom rap: Ballroom culture and, 15, 45, 50–52; as genre, 63–66; lyrics and, 52–56; musical references in, 56–60; visibility of, 130; visual references in, 60–63

Bambaataa, Afrika, 33–35
Banks, Azealia, 15, 42, 45, 57–60, 64
"Barbie Dreams" (Minaj), 40
Baton Rouge, Louisiana, 99
Battan, Carrie, 42
BBC Radio One, 128
b-boy movement, 32–33
"Beats Knockin'" (Diplo), 114
Beautiful Thugger Girls (Young Thug), 128
Berlant, Lauren, 31
Beyoncé, 16, 74, 93, 94–95, 114–15
Big Daddy Kane, 3
Big Day Out festival, 82
Big Freedia: bounce music and, 44; COVID-19 pandemic and, 122; Drake and, 117–18; Kesha and, 120–21; kinship networks and, 105–6; mainstream success and, 94–95, 113–14; shade and, 119–20; "sissy bounce" and, 109–11; touring and, 108; visibility and, 16
Big Freedia: Queen of Bounce, 113–14
Billboard, 10, 117, 126–28
bisexuality, 58–59
Black artists: Ballroom rap and, 45, 50–51; Banks and, 59–60; disco and, 18–25; diversity of, 5–6; hip hop and, 15, 129–30; homophobia and, 14; house music and, 30–31; kinship networks and, 105–7; in New Orleans, 96–97; performance labor and, 63–66; queer literature and, 65; queer rap and, 43; shade and, 120; women as, 69–71; Young M.A and Syd and, 90–93; Young M.A as, 80–81

Black communities: Ballroom culture and, 45–49, 56–57; Ballroom rap and, 50–55; "Black homophobia" and, 12–14; disco and, 20–25, 27; hip hop and, 40; homophobia and, 9–13; house music and, 29–31, 59; in New Orleans, 96–97, 99; queerness and, 9
Blackness: heterogeneity of, 35; invented pathologies and, 13–14; Leif and, 52; queerness and, 7–8; sexuality and, 87–88; Sylvester and, 23–24
Black women: butchness and, 67–68; female masculinity and, 71–74, 90–92; house music and, 30; musical lineages and, 76–77; as rappers, 69–71; sexuality and, 87–89. See also blues women; butch women; women; women rappers
Blanco, Mykki, 42, 61–64
BlaqNmilD, 117
blues women, 64–65, 76–77. See also Black women; women
"B/M/F (Black Model Famous)" (House of LaDosha), 59
"B.M.F (Blowin' Money Fast)" (Ross), 59
Boody, 56
"BOP" (DaBaby), 126
"Born This Way" (Lady Gaga), 10
Bouie, Jamelle, 13
"Bounce It Biggity Bounce It" (Ha Sizzle), 100–101, 116
bounce music: Big Freedia and, 94–95, 113–14; emergence of, 96–99; exploitation of, 119–20; kinship networks and, 105–8; mainstream and, 16, 93, 114–18, 130; post-Katrina diaspora and, 99–105; "sissy bounce" and, 108–13
Bradley, Regina N., 70
braggadocio, 39, 52, 54, 57, 75
Brathwaite, Fred, 33
"Brooklyn Chiraq" (Young M.A), 74
"Brown's Beat" (Paul), 98–99
Bucano, Rocky, 31
Buckland, Fiona, 31
"Buckle Your Knees" (Ha Sizzle), 100
burden of liveness (Muñoz), 72–73, 91–92
"Burning Like Paris" (House of LaDosha), 59

Butch Queens, 47–48, 52, 56, 61
butch women, 6, 16, 67–68, 73–80. See also Black women; female masculinity; women; women rappers

Cakes da Killa, 15, 42, 45, 50, 55–58, 64
Call Me by Your Name, 124
camp, 128
Carnival, 97
Cash Money Records, 112
Catholic Church, 12
Channel Orange (Ocean), 1
Chapman, Alex, 86
Chapman, Alix, 97
Charnas, Dan, 31–33
"Chasing Rainbows" (Big Freedia), 120
"Chasing Time" (Banks), 58
Cheeky Blakk, 98
Chic, 14
Chicago, Illinois, 28–29, 35–36
"Child's Play" (Drake), 116–17
chosen families, 46–47
Christgau, Robert, 10
Chuck D, 20
civil rights, 11, 63
closeted artists, 8
clubs, 22–27, 28–31. See also cultural spaces
"Cocaine" (Internet), 83–87
Cockettes, 24
"Coke White, Starlight" (Blanco), 62
"Come into My House" (Queen Latifah), 38–39
coming out, 1–4, 86, 92, 125–26
Cominsky Park, 27–28
Common, 43
Considine, Clare, 42
Copland, Aaron, 27
Corey, Dorian, 120
country music, 127–29
COVID-19 pandemic, 121–22
Crawford, Cunty, 59
cultural spaces, 21–23, 28–31, 34–35, 37–38. See also clubs
cunt, 53, 56, 58–59
Currid, Brian, 30
Cyrus, Billy Ray, 128

DaBaby, 126
Dahl, Steve, 27, 33
Dallas, Texas, 99–101
dance music, 18–20, 21, 94–95, 122. *See also* disco; electronic dance music (EDM); house music
Darden, Ebro, 57
decolonization, 6–7
Defense of Marriage Act, 10
Def Jam, 18
DeJ Loaf, 78
De La Soul, 38
DePino, DJ David, 46
Derek B, 98
Detroit sound, 26
Dew Drop Inn, 97
diaspora, post-Katrina, 99–104, 107, 113–14
Dickel, Simon, 65
Dinerstein, Joel, 105
Diplo, 93, 95, 114
"Dirt Road Anthem" (Aldean), 128
disco: backlash against, 27–28; Ballroom rap and, 56–57; Black queer artists and, 21–22; Black queer community and, 25–26; distancing from rap and, 31–34; hip hop and, 14, 39; house music and, 28–30, 36–38, 49–50; LGBTQ rights movement and, 23; queer subcultures and, 34–35; rap and, 18–20; Sylvester and, 24
Disco Demolition Night, 27
disidentification, 9
distancing, 32–39
DJ Dickie, 98
DJ Doug beat, 98
DJ Hollywood, 31–33
DJ Irv, 97
DJ Jubilee, 105
DJ Kool Herc, 33
DJ Lil Man, 100–101
DJ Quick, 36–37
DJs, 26–27, 29, 31–32, 36
"down low" men, 37
Downstairs Records, 36
drag, 45, 47, 60–62, 97
"Drag Rap" (Showboy), 97–99

Drake, 16, 93, 94–96, 116–19, 123
Drott, Eric, 51, 59, 64
drug use, 84–85
Dupree, Paris, 46

Echols, Alice, 14, 19, 21, 25
effeminacy, 4, 53, 65
electronic bounce music (EBM), 114
electronic dance music (EDM), 114. *See also* dance music
Elliott, Missy, 78, 93, 95, 115–16
Eminem, 40
Ethnic Stew (Tribe), 36
Eulogy, The (Cakes da Killa), 56–57
Ewoodzie, Joseph C., Jr., 40–41
"Ex-Factor" (Hill), 117
exploitation, 119–20
"Express Yourself" (Diplo), 114

Fader, The, 120
Fajardo, Kale Bantigue, 71
fashion, 37–38, 60
female masculinity, 67–74, 75–76, 90–93. *See also* butch women; masculinity
femininity: Ballroom culture and, 47–49, 53, 56; hip hop and, 70; as passive, 79–80; realness and, 61–62
feminism, 90
femmephobia, 33–35
Femme Queens, 47, 49, 61
Fensterstock, Alison, 96–97
Fin (Syd), 89
First Choice, 57
Five Percenter rap, 51
Flamingo, 23, 26
Fly Boi Keno. *See* Keno
"Formation" (Beyoncé), 16, 94, 114–15
Foxxx, Njena Reddd, 54
Frank, Gillian, 23, 25, 27–28
Fresco, Michael, 26
"Fuck Katrina" (5th Ward Weebie), 103–4
funerals, second line, 103–5

Gamble, Kenneth, 26
gangsta rap, 5. *See also* rap
Garber, Eric, 22
Gate, 37

gay rap. *See* queer rap (and queer rappers)

gender: Ballroom culture and, 45–49, 56; Ballroom rap and, 50–52, 63–64; Banks and, 58–59; in Blanco's work, 62–63; female masculinity and, 67–71; in Ha Sizzle's music, 117; heteronormative disidentification and, 9; identity vs. expression and, 79–80; in Leif's lyrics, 54; race and, 7–8; rap and, 2–6, 40–41, 92; realness and, 61–62; vocal performance and, 76; women rappers and, 130

gender nonconformity, 6, 16, 61–63, 86, 96–97, 117, 118

genres: Ballroom rap and, 50–51, 63–66; dance music and, 18–19; disco and rap and, 31–34; distancing and, 39; gender in Ballroom culture and, 48–50; Lil Nas X and, 127–30; queer rap and, 43–44

"Get 2 Werk" (Cakes da Killa), 56

ghettocentric films, 68

ghosting, 118–19

Gibsone, Harriet, 82, 88

"Girlfriend" (Queen Pen), 70

God-des, 6

"Goodie Goodies" (Cakes da Killa), 56

"Good Times" (Chic), 14

Grae, Jean, 73

Grandmaster Flash, 33

Grandmaster Flash and the Furious Five, 40

Gray, F. Gary, 67

Great Migration, 22

grief, 103–5, 108

Guardian, 42, 82, 85

"Ha Dance, The" (Masters at Work), 56

Halberstam, Jack, 67, 71, 73, 75

Hammonds, Evelynn M., 71–72, 87

hampton, dream, 2–3

Harlem, New York, 15, 22, 45

Harlem Renaissance, 65

Harlow, Jack, 127

Ha Sizzle, 100–102, 105–8, 110–12, 116–17, 122

Hawkins, Stan, 62–63

Head Bangas Tour, 94, 121

"Hello" (Adele), 94

heteronormativity, 8–9, 50–51, 73

heterosexuality: bounce music and, 108–9; decentralization of, 130; disco backlash and, 27–28; disco and rap and, 31–34; hip hop and, 38; house music and, 37; "INDUSTRY BABY" and, 127; queer appropriation and, 121–23; queerness and, 7–8; queer subcultures and, 34–35; rap and, 2, 5, 20, 39–41; "Same Love" and, 12–14; women rappers and, 73

"Hey" (Leif), 53–54

High Road (Kesha), 120

"High School Never Ends" (Blanco), 62

Hill, Lauryn, 117

hip hop: authenticity and, 16–17; Ballroom culture and, 48–50; Ballroom rap and, 54, 65–66; Black queer women and, 69–72; bounce music and, 95–97, 110–13, 118–19; country music and, 128; disco and, 26; distancing from disco and, 31–33; distancing from house music and, 35–39; homophobia and, 9–14, 39–40, 86–89; Lil Nas X and, 4, 126–27; masculinity and, 40–41, 68–69; Ocean's coming out and, 1–3; queer foundations of, 14–15, 18–19; queerness and, 34–35, 123, 129–30; queer readings of, 7–9; *Set It Off* and, 67–68; white appropriation and, 121; women rappers and, 73; Young M.A and, 74–77. *See also* rap

Hobbs, Holly, 102

Holman, Felicia, 36

homophobia: Ballroom rap and, 50; Black queer women and, 15–16, 72, 73; disco and, 18–21, 24–27; disco and rap and, 33–34; in ghettocentric films, 68; house music and, 29–30, 35–37; Kodak Black and, 77–79; Lil Nas X and, 126; Odd Future and, 82, 88–90; queer rap and, 43–44; racial politics and, 9–14; rap and, 5–6, 39–40, 86–87, 123; "sissy bounce" and, 110–11

house music: Ballroom culture and, 45, 48–50; Ballroom rap and, 56–58; dis-

tancing from hip hop and, 35–39;
emergence of, 28–29; hip hop and, 15,
18–20; whitewashing of, 30; world-
making and, 31
House of Dupree, 46
House of LaDosha, 59
houses, 45–47, 54
Houston, Texas, 99, 101
Hubbs, Nadine, 19, 21, 27–28, 129
Huff, Leon, 26
Huffington Post, 86
Hughes, Walter, 21
Hunger Pangs (Cakes da Killa), 56–57
Hurricane Katrina, 99–105, 107, 122
hypervisible/invisible paradox, 15–16, 71–
73, 79–81, 87–90, 91

identity politics, 7–9, 90–93, 109–12
"I'll House You" (Jungle Brothers), 38–39
"Ima Read" (Katz), 54–55
"INDUSTRY BABY" (Lil Nas X),
126–27
"In My Feelings" (Drake), 94, 118, 123
Internet, 73, 82–86, 88–89
intersectionality, 5–9, 25, 43, 52–53, 92
invisibility, 72, 79
"I Run This Club" (Cakes da Killa), 55
"It's Not Ovah" (Cakes da Killa), 56–57

Jay Z, 2, 43
jazz funerals. *See* funerals, second line
Jeffries, Michael P., 68–69
JenRo, 6, 44
Johnson, E. Patrick, 48
Johnson, Myles, 118
"Jolene" (Parton), 16, 128–29
Joshi, Tara, 85, 90
Jungle Brothers, 3, 38

Kajikawa, Loren, 18, 32
Katz, Zebra, 15, 42, 45, 50, 54–55, 57–58,
60, 64
Keeling, Kara, 67–68
Keno, 102, 104, 106–8, 110–11, 114
Kesha, 94, 120–21
Keyes, Cheryl L., 64–65, 69–70, 76–77
"Kicked Out the House" (De La Soul), 38

kinship networks, 46–47, 54–56, 105–8,
113–14
Kitwana, Bakari, 43
Knuckles, Frankie, 22, 29, 35, 57
Kodak Black, 73, 77–80
"Koi" (Leif), 60

LaDosha, La'fem, 59
Lady Gaga, 10
Late Show with David Letterman, 42
Latinx artists, 5, 15, 18–19, 25
Latinx communities, 40, 45–48, 53
LA Weekly, 85
Lawrence, Tim, 22–23, 27, 32–33
Leif, 15, 42–45, 50, 52–54, 56, 60, 64
lesbians: Black queer women and, 73–74;
as hip hop archetype, 70; Kodak Black
and, 77–79; sexuality and, 72; Syd's dis-
identification with, 82–86; Young M.A
and, 80; Young M.A and Syd and, 90,
93
"Let No Man Put Asunder" (First
Choice), 57
Levan, Larry, 22, 29, 36–37
Lewis, Ryan, 10–11
LGBTQ community: backlash against
Syd and, 84–85; Ballroom culture and,
45–48; Big Freedia and, 113–14; bounce
music and, 105–8; hip hop and, 35; rap-
pers and, 43; "She Gutta" and, 62–63;
Syd and, 88–89
LGBTQ rights movement: disco and, 23;
racial politics and, 12–14
"Life Alert" (Cakes da Killa), 57
Lil Jon, 114
Lil Nas X, 4, 16, 19, 92, 124–30
Lil Wayne, 99
Liquid (Leif), 56
literature, 65
Little Richard, 97
Live Lounge, 128
"Living Gud, Eating Gud" (Cakes da
Killa), 56
Livingston, Jennie, 46
LL Cool J, 128
Loft, 21–22, 29, 31
Logitech, 124, 128

Love, Bettina, 96
"Love Hangover" (Ross), 49
"Love Is the Message" (MFSB), 49
lyrics, 40, 52–58, 74–76, 82, 84, 109–10, 116–18, 125

Ma, Remy, 74
"MacArthur Park" (Summer), 57
Macklemore, 10–15, 18, 43
Madonna, 46, 60
mainstream: Big Freedia and, 122; Black queer women in, 91–92; bounce music and, 16, 94–95, 99, 110–18; exploitation of bounce music and, 119–20; Lil Nas X and, 124–26; non-normative identities and, 2–5; queering of, 7–9; queer rap and, 43; Young M.A and, 72–77
Mancuso, David, 21–22, 31
Mannie Fresh, 98, 111–12, 122
Marchan, Bobby, 97
marriage equality, 10–13
Marriage Equality Project, 10
Martians, Matt, 82
masculinity: Ballroom culture and, 47–49; Ballroom rap and, 50, 65–66; Black queer women and, 15–16, 67–68, 70–72; decentralization of, 130; disco backlash and, 27–28; disidentification and, 9; in hip hop, 90; hip hop and, 37–38, 40–41; hip hop authenticity and, 17, 68–69; Odd Future and, 89; rap and, 2–5; realness and, 61–62; Syd and, 82–83; women rappers and, 73. *See also* female masculinity
Masters at Work, 56
Mayfield, Curtis, 11
McCune, Jeffrey Q., 37–38, 129–30
McDonald, Natalie Hope, 43
MC Hammer, 5
McNally, James, 58–60
Medusa, 6
Megan Thee Stallion, 130
Melpomene housing projects, 99, 116
men, 21–25, 68–71
mental health, 89–90
"Mermaid Ball," 59
"Message, The" (Grandmaster Flash and the Furious Five), 40
Messy Mya, 16, 114–15
MFSB (Mother Father Sister Brother), 26
Michigan Womyn's Music Festival (MWMF), 6
Miller, Matt, 97–98, 109
Minaj, Nicki, 40, 73–74
Mincher, Chris, 10
minoritarian identities, 9
misogyny, 5–6, 79
Miyakawa, Felicia M., 51
"MONTERO (Call Me By Your Name)" (Lil Nas X), 124–26
MONTERO (Lil Nas X), 16
Motown, 26
Mr. Meana, 108
multiculturalism, 24–25
Muñoz, José Esteban, 8–9, 72, 91
musical lineages: Ballroom culture and, 44–45, 56–60; Ballroom rap and, 63–64; Black queer artists and, 5, 9, 41, 130; Black queer women and, 66, 76–77; disco and, 14–15, 19–22, 27; house music and, 49–50; Lil Nas X and, 16
musical references, 56–60
music videos: "Cocaine" and, 83–87; "Formation" and, 114–15; "INDUSTRY BABY" and, 127; "MONTERO" and, 124–25; "Nice For What" and, 117–18; "Old Town Road" and, 128; as visual references, 60–63
MySpace, 100–101

"Na" beat, 98
"Nasty Girl" (Vanity 6), 49
National Gay and Lesbian Task Force, 13
Native Tongues, 38
New Orleans, Louisiana: Big Freedia and, 121–22; Black queer rappers and, 5; bounce music and, 16, 93, 95–99, 116–19; gay rappers in, 109–13; post-Katrina diaspora and, 99–105; sissy bounce and, 106–8
New Way Vogue, 49, 56
New York City, New York: Ballroom rap and, 50–52, 66; Black queer rappers and, 5, 15; house music and, 29, 31, 45;

New Orleans and, 98; queer rap and, 42–44
New York Times Magazine, 82–83, 89
"Nice For What" (Drake), 16, 94, 117–18, 120
Nichols, Eboni, 38
Nicky da B, 111, 114
Nine Inch Nails, 128
normativity, 88

Obama, Barack, 12
Ocean, Frank, 1–4, 86, 92, 123, 125
Odd Future, 73, 81–83, 86–90
"Old Town Road" (Lil Nas X), 16, 124, 127–29
"Ooouuu" (Young M.A), 74–77
outing, 23
"Oven Ready" (Cakes da Killa), 56

Paisley, Brad, 128
Palimpsest: A Journal on Women, Gender, and the Black International, 7
Paradise Garage, 36–37
Parents Music Resource Center, 5
Paris Is Burning (Livingston), 46, 57, 120
Partners-N-Crime (PNC), 108
Parton, Dolly, 16, 129
Patterson, Rahsaan, 3
Paul, Cameron, 98
Pennington, Stephan, 76
"People Get Ready" (Mayfield), 11
"Pep Rally" (Elliott), 115–16
performance, 61–62, 63, 66, 69, 91, 130
Perry, Imani, 7–8, 68–70
Philadelphia International Records, 26
Philly sound, 26
"Pimpin Ain't Eazy" (Black), 77–78
Pitchfork, 42, 44, 81
Plaquemines Parish, Louisiana, 99
pop music, 2, 10–11, 120–21
POSE, 46
Powell, Elliott H., 7, 119
Powers, Ann, 128
Price, Phillip "Triggerman," 98
pride, politics of, 88
Prop 8, 12–13

Public Enemy, 20
punk, 64

Quattlebaum, Michael, Jr. *See* Blanco, Mykki
Queen Latifah, 3, 38–39, 67–68
Queen Pen, 70, 77
queerness: Ballroom rap and, 65–66; bounce music and, 95–97, 117–19; camp and, 128; disco and, 27; hip hop and, 14, 34–35, 129–30; house music and, 29–30, 36–38; in Katz's lyrics, 55; Lil Nas X and, 124–26; Ocean and, 1–3; Queen Latifah and, 67; racial politics and, 18; rap and, 4–6, 39–41; readings of heterosexual artists and, 7–8; Syd and, 83–88; Sylvester and, 23–24; Young M.A and Syd and, 90–92
queer rap (and queer rappers): appropriation and, 121–23; Ballroom rap and, 42–45, 66; bounce music and, 96–97, 99–100, 114, 118–19; mainstream success and, 126; "sissy bounce" and, 108–12; sissy bounce and, 105–7; Young M.A and, 80–81; Young M.A and Syd and, 91–93
queer studies, 8

R&B, 2, 10–11, 48–49
race: in Blanco's work, 62–63; disco and, 18–19; disco and rap and, 32–33; female masculinity and, 71–72; gender and, 7–8, 48; house music and, 29–30; "lesbian" and, 85, 91; queer rap and, 43; rap and, 5–6; realness and, 61; "Same Love" and, 12–14; sexuality and, 87–88
racism, 23–28, 128
Rainey, Ma, 76–77
"Raising Hell" (Kesha), 94, 120
rap: dance music and, 18; disco and, 14, 19–20; distancing from disco and, 31–35; gay rappers and, 15; homophobia and, 39–40; queerness and, 2–6. *See also* gangsta rap; hip hop; queer rap (and queer rappers)
rap collectives, 81–82, 90
"Rapper's Delight" (Sugarhill Gang), 14, 39

Rapsody, 130
reading, 54–55
realness, 61–62
Realness with a Twist, 61
reception history, 17
Red, Katey, 99
Referendum 74, 10, 12
Regis, Helen A., 104–5
religious conservativism, 12, 125
"Rent" (Big Freedia), 122
rent parties, 22
respectability politics, 88, 96, 125–26
Riot Boi (Leif), 60
rock and roll, 18
"Rock the Beat" (Derek B), 98
"Roll Call" beat, 98
Rolling Loud Miami, 126
Rolling Stone, 127
Rose, Tricia, 69
Rosenberg, Peter, 57
Rubin, Rick, 18
Rusty Lazer, 99, 105, 107, 113

Salkind, Micah E., 35
Salt 'n Pepa, 73
"Same Love" (Macklemore and Lewis),
    10–14, 18, 125
samples: bounce music and, 16, 93, 95–96,
    98–99; in Drake's music, 116–18; in
    "Formation," 114–15; ghosting and,
    118–19; musical references and, 56–57;
    in "Pep Rally," 115–16
Saturday Night Live, 124, 126
Savage, Dan, 13
Schooly, Magnolia, 102
self-fashioning, 63
Set It Off (Gray), 67–68, 74, 93
sexism, 68
sexual abuse, 35
sexuality: Ballroom culture and, 45–48;
    Ballroom rap and, 63–64; in Banks's
    lyrics, 58; Black queer women and, 72,
    92; in Blanco's videos, 62–63; blues
    women and, 77; gay rappers and, 122–
    23; gender and, 4; heteronormative dis-
    identification and, 9; in Leif's lyrics,
    52–53; rap and, 5; realness and, 61;

"sissy bounce" and, 109–12; Syd and,
    83–87; Young M.A and, 74, 78–80
shade, 46, 120
Sharpley-Whiting, Tracy, 70
She, 6
"She Gutta" (Blanco), 62–63
"She Rode That Dick Like a Soldier" (Ha
    Sizzle), 100–101, 116–17
Showboy, 97
Simmons, Russell, 2, 86
sissy bounce, 96, 99–100, 105–13. See also
    bounce music
Sissy Nobby, 96, 98, 102–3, 105–7, 109–11
Skim, 6
Smalls, Shanté Paradigm, 7–8, 40, 73
Smith, Anna Marie, 79–80
Smith, Troy L., 36
Snoop Dogg, 2–3
Snorton, C. Riley, 4, 88
social media, 81–82, 99–102, 126–27
social practices, 19–20
"Soda" (Leif), 56, 60
Spillers, Hortense, 72
Stardust Ballroom, 31
St. Bernard Parish, Louisiana, 99
Stonewall riots, 22–23
subcultures: Ballroom culture and, 44–
    45; Ballroom rap and, 51, 63–64; disco
    and, 18–22; heterosexuality and, 37; hip
    hop and, 34–35, 39. See also
    underground
Sugarhill Gang, 14
Sullivan, Andrew, 13
Summer, Donna, 57
"SUN GOES DOWN" (Lil Nas X), 124,
    126
Syd (Tha Kid): "Cocaine" and, 83–85;
    hampton and, 3; masculinity and, 66,
    72–73; Odd Future and, 81–83; as
    queer rapper, 15–16; resistance to labels
    and, 90–91; sexuality and, 85–90, 92–
    93; visibility and, 118
Sylvester, 23–24

Tank and the Bangas, 94
Tavakoli, Mina, 75
Tavia, Mark, 106

"Tear the House Up" (Katz), 57, 60
technological innovations, 18, 26, 29
"Thank You, Frank Ocean" (hampton), 2–3
That B.E.A.T., 115
"That Big Big Beat" (Banks), 58
Thomas, Anthony, 29–30
Thomson, Virgil, 27
"Thrift Shop" (Macklemore and Lewis), 10
Thug Life: Race, Gender, and the Meaning of Hip-Hop (Jeffries), 68–69
TikTok, 127
Time, 109, 128
TLC, 73
tomboys, 73
Torain, Troi "STAR," 34–35
trans artists, 4–5, 95–97, 108–14, 118–19, 126
trans men, 47
trans women, 47
Trapped in a Culture, 34–35
"Triggerman" beat, 98–99. *See also* "Drag Rap" (Showboy)
Tucker, MC T., 97
"Tutti Frutti" (Little Richard), 97
Tyler, The Creator, 2–3, 81–82, 86–89

underground, 4, 28. *See also* subcultures
Universal Hip Hop Museum, 31
US Supreme Court, 10

Vandross, Luther, 3
Vanilla Ice, 5
Views (Drake), 116
visibility, 16–17, 118–20, 130
visual references, 60–63, 118–19, 124–25, 128
vocal performance, 76
"Vogue" (Madonna), 46, 60
voguing, 46, 49, 56, 60–61. *See also* New Way Vogue

Warehouse, 28
Warner, Michael, 31

Watkins, S. Craig, 68
"Wavvy" (Blanco), 62
West, Kanye, 43
"Where Dey At" (MC T. Trucker and DJ Irv), 97, 99
White, Miles, 65, 69
whiteness: Black homophobia and, 12–14, 18; disco and, 23–26; disco backlash and, 27–28; "lesbian" and, 85, 91; queer studies and, 8; rap and, 5–7, 32–33
whitewashing, 29–30
Wills, Leila, 35
women: as Black queer artists, 66; gender performance in rap and, 4; hip hop and, 41; homophobia in rap and, 39–40; masculinity and, 71–72; musical lineages and, 64–65; "Nice For What" and, 117–18; queer hip hop and, 6–7, 15–16. *See also* Black women; blues women; butch women; women rappers
women rappers: Banks and, 58; blues women and, 65, 76–77; hypervisible/invisible paradox and, 15–16, 72–73; male rappers and, 69; masculinity and, 73; Young M.A and, 80–81
world-making, 31, 38, 129–30
Wortham, Jenna, 82–83, 89
"Wut" (Leif), 42, 52–53

"You Make Me Feel (Mighty Real)" (Sylvester), 24
Young, Earl, 26
Younger, Briana, 81–82
Young M.A: Kodak Black and, 77–80; masculinity and, 66, 72–73; "Ooouuu" and, 75–77; as queer rapper, 15–16; resistance to labels and, 80–81, 90–91; sexuality and, 74–75, 92–93
Young Thug, 128
YouTube, 102, 127

Zulu Nation, 34–35